EMPOWERED EDUCATORS IN AUSTRALIA

How High-Performing Systems Shape Teaching Quality

Dion Burns and Ann McIntyre

JB JOSSEY-BASS™

A Wiley Brand

Published by Jossey-Bass
A Wiley Brand
One Montgomery Street, Suite 1000, San Francisco, CA 94104-4594—www.josseybass.com

Jossey-Bass books and products are available through most bookstores. To contact
Jossey-Bass directly call our Customer Care Department within the U.S. at 800-956-7739,
outside the U.S. at 317-572-3986, or fax 317-572-4002.

Wiley publishes in a variety of print and electronic formats and by print-on-demand.
Some material included with standard print versions of this book may not be included in
e-books or in print-on-demand. If this book refers to media such as a CD or DVD that
is not included in the version you purchased, you may download this material at http://
booksupport.wiley.com. For more information about Wiley products, visit www.wiley.com.

ISBN: 9781119369646
ISBN: 9781119369677
ISBN: 9781119369707

Cover design by Wiley
Cover image: © suriya9/Getty Images, Inc.

FIRST EDITION
PB Printingg   10 9 8 7 6 5 4 3 2 1

CONTENTS

In loving memory of Dr. Paul Brock, educator, researcher, mentor, and friend. For Melissa, Aramaia, and Anika with love and gratitude.

FOREWORD

FEW WOULD DISAGREE THAT, among all the factors that affect how much students learn, the quality of their teachers ranks very high. But what, exactly, do policy makers, universities, and school leaders need to do to make sure that the vast majority of teachers in their jurisdiction are *literally* world class?

Perhaps the best way to answer that question is to look carefully and in great detail at what the countries whose students are performing at the world's top levels are doing to attract the highest quality high school students to teaching careers, prepare them well for that career, organize schools so teachers can do the best work of which they are capable, and provide incentives for them to get better at the work before they finally retire.

It was not hard for us to find the right person to lead a study that would do just that. Stanford professor Linda Darling-Hammond is one of the world's most admired researchers. Teachers and teaching have been lifelong professional preoccupations for her. And, not least, Professor Darling-Hammond is no stranger to international comparative studies. Fortunately for us and for you, she agreed to lead an international comparative study of teacher quality in a selection of top-performing countries. The study, *Empowered Educators: How High-Performing Systems Shape Teaching Quality Around the World*, took two years to complete and is unprecedented in scope and scale.

The volume you are reading is one of six books, including case studies conducted in Australia, Canada, China, Finland, and Singapore. In addition to the case studies and the cross-study analysis, the researchers have collected a range of videos and artifacts (http://ncee.org/empowered-educators)—ranging from a detailed look at how the daily schedules of teachers in Singapore ensure ample time for collaboration and planning to a description of the way Shanghai teachers publish their classroom research in refereed journals—that we hope will be of great value to policy makers and educators interested in using and adapting the tools that the top-performing jurisdictions use to get the highest levels of teacher quality in the world.

Studies of this sort are often done by leading scholars who assemble hordes of graduate students to do the actual work, producing reams of reports framed by the research plan, which are then analyzed by the principal investigator. That is not what happened in this case. For this report, Professor Darling-Hammond recruited two lead researcher-writers for each case study, both senior, one from the country being studied and one from another country, including top-level designers and implementers of the systems being studied and leading researchers. This combination of insiders and external observers, scholars and practitioner-policy makers, gives this study a depth, range, and authenticity that is highly unusual.

But this was not just an effort to produce first-class case studies. The aim was to understand what the leaders were doing to restructure the profession of teaching for top performance. The idea was to cast light on that by examining what was the same and what was different from country to country to see if there were common threads that could explain uncommon results. As the data-gathering proceeded, Professor Darling-Hammond brought her team together to exchange data, compare insights, and argue about what the data meant. Those conversations, taking place among a remarkable group of senior policy actors, practitioners, and university-based researchers from all over the world, give this work a richness rarely achieved in this sort of study.

The researchers examined all sorts of existing research literature on the systems they were studying, interviewed dozens of people at every level of the target systems, looked at everything from policy at the national level to practice in individual schools, and investigated not only the specific policies and practices directly related to teacher quality, but the larger economic, political, institutional, and cultural contexts in which policies on teacher quality are shaped.

Through it all, what emerges is a picture of a sea change taking place in the paradigm of mass education in the advanced industrial nations. When university graduates of any kind were scarce and most people had jobs requiring only modest academic skills, countries needed teachers who knew little more than the average high school graduate, perhaps less than that at the primary school level. It was not too hard to find capable people, typically women, to do that work, because the job opportunities for women with that level of education were limited.

But none of that is true anymore. Wage levels in the advanced industrial countries are typically higher than elsewhere in the world. Employers who can locate their manufacturing plants and offices anywhere in the world and who do not need highly skilled labor look for workers who have the basic skills they need in low-wage countries, so the work available to workers with only the basic skills in the high-wage countries is drying up. That process is being greatly accelerated by the rapid advance of automation. The jobs that are left in the high-wage countries mostly demand a higher level of more complex skills.

These developments have put enormous pressure on the governments of high-wage countries to find teachers who have more knowledge and a deeper command of complex skills. These are the people who can get into selective universities and go into occupations that have traditionally had higher status and are better compensated than school teaching. What distinguishes the countries with the best-performing education systems is that: 1) they have figured this out and focused hard on how to respond to these new realities; and 2) they have succeeded not just in coming up with promising designs for the systems they need but in implementing those systems well. The result is not only profound changes in the way they source, educate, train, and support a truly professional teaching force, but schools in which the work of teachers is very differently organized, the demands on school leaders is radically changed, teachers become not the recipient of a new set of instructions from the "center," but the people who are actually responsible for designing and carrying out the reforms that are lifting the performance of their students every day. Not least important, these systems offer real careers in teaching that enable teachers, like professionals in other fields, to gain more authority, responsibility, compensation, and status as they get better and better at the work, without leaving teaching.

This is an exciting story. It is the story that you are holding in your hand. The story is different in every country, province, and state. But the themes behind the stories are stunningly similar. If you find this work only half as compelling as I have, you will be glued to these pages.

MARC TUCKER, PRESIDENT
NATIONAL CENTER ON EDUCATION AND THE ECONOMY

ACKNOWLEDGMENTS

WE WISH TO ACKNOWLEDGE and thank the many individuals and organizations who so generously donated their time and energy for helping us with the planning and implementation of the study, and who shared with us their knowledge and experiences in the preparation of this book.

Firstly, we'd like to thank Marc Tucker and Betsy Brown-Ruzzi at the National Center on Education and the Economy, as well as Barry McGaw, Tony Mackay, and advisers at the Center on International Education Benchmarking who provided their feedback and suggestions in the preparation of the draft. We also thank the Center for Teaching Quality and their network of teachers, several of whom contributed to this project. We also offer our thanks to Barnett Berry and the Center for Teaching Quality, whose teachers contributed their experiences and perspectives to this work.

We would like to give our sincere appreciation to the study's principal investigator, Linda Darling-Hammond, for the opportunity to be involved in such a valuable project, and for her guidance throughout. And we thank the members of the project team—Jon Snyder, Sonya Keller, Maude Engström—as well as the other country case authors—Misty Sato, Carol Campbell, Ann Lieberman, Pamela Osmond-Johnson, Ken Zeichner, Lin Goodwin, and Ee Ling Low—for their communication, advice, and feedback.

We'd also like to thank the many educational experts with whom we spoke. We acknowledge the faculty and staff of the Universities of Melbourne, Sydney, and Wollongong, and of La Trobe University. Among these, we are particularly thankful to Stephen Dinham, Robyn Ewing, Patrick Griffin, John Hattie, Larissa McLean-Davies, Field Rickard, Sharon Tyndall-Ford, and Roger Wander.

We are grateful to the many individual policymakers who gave their time to this project. We acknowledge the Victoria Department of Education and Training and the NSW Department of Education and Communities for their assistance in conducting this research, and to the many senior staff who provided important information on the context and goals of policy reforms. We are particularly thankful to Michele Bruniges at the NSW Department of Education and Communities, Ross Fox at the National Catholic Education Commission in Sydney, Don Paproth and Fran Cosgrove at the Victorian Institute of Teaching, Patrick Lee at the NSW Institute of Teachers, and Bruce Armstrong and Chris McKenzie of the Bastow Institute of Educational Leadership for their generosity with their time and very thoughtful perspectives.

We would also like to thank the members of the federal and Victorian branches of the Australian Education Union, and the NSW Teachers' Federation. Particular thanks to Angelo Gavrielatos, Denis Fitzgerald, Susan Hopgood, Maurie Mulheron, and Justin Mulally, and to Michael Victory of the Teachers Learning Network.

Special thanks go to the many schools, principals, teachers, staff, and students who so generously opened their doors to us, provided us with information and materials, and allowed us to enter and observe their classes. In New South Wales, we thank Principals Joanne Jarvis, David Smith, Estelle Southall, and Annette Udall, Assistant Principal Ian Casey, and teachers Antonella Albini, Rachel Clapham, Heather Crawford, Jeff Debnam, Samson Fung, Steven Holz, Roxanne Marnios, Daniel McKay, and Michelle Tregoning. In Victoria, we add our thanks to Sara-Kate Allen, Seona Aulich, Mary Dowling, Tania Ellul, Olivia Ha, and Aaron Vreulink.

Finally, we particularly acknowledge the late Paul Brock who sadly passed away before the publishing of this book. Paul introduced the two study authors and provided important feedback that informed the work. We thank him for his friendship, and his nearly 50 years of work dedicated to the betterment of education in NSW and Australia.

We are grateful to all those who contributed their time, energy, and expertise towards this research. Ultimately, any errors or omissions are the responsibility of the authors.

This study has been designed to gather evidence regarding the systems that create opportunities to promote excellence and equity in educational outcomes. We trust that this study will inform future policies to enable teachers to have the greatest impact on their students' learning.

DION BURNS AND ANN MCINTYRE

ABOUT THE SPONSORING ORGANIZATIONS

THIS WORK IS MADE possible through a grant by the Center on International Education Benchmarking® of the National Center on Education and the Economy® and is part of a series of reports on teacher quality systems around the world. For a complete listing of the material produced by this research program, please visit www.ncee.org/cieb.

CENTER ON INTERNATIONAL
EDUCATION BENCHMARKING
LEARNING FROM THE WORLD'S HIGH PERFORMING EDUCATION SYSTEMS

The Center on International Education Benchmarking®, a program of NCEE, funds and conducts research around the world on the most successful education systems to identify the strategies those countries have used to produce their superior performance. Through its books, reports, website, monthly newsletter, and a weekly update of education news around the world, CIEB provides up-to-date information and analysis on those countries whose students regularly top the PISA league tables. Visit www.ncee.org/cieb to learn more.

The National Center on Education and the Economy was created in 1988 to analyze the implications of changes in the international economy for American education, formulate an agenda for American education based on that analysis, and seek wherever possible to accomplish that agenda through policy change and development of the resources educators would need to carry it out. For more information visit www .ncee.org.

Research for this volume was coordinated by the Stanford Center for Opportunity Policy in Education (SCOPE) at Stanford University. SCOPE was founded in 2008 to foster research, policy, and practice to advance high quality, equitable education systems in the United States and internationally.

ABOUT THE AUTHORS

 **Dion Burns, M.Ed, M.IR,** is a senior researcher with the Learning Policy Institute and Research Analyst at the Stanford Center for Opportunity Policy in Education. With a background in policy and quantitative analysis, his research has focused on international education policies, particularly those that promote high-quality and equitable learning opportunities.

Over the past 20 years, Dion has variously worked as a teacher in Japan, a higher education policy analyst in New Zealand, and an education diplomat with roles in Latin America and the Republic of Korea.

 **Ann McIntyre, MLitt, BA, DipT, GDipOLCD, FACEL, FACE,** is recognized for her work in quality teaching, leadership, and school and system improvement. She provides powerful professional learning that draws together research, policy, and school practice.

Ann's work explores the power of the alignment of teacher, leader, and school and system learning, and their impact on student outcomes. As the director of Professional Learning and Leadership Development in NSW she led the development of professional frameworks, programs, and research.

As superintendent of schools and school principal, she received numerous excellence awards, and while principal received a school quality assurance report stating "this school is on the leading edge of best practices in teaching and learning."

As a result of her contribution to educational leadership, Ann has been recognized through many awards including the Churchill Fellowship, the Sydney Leadership Award, and national Australian Council for Educational Leaders and Australian College of Educators Fellowships.

ONLINE DOCUMENTS AND VIDEOS

Access online documents an videos at
http://ncee.org/empowered-educators

Link Number	URL	Title
1–1	http://ncee.org/2016/12/national-declaration-on-the-educational-goals-for-young-australians/	Melbourne Declaration on Educational Goals for Young Australians
1–2	http://ncee.org/2016/12/australian-professional-standard-for-teachers/	Australian Professional Standard for Teachers
1–3	http://ncee.org/2016/12/australian-professional-standard-for-principals/	Australian Professional Standard for Principals
1–4	http://ncee.org/2016/12/students-first-temag-report/	Students First (TEMAG Report)
1–5	http://ncee.org/2016/12/review-of-funding-for-schools-gonski/	Review of funding for schools – Gonski
2–1	http://ncee.org/2016/12/nsw-5-year-strategic-plan/	NSW 5 Year Strategic Plan
2–2	http://ncee.org/2016/12/video-michele-bruniges-on-teacher-quality/	Video: Michele Bruniges on Teacher Quality
2–3	http://ncee.org/2016/12/review-of-funding-for-schools-gonski/	Review of funding for schools – Gonski
2–4	http://ncee.org/2016/12/great-teaching-inspired-learning/	Great Teaching, Inspired Learning
2–5	http://ncee.org/2016/12/students-first-temag-report/	Students First (TEMAG Report)
2–6	http://ncee.org/2016/12/professional-teaching-standards/	Professional Teaching Standards
2–7	http://ncee.org/2016/12/australian-professional-standard-for-teachers/	Australian Professional Standard for Teachers

Link Number	URL	Title
2–8	http://ncee.org/2016/12/video-daniel-mckay/	Video: Daniel McKay on Supporting Teacher PD
2–9	http://ncee.org/2016/12/video-steven-holz/	Video: Steven Holz on Teachers in Schools and Communities
2–10	http://ncee.org/2016/12/nsw-performance-and-development-framework/	NSW Performance and Development Framework
2–11	http://ncee.org/2016/12/video-gonski-funding-model/	Video: Gonski Funding Model
3–1	http://ncee.org/2016/12/deecd-principals-for-health-and-well-being/	DEECD Principals for Health and Well Being
3–2	http://ncee.org/2016/12/victorian-early-years-learning-and-development-framework/	Victorian Early Years Learning and Development Framework
3–3	http://ncee.org/2016/12/blueprint-for-government-schools/	Blueprint for Government Schools
3–4	http://ncee.org/2016/12/deecd-2013--17-strategic-plan/	DEECD 2013-17 Strategic Plan
3–5	http://ncee.org/2016/12/towards-victoria-as-a-learning-community/	Towards Victoria as a Learning Community
3–6	http://ncee.org/2016/12/from-new-directions-to-action/	From New Directions to Action
3–7	http://ncee.org/2016/12/education-state-schools/	Education State – Schools
3–8	http://victoriancurriculum.vcaa.vic.edu.au/	The Victorian Curriculum F–10
3–9	http://ncee.org/2016/12/roles-and-responsibilities-of-teaching-service/	Roles and Responsibilities of Teaching Service
3–10	http://ncee.org/2016/12/victorian-government-schools-agreement-2013/	Victorian Government Schools Agreement 2013
3–11	http://ncee.org/2016/12/remuneration-teaching-service/	Remuneration Teaching Service
3–12	http://ncee.org/2016/12/recruitment-in-schools/	Recruitment in Schools

Link Number	URL	Title
3–13	http://ncee.org/2016/12/guide-to-the-accreditation-process-of-ite-programs/	Guide to the Accreditation Process of ITE Programs
3–14	http://ncee.org/2016/12/course-map-monash-2015/	Course Maps for Monash University, 2015
3–15	http://ncee.org/2016/12/pre-and-post-test-zpd/	Pre- and Post-Test ZPD
3–16	http://ncee.org/2016/12/team-meeting-minutes/	Wilmott Park Primary School Grade 4 Team Meeting Minutes
3–17	http://ncee.org/2016/12/deecd-school-accountability/	DEECD School Accountability
3–18	http://ncee.org/2016/12/professional-learning-in-effective-schools/	Professional Learning in Effective Schools
3–19	http://www.bigandsmallmedia.com.au/DEECD/?view=featured	Evidence Based Professional Learning Cycle
3–20	http://ncee.org/2016/12/wpps-improvement-goals/	WPPS Improvement Goals
3–21	http://ncee.org/2016/12/professional-learning-reflections/	Professional Learning Reflections
3–22	http://ncee.org/2016/12/developmental-learning-framework-for-school-leaders/	Developmental Learning Framework for School Leaders

A NATIONAL FRAMEWORK TO SUPPORT TEACHING QUALITY IN AUSTRALIA

Dion Burns and Ann McIntyre

THE MOST SIGNIFICANT DEVELOPMENT influencing teaching quality in Australia over the past decade has, without question, been the establishment of nationally agreed policies for education. The wide-ranging policies, influencing what is taught, how it is taught, and who teaches it, have occurred under the auspices of two national organizations: ACARA (the Australian Curriculum, Assessment and Reporting Authority), and AITSL (the Australian Institute for Teaching and School Leadership).

In the first chapter of this volume, we look at each organization, their policies, and how they are intended to frame improvements in the quality of education in Australia. We also look at the issue of educational funding—a third plank of national reforms. In particular, we survey the Gonski reforms, which aims to equalize funding across states and school systems, and which is influencing states' approach to the more equitable resourcing of education.

Preceding this, we discuss the context for education in Australia, including its school system in international comparison. We also highlight some of the challenges, in particular those related to achieving an equitable education for all students.

We begin however by briefly looking firstly at the governmental arrangements for education, and then the Melbourne Declaration—the statement that sets the long-term vision of a high-quality and equitable education for young Australians, and which has provided the impetus for powerful national reforms in a federal education system.

Australia, Its Constitution, and Federalism in Education

Education policy in Australia is formally the responsibility of the governments of each of its six states and two territories. Originally a series of independent colonies, the states federated to became the country of Australia with the establishment of a federal constitution in 1901. The states and territories retain constitutional independence from the parliament of the federal government over many important policy functions, including responsibility for education.[1] Thus each state in Australia operates its own set of government schools, and trains and registers its own teachers.

Federal influence over state policy is however permitted under the federal constitution's Section 96:

> During a period of ten years after the establishment of the Commonwealth and thereafter until the Parliament otherwise provides, the Parliament may grant financial assistance to any State on such terms and conditions as the Parliament thinks fit.

(Section 96, Commonwealth of Australia Constitution Act, 1901)

This allows the federal government to provide funding to states, and tie it to specific initiatives, including in education. Successive federal governments have made use of this provision for the past 40 years, such as the assumption of responsibility for the funding of Australian universities in the 1970s. Its use as a legislative tool in school education has also grown, particularly over the past decade. This effectively means that where federal funds are provided, federal policy applies.

The increasing influence of this provision is facilitated by the nature of taxation and funding in Australia. Income and general taxes (such as GST—a value-added tax on goods and services) are collected by the federal government and subsequently dispersed to state governments in order to fund their agendas. Funding may also be directed towards school systems and specific activities. Policy matters in states and territories are thus both directly and indirectly funded by the Australian government.

Despite constitutional independence, this imbalance in funding power (known as a vertical fiscal imbalance) discourages states from declining federal funds, particularly in expensive policy areas such as education, and gives the federal government an influential voice in policy. Agreement between state and federal governments has predominated in education policy in recent years, but at times during 2003–2007, the Australian government used the specter of a reduction of funding to move states towards national policies, a period described as "coercive federalism" (Harris-Hart, 2010; Reid, 2009).

Although center-right governments have in general tended to favor a states-based approach to education policy, attempts to create national policy in areas such as curriculum over the last 40 years have been led by both Liberal (center-right) and Labor (center-left) parties. The discourses and stated rationales for national-level policies in education have thus shifted over time. These have included equity issues, national identity and cohesion, the inefficiencies of misalignment between states (the so-called railway gauge phenomenon),[2] and human capital and economic growth imperatives (Gable & Lingard, 2013; Harris-Hart, 2010).

More recently, flagging international education competitiveness and the risk of "losing the education race" has been articulated as a primary driver (Franklin, 2012; Reid, 2009). Gable and Lingard (2013) have contended that Australia's increased participation in international organizations, such as the Organisation for Economic Co-operation and Development (OECD), have led it to increasingly accept a knowledge economy and productivity growth rationale, and thus to focus on education governance centered on addressing systemic issues through national level policies, rather than local issues of instruction and learning.

The most significant developments in federal education policy occurred following the election of a center-left Labor party to the federal government in 2007. The Rudd-Gillard government sought to enact its reform agenda in three key areas:

1. "Raising the quality of teaching in our schools.
2. Ensuring all students benefit from schooling through strategies based on high expectations of attainment, engagement and transitions for every student, especially in disadvantaged school communities.
3. Improving transparency and accountability of schools and school systems at all levels." (Rudd & Gillard, 2008)

The success in achieving national-level policies has largely been achieved through a "co-operative federalism" (Harris-Hart, 2010). With the signing of the Melbourne Declaration in 2008 (described below), the Australian government pursued national policies largely through a series of National Partnerships agreements between federal and state governments in areas including numeracy and literacy, and teaching quality. This took place through two main organizations, the Council of Australian Governments (COAG) (representing both Commonwealth and state governments) and its related body, the Education Council.[3] The process has relied on consensus, and although now well-entrenched, with subsequent changes of leadership at state and federal levels, its success is still potentially subject to political forces. The challenges in implementing national funding reforms (discussed later in this paper) provide one such example.

The Australian government has established several national level bodies—most prominently the Australian Institute of Teaching and School Leadership (AITSL) and the Australian Curriculum, Assessment and Reporting Authority (ACARA)—to develop and promulgate national policies in specific areas, the majority of which are enacted at the state level. The federal government's role in education takes the form of policy leadership, the establishment of standards, recurrent school funding (including to nongovernment schools), funding specific initiatives for innovation and change, and assessment monitoring and reporting (Gable & Lingard, 2013; Zanderigo, Dowd, & Turner, 2012). A schematic of the key documents and organizational relationships is shown in Figure 1.1.

A Pivot Point—The Melbourne Declaration

A key transition point towards the adoption of national-level policies in education was the signing in 2008 of the Melbourne Declaration on Educational Goals for Young Australians (Link 1-1). Issued by the then

Figure 1.1 National School Education Policy and Reporting Framework.

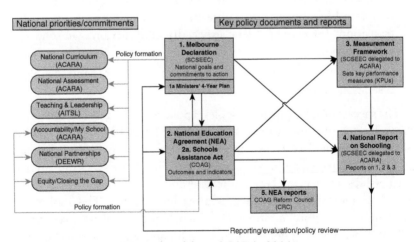

Reproduced from ACARA, 2014.

Ministerial Council on Education, Employment, Training and Youth Affairs (MCEETYA), and signed by all eight federal, state, and territory education ministers, it came at a time when both the federal government, and all but one Australian state, were led by center-left Labor governments.

The two broad goals of the Melbourne Declaration are:

○ Goal One: Australian schooling promotes equity and excellence

○ Goal Two: All young Australians become:

- successful learners
- confident and creative individuals
- active and informed citizens (MCEETYA, 2008)

Endorsed by all Australian education ministers, the MCEETYA plan outlines key strategies and initiatives that Australian governments will commit to in eight interrelated areas in order to support the achievement of the educational goals for young Australians. These eight areas are:

○ developing stronger partnerships

○ supporting quality teaching and school leadership

○ strengthening early childhood education

○ enhancing middle years development

○ supporting senior years of schooling and youth transitions

○ promoting world-class curriculum and assessment

○ improving educational outcomes for indigenous youth and disadvantaged young Australians, especially those from low socioeconomic backgrounds

○ strengthening accountability and transparency

Building on the earlier Hobart and Adelaide declarations (1989 and 1999 respectively), which established a framework for national cooperation, the Melbourne Declaration represents an important and symbolic pivot point in increasing the influence of national-level education policy, and its effects are dramatically shaping teaching quality in Australia.

In particular, the Declaration drew important attention to issues of educational equity. This includes disparities in education experienced by indigenous students, by students with disabilities, and by students from lower socioeconomic backgrounds. It also brought attention to differences in educational provision between states, and between the government and nongovernment school sectors. The document thus provided important context and momentum for developments in teaching standards and curriculum, and highlighted the need for funding reform.

As a consequence, there has been increased federal engagement and cross-state collaboration on educational issues. Key amongst these are: the Schools Assistance Act (2008), providing funding to Catholic and independent schools; the National Education Agreement, with a student performance and assessment measurement framework (Council of Australian Governments, 2010); the Smarter Schools National Partnership for Improving Teacher Quality (Council of Australian Governments, 2013); new initiatives in initial teacher education (ITE) programs; and the Gonski report (Gonski et al., 2012), recommending an increased federal role in education funding; and the Australian Curriculum.

These were further strengthened by the Australian Education Act 2013 that took effect from 1 January 2014. The Act made Commonwealth funding to states and territories contingent upon the implementation of the Australian Curriculum and participation in the National Assessment Program—Literacy and Numeracy (NAPLAN). It is focused on improving teacher quality through the adoption by states and territories of the *Australian Teacher Performance and Development Framework* and the *Australian Charter for the Professional Learning of Teachers and School Leaders*, each of which is underpinned by the *Australian Professional Standards for Teachers (APST)* and the *Australian Professional Standard for Principals*.

About Australia

A look at Australia's geography and demography provides useful insights to key developments in education policy. Australia is a vast country, with a comparatively small population. It has a land mass of around 2.9 million square miles, comparable to that of the United States, yet its total population is around just 23.5 million. Australia's population distribution is heavily skewed towards the south-east of the country. The two most populous states, Victoria and New South Wales, account for over half the national population, and with two-thirds of these people living in the cities of Melbourne and Sydney. As described by one of the authors of this report: "If you considered Australia to be a house, everyone would be sitting on the front verandah."

The country has a very diverse population. Among its 23.5 million residents, around 1 in 4 was born overseas, and nearly 1 in 5 speak a language other than English at home. The most common non-English languages are (in order) Mandarin, Italian, Arabic, Cantonese, Greek, and Vietnamese. A little over half a million Australians, around 3%, identify as being of Aboriginal or Torres Strait Islander origin, the largest

Figure 1.2 Population Density of Australia.

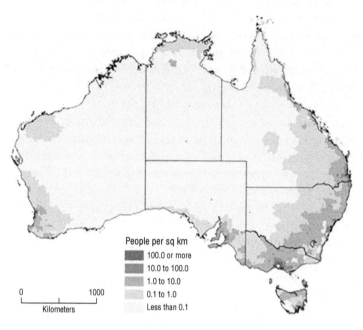

Reproduced from ABS, 2014b.

proportion of which live in New South Wales (32%) and Queensland (28%). Although just 10% of Aboriginal and Torres Strait Islanders live in the Northern Territory, they comprise 27% of the territory's population (see Figure 1.2, ABS, 2012b).

This combination of geography and demography gives states and territories different characteristics and contexts for learning, and provides challenges for the development of nationally consistent education. For example, NSW is the most populous state, has around one third of Australia's indigenous population, a large proportion of rural and remote schools, and around 30% of its students speak a language other than English at home. The Northern Territory is sparsely populated, with a median age lower than that of the national median, and the largest indigenous population per capita. Western Australia comprises a third of the land mass of Australia, and has a mix of petroleum, mining, and agricultural interests, and many small remote communities. By contrast, Victoria has an immigrant population much greater than that of the national average, with greater than one-third born abroad, very small remote and indigenous populations, and a diverse economy largely dominated by the services sector.

Aboriginal and Torres Strait Islanders tend to face greater challenges and fewer opportunities than their non-indigenous counterparts. For example, unemployment among indigenous Australians is considerably greater than among the non-indigenous population (17.2% versus 5.5%), while labor force participation is 20 percentage points lower (ABS, 2014d). Aboriginal and Torres Strait Islanders are also twice as likely to report fair or poor health (23.1% versus 11.8%), and face higher rates of mortality, heart disease, and other serious illnesses.

Remoteness plays a role in this. Around one-third of Australians live in regional and remote areas, which offer less diverse labor markets and access to fewer resources. In regional and remote areas, indigenous people make up a relatively large percentage of the population. Of all people who live in very remote areas, almost half (47%) are indigenous people while of those living in remote areas, 15% are indigenous (AIHW, 2014). However, this is less the case in NSW, where the great majority of Aboriginal and Torres Strait Islanders live in cities or regional towns.

Education is viewed as playing a very important role in increasing opportunities for indigenous Australians. For example, the Australian Bureau of Statistics found that closing the education gap would decrease the gap in labor force participation by half (ABS, 2014c). This is particularly important given that Aboriginal people make up a higher proportion of Australia's children and young people with a median age of 21, compared to that of 38 for the non-Aboriginal population.

Social Democratic Systems in Australia

The Melbourne Declaration reflects the importance placed on education in building and sustaining a democratic, equitable, and just society that is well placed to contribute to the global knowledge economy. The focus on developing students who are "successful learners, confident and creative individuals, and active and informed citizens" (MCEETYA, 2008), is a key role of education but there is also a strong awareness that the well-being of the whole child is essential and is a fundamental requirement of social policy.

Core national services that are designed to provide a safety net to underpin child well-being in Australia include health and social security support services. The nation has a system of legislation, policies, regulation, and funding to enable all people to access quality health services. Since the 1970s, the Australian government has funded a universal public health insurance scheme to provide free or subsidized health treatment (DHS, 2014). The program is supplemented by social welfare arrangements, such as smaller out-of-pocket costs and more generous safety nets for those who receive certain income-support payments (AIHW, 2012).

The Australian government also provides a range of social security payments and services, including income support payments, disability support, age pension support, youth allowances and study allowances, and rental assistance. Together, Australian social welfare contribution in 2014 represented 19% of GDP.

Australian Education in International Comparison

Schooling in Australia

Education in Australia is publicly funded, with all students having the right to a free education. Schooling is comprised of both government and nongovernment schools, the latter being further divided into Catholic and independent schools. Unlike many countries, all three systems receive public funding. The majority of students (65.1%) attend government schools, while around 20.6% and 14.3% attend Catholic and independent schools respectively (ABS, 2013). The percentage of students in nongovernment schools is higher at the secondary level.

Education in government schools is administered at the state level, and thus there is policy difference, such as the degree of centralization, that occur between states and territories. Nongovernment schools are also typically affiliated to systems administered at the state level. For example, Catholic schools in NSW are connected to the Catholic Education Commission of New South Wales, and are administered through 11 state level dioceses. Many independent schools in NSW have an affiliation with the Association of Independent Schools of NSW.[4] This organization of schooling facilitates the dissemination and implementation of policy and dispersion of funds across the systems.

Teaching and Teachers' Time in Australia

International data suggest that teachers in Australia work hours that are longer than average when compared to other OECD countries, but that this time favors greater involvement with colleagues in teaching and planning, and school management. The Teaching and Learning International survey (TALIS) found that Australian teachers worked an average of 42.7 hours a week, slightly longer than the TALIS average, but that the number of teaching hours was slightly fewer, at 18.6 a week. Australian teachers spent nearly twice the average number of weekly hours participating in school management (3.1 hours), and considerably more weekly hours than average working and in dialog with colleagues (3.5 hours) (OECD, 2014c, p. 387). Perhaps as a consequence, the TALIS report found that teachers in Australia were more likely to incorporate active teaching strategies— small group problem-solving, the use of ICT, and projects of longer than a week—into their teaching practices (OECD, 2014c, p. 155).

TALIS also surveyed teachers' views of the teaching profession. It found that nationwide, just 38.5% of lower secondary teachers thought that the teaching profession was valued in society (OECD, 2014c, p. 408). While this was greater than the TALIS average (30.9%), it shows that there is much that can be done to raise the attractiveness of teaching in Australia. Many of the national reforms outlined later in this report are intended to contribute to the professionalization and raise the status of teaching.

Teachers in Australia are paid reasonably competitively for their work. When compared with other countries, their salary is above the OECD mean, on a level comparable with teachers in Canada and the United States. However, the range of possible salaries is much narrower than in these countries. It takes as few as eight years to reach the top of the teacher salary scale in Australia, compared with an OECD average of twenty-four, and the ratio of the top-of-scale to starting salaries is just 1.44 in Australia, lower than the 1.68 in Canada, and 1.52–1.61 for teachers in the United States (OECD, 2015).

When compared with other occupations, overall, the teaching profession in Australia is paid slightly less than other professions with similar levels of education (around 90%) (OECD, 2015), a level similar to teachers in Canada and Finland, but above that of the OECD average. Teachers are well paid at the start of their careers, a factor which has helped maintain high levels of recruitment of teachers into the profession. A government-supported survey of occupations in 2012 found that new graduate teachers ranked 7th among 27 professional occupations in their level of compensation, behind several medical fields and engineering, but ahead of law, sciences, and accounting (Graduate Careers Australia, 2013).

However, the low salary ceiling means that teacher salaries have tended to fall behind those of other professions later in the career, with overall, teaching paid at around 90% of that of similarly qualified professions. This is a rate similar to that in high-performing countries such as Canada and Finland, and above the OECD average (see Figure 1.3). In response, several states have recently revised their salary structures to significantly increase the pay of veteran teachers who meet standards of accomplishment aligned with professional teaching standards.

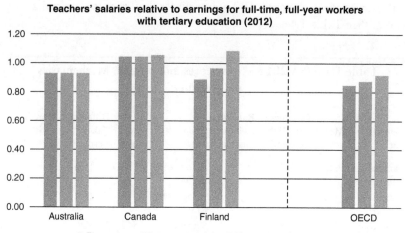

Figure 1.3 Teacher Salaries Relative to
Other Occupations.

Teachers' salaries relative to earnings for full-time, full-year workers
with tertiary education (2012)

■ Elementary   ■ Lower secondary   ■ Upper secondary

Source: OECD. (2014). *Education at a Glance 2014*. OECD Publishing.

International Educational Performance and Comparisons

Australia's relative education performance has had an important bearing on educational policy discussion. As a nation, Australia's performance on international assessments such as the Programme for International Student Assessment (PISA) has been comparatively strong. In PISA 2012, Australia scored well above the OECD average, placing it among the top 20 jurisdictions in each of mathematics, reading, and science. It had an above average share of top performers, with 14.7% scoring in Bands 5 and 6 on PISA mathematics (c.f. OECD mean of 11.9%), and a smaller than average share of low performers, with 19.6% performing below Band 2 (c.f. OECD mean of 26.0%) (OECD, 2014b, p. 298).

However, Australia's performance on PISA has also declined over time. From 2003 to 2012, the mean score in PISA mathematics dropped by 20 points. This included a decrease in the proportion of top performers (Bands 5 and 6), and an increase in low performers (those scoring in below Band 2) (OECD, 2014b; Thomson, De Bortoli, & Buckley, 2014).

Furthermore, within Australia, there are important differences in performance across states and territories. In PISA Reading, five states (the Australian Capital Territory, Western Australia, Victoria, New South Wales, and Queensland) scored statistically significantly higher than the

OECD average, while Tasmania and the Northern Territory scored significantly lower. The spread of reading scores was especially large in the Northern Territory. At 413, the difference between those of the 5th and 95th percentiles was nearly 100 points wider than that for Australia as a whole. (See Table 1.1).

Table 1.1 PISA 2012 Mean Scores and Spread: Mathematics and Reading.

Country/ state	Mean score	Difference 5th–95th percentile	Ranking within Australia	Country/ state	Mean score	Difference 5th–95th percentile	Ranking within Australia
Shanghai-China	613	331		Shanghai-China	570	259	
Singapore	573	344		Hong Kong-China	545	281	
Hong Kong-China	561	318		Singapore	542	329	
Finland	519	281		Australia Capital Territory	525	339	1
Canada	518	293		Finland	524	309	
Australia Capital Territory	518	319	1	Canada	523	305	
Western Australia	516	303	2	Western Australia	519	307	2
New South Wales	509	336	3	Victoria	517	302	3
Australia	504	315		New South Wales	513	332	4
Queensland	53	305	4	Australia	512	318	
Victoria	501	299	5	Queensland	508	317	5
OECD average	494	301		South Australia	500	301	6
United Kingdom	494	312		United Kingdom	499	320	
South Australia	489	299	6	United States	498	303	
United States	481	295		OECD average	496	310	
Tasmania	478	317	7	Tasmania	485	329	7
Northern Territory	452	368	8	Northern Territory	466	413	8

Thomson, De Bortoli, & Buckley, 2014.

Educational performance over time has also varied by state. Victoria was the only Australian jurisdiction in which scores did not decline from 2000 to 2012. Although PISA mathematics scores from 2003 to 2012 fell for all Australia jurisdictions, these declines were less precipitous in Victoria and NSW than in most other Australian jurisdictions (Thomson, De Bortoli, & Buckley, 2014).

Concern regarding flagging international education competitiveness has provided impetus to federal policy initiatives in Australia (Patty, 2013), including a renewed focus on teaching quality and standards (Dinham, Ingvarson, & Kleinhenz, 2008). Raising its performance on international assessments such as PISA have become a national education goal, embedded both in the rationale for, and the wording of, the Australian Education Act 2013 (*see also* Box 1.1.), as noted by then Prime Minister Julia Gillard:

> This is why I announce today that before the end of this year, I will introduce a bill to our Parliament: To enshrine our nation's expectations for what we will achieve for our children, our vision of the quality of education to which our children are entitled and our preparedness to put success for every child at the heart of how we deliver and fund education.
>
> By 2025, I want Australian schools to be back in the top five schooling systems in the world.
>
> By 2025, Australia should be ranked as a top 5 country in the world in Reading, Science and Mathematics—and for providing our children with a high-quality and high-equity education system.
>
> (Gillard, 2012)
>
> [T]he Australian schooling system is [defined to be] highly equitable if there is a limited relationship between a student's socioeconomic status and his or her educational performance, as measured by the Programme for International Student Assessment.
>
> (Commonwealth of Australia, 2013)

PISA and TIMSS (together with Australia's NAPLAN assessment) were specifically listed as performance and assessment requirements in the National Education Agreement (2010) between the Australian government and the states.

Box 1.1 Goals of the Australian Education Act 2013

3. Objects of this Act
   1. The objects of this Act are the following:
      a. to ensure that the Australian schooling system provides a high quality and highly equitable education for all students by having regard to the following national targets:
         i. for Australia to be placed, by 2025, in the top 5 highest performing countries based on the performance of school students in reading, mathematics and science;
         ii. for the Australian schooling system to be considered a high quality and highly equitable schooling system by international standards by 2025;
         iii. lift the Year 12 (or equivalent) or Certificate II attainment rate to 90% by 2015;
         iv. lift the Year 12 (or equivalent) or Certificate III attainment rate to 90% by 2020;
         v. at least halve the gap between Aboriginal and Torres Strait Islander students, and other students, in Year 12 or equivalent attainment rates by 2020 from the baseline in 2006;
         vi. halve the gap between Aboriginal and Torres Strait Islander students, and other students, in reading, writing and numeracy by 2018 from the baseline in 2008;
      b. to acknowledge the matters referred to in the Preamble;
      c. to provide a needs-based funding model for schools applied consistently across all schools which includes:
         i. a base amount of funding for every student; and
         ii. additional loadings for students and schools who need extra support;
      d. to implement the National Plan for School Improvement.

Source: Australian Education Act, 2013.

Comparative performance has also influenced policy discussions at the state level. In Victoria, lack of growth in international scores despite investments in capacity building during the same period informed the state's thinking in making the case for increasing school autonomy, identifying central direction inhibiting local decision-making around teaching practice, curriculum, assessment, and reporting as factors hindering growth in student outcomes (DEECD, 2012c). Interestingly, this movement in Victoria towards further decentralization at the state level occurred simultaneously with a countertrend towards centralization of policies at the national level in key areas of curriculum, assessment, and teacher registration, discussed later in this chapter.

Education and Equity

Australia is regarded as a high-equity country by some measures. The country has lower than average between-school variance, and the strength of the relationship between students' socioeconomic background (SES) and mathematics performance on PISA is relatively low. Nationally, SES explained just 12.3% of the variation in PISA mathematics scores, lower than the 14.6% average for all OECD countries. Among states, the strength of relationship in Victoria was weakest, with SES explaining just 9% of the variation in mathematics scores, placing it line with other high-equity jurisdictions, such as Canada, Finland, and Hong Kong (Thomson, De Bortoli, & Buckley, 2014). See Figure 1.4.

Figure 1.4 Quality and Equity of Performance in Mathematical Literacy Internationally.

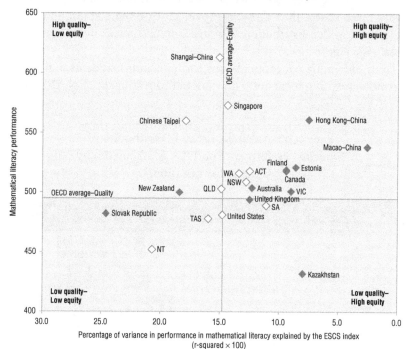

Note: Shaded diamonds represent countries in which the strength of the relationship is significantly different to the OECD average.

Reproduced from Thomson, De Bortoli, & Buckley, 2014.

However, these data mask important equity challenges that exist across five principal axes: school sector, indigenous status, immigrant status, remoteness, and socioeconomic status. Students in Catholic and Independent schools, for example, tend to perform comparatively better on international assessments than their counterparts in government schools (Thomson, De Bortoli, & Buckley, 2014), although analysis of PISA data indicate this is largely attributable to the higher SES of private school students (Mahuteau et al., 2010). While first-generation students, interestingly, tend to perform better than those from nonimmigrant backgrounds, there is also wide variance across subgroups (ACARA, 2013a; Thomson, De Bortoli, & Buckley, 2014).

The greatest disparities in educational outcomes occur across indigenous status. Despite recent improvements in retention and achievement—the proportion of Aboriginal and Torres Strait Islander students completing Year 12 or higher qualifications increased from 30% to 37% from 2006 to 2011 (ABS, 2012a, 2013; ACARA, 2013a)—PISA data show a 90-point difference between indigenous and non-indigenous students, estimated to be equivalent to more than two-and-a-half years of schooling (Thomson, De Bortoli, & Buckley, 2014). Remoteness contributes to these gaps. Students in metropolitan areas had significantly higher mean scores than those in provincial or remote areas, and there was a much wider distribution of scores among students living in remote areas. (See Figure 1.5).

Thus addressing educational gaps for indigenous students and those in remote areas is a focal point for national educational policy. Different

Figure 1.5 Mean Scores and Distribution of Students' Performance on PISA Mathematics by Geographic Location.

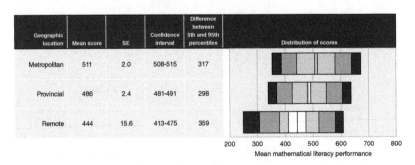

Geographic location	Mean score	SE	Confidence interval	Difference between 5th and 95th percentiles	Distribution of scores
Metropolitan	511	2.0	508-515	317	
Provincial	486	2.4	481-491	298	
Remote	444	15.6	413-475	359	

Reproduced from Thomson, De Bortoli, & Buckley, 2014.

emphases may be placed on their implementation at the state level, given the great differences in indigenous populations and remoteness among states and territories. For example, just 2% of students in Victoria identify as Aboriginal or Torres Strait Islander, compared with over 40% in the Northern Territory (ABS, 2013).

The Melbourne Declaration underscores the need to address both excellence and equity, and emphasis over the past decade has been on nationally agreed policies. Yet within each state the diversity of student needs and educational priorities influences the way these policies become manifest in the state-based education systems across Australia. These national and state policies are addressed in the remainder of this volume.

Professional Teaching Standards and the Role of AITSL

Much of the emphasis of education policy to achieve the goals of the Melbourne Declaration, and address the above challenges, has been directed at improving teaching quality. The formation of AITSL (the Australian Institute for Teaching and School Leadership), and with it the introduction of the national professional standards for teaching (Link 1-2), is perhaps the most significant development shaping teaching quality and the nature of the teaching profession in Australia.

Progressively phased in from 2010, the standards influence those who graduate as teachers and enter the classroom, how they are trained, the induction they receive upon graduation, and their ongoing professional development. In the coming years, they will also influence those who apply to become teachers, and their ongoing career pathway in teaching. The implementation of standards nationally is also intended to contribute to a more equitable foundation for teaching quality through the development of high quality systems through each state and territory.

Development of the Professional Teaching Standards

The process by which AITSL and the standards were developed has played a role in their influence. Firstly, prior to 2010, teacher registration was solely a state level responsibility, with significant variability. States such as Victoria and NSW already had in place professional teaching standards: Victoria required registration for all teachers; NSW required registration only for those beginning after 1 October 2004 with evidence of their teaching proficiency. Meanwhile, states such as South Australia had teacher registration, but this was not backed by an established set of state teaching standards.

Early foundational work in the development of national teaching standards was carried out by a predecessor body to AITSL—Teaching Australia—originally established as the National Institute for Teaching and School Leadership. Its mandate was to consult nationally with the teaching profession and to build a set of national standards based on those already developed by various teacher professional associations (Thomas & Watson, 2011). However, parallel efforts were also being simultaneously undertaken by other organizations, including state employing authorities, which were seeking to achieve national consensus on teaching standards through the Ministerial Council (MCEETYA) (Thomas & Watson, 2011).

AITSL was established by the Ministerial Council in agreement with the federal government in late 2009 as a government agency, disestablishing Teaching Australia and taking on the role of developing and validating the national teaching standards (Thomas & Watson, 2011). This was done through a process of broad consultation with teacher regulatory authorities, unions and professional associations, and through surveys and focus groups with teachers and principals from around Australia. Thus the standards drew heavily on knowledge from within the teaching profession. As a result, the standards were seen as having strong validity and efficacy by the teaching profession.

Secondly, AITSL itself draws on expertise from educators. Its board at formation represented a broad cross-section of education stakeholders, including universities, schools, departments of education, Catholic and independent education offices, the Australian Education Union, and principal professional associations. More recently it has been streamlined to a smaller group. This unique governance structure connects federal and state education ministers with institutes of teaching and members of the teaching profession, providing the potential for knowledge sharing throughout the system.

Some education commentators have contended that the establishment of AITSL signaled a move from a purely teacher-led set of standards to one that combines these with the interests of government as employing authorities, and therefore represents a fusion of the discourse around teaching quality with that of quality assurance and accountability (Thomas & Watson, 2011), a fact that is noted in the preamble to the standards themselves (AITSL, 2011b). Others, such as former AITSL Chair Tony Mackay, have noted that developing the standards in this way represents an important step in engaging a more comprehensive and representative scope of the profession, and thereby strengthening the authority and legitimacy of both AITSL and the standards.

> The way which [AITSL has] gone about the work has been through really strong collaborative activity, strong cooperation across the states and territories in the sectors, [and] full partnership of the profession... If you ever think that you can (be legitimized) without the profession seeing themselves as being absolutely fundamental to both the development of the policy as well as the implementation,... it's impossible.

The Australian Professional Standards for Teachers (APST)

The standards are informed by evidence describing the key areas of teachers' work. The standards describe action across three teaching domains: professional knowledge, professional practice, and professional engagement. The seven standards and 37 focus areas under the APST outline what teachers are expected to know and be able to do at each of four different career levels: Graduate, Proficient, Highly Accomplished, and Lead. The seven standards are:

1. Know students and how they learn
2. Know the content and how to teach it
3. Plan for and implement effective teaching and learning
4. Create and maintain supportive learning environments
5. Assess, provide feedback and report on student learning
6. Engage in professional learning
7. Engage professionally with colleagues, parents/careers and the community

The standards have several declared purposes. Among them is to make explicit the elements that constitute high-quality and effective teaching that will improve student outcomes, and to provide a common discourse to describe the expectations for teachers both within the teaching profession, and among other education stakeholders (AITSL, 2011b). The standards may also contribute to the professionalization of teaching, as the document itself notes:

> Developing professional standards for teachers that can guide professional learning, practice and engagement facilitates the improvement of teacher quality and contributes positively to the public standing of the profession.

> (AITSL, 2011b)

The Graduate level of the standards plays an important role in the accreditation of initial teacher education (ITE) programs. It establishes the standards that graduates from ITE are expected to achieve by the completion of their course. Similarly, the Proficient level of the standards provides the basis for teacher registration. It sets a pathway for graduate teachers to move from provisional to full registration in their first years of teaching, and in doing so helps establish expectations for the outcomes of teacher induction. Highly Accomplished teachers are those that demonstrate a high level of capability in the standards, while Lead teachers are those that demonstrate these capabilities not just individually, but show leadership across the school. These higher levels of the standards—not yet adopted by all states–inform voluntary certification, but three jurisdictions have now tied them to salary increases.

One of the most important functions of the standards is to provide a common framework to inform teacher conversations around professional learning centered on student learning. It is intended that the standards be used as a basis for teachers to "judge the success of their learning and assist self-reflection and self-assessment" (AITSL, 2011b).

Implementation and Impact of the Standards

All states and territories in Australia are now required to implement the Australian Professional Standards for Teachers, although the extent of functional implementation varies across states. The Australian standards were well informed by those in place in NSW and Victoria, and these states were thus better positioned to adapt their systems to national standards.

The standards have had four important impacts upon teaching and teaching quality. Firstly, they have provided a common language to describe teaching quality. As they have been progressively adopted by the profession, it has helped shape the nature of conversations between early career and more experienced teachers to help inform improvement in their teaching practice.

Secondly, it has helped bridge differences between states in the required standards for teachers. Although registration remains a state responsibility, the standards now underpin a nationally consistent approach.

Thirdly, the standards help link initial teacher education with in-service professional development and career development. Establishing the first level as Graduate Teacher, the standards connect expectations in teacher knowledge, practice, and engagement for new graduates with that of the profession. The Proficient Teacher level lays the foundation for standards-based induction and mentoring for early career teachers, setting up a pattern of ongoing professional learning beyond graduation. The higher levels offer a pathway for teachers to continue developing their expertise and advance their career while remaining in the classroom. As illustrated by former AITSL Chair Tony Mackay, finding coherence among policies that drive each of the phases of the teaching career is important in raising learning outcomes:

> If you don't get a system of teacher quality and leadership quality thinking about all of the dimensions of that (initial teacher education, pedagogy, leadership development), it's very hard to be able to drive forward an agenda that really is going to have some leverage over quality learning for all young people.

Fourthly and relatedly, it has facilitated increased consistency of teacher training programs. The majority of initial teacher education in Australia takes place in universities, which must now demonstrate that their programs meet certain content requirements consistent with the standards. This is necessary if their graduates are to be permitted to become registered to teach in schools (see below).

Australian Professional Standard for Principals

The development of the teaching standards is part of a systemic approach to influencing teaching quality in Australia. Together with these teaching standards has been the development of a national standard for principals (Link 1-3).

In recognition of the critical relationship between effective school leadership and teacher quality, in 2011, AITSL developed the *Australian Professional Standard for Principals*. In developing the standard, AITSL drew upon both research evidence regarding the characteristics of effective school leadership and significant national consultation with school leadership associations and state and jurisdictional employers. As a result the standard has been ratified by each state and territory education minister as well as being widely accepted within the profession.

The standard has provided a professionally agreed-on public statement describing what principals are required to know, understand, and do to succeed in leading improvement within their school. It is represented as an integrated model that recognizes three leadership requirements that a principal draws upon, within five areas of professional practice. (See Figure 1.6.)

Figure 1.6 Conceptual Framework for the
Australian Professional Standard for Principals.

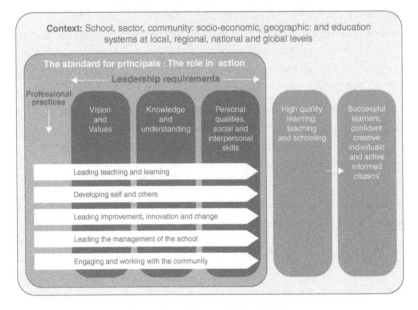

Reproduced from AITSL, 2011c.

Much like the professional teaching standards, the *Australian Professional Standard for Principals* has provided clarity of understanding and a common language to describe and promote effective school leadership. The standard has also enabled the development and sharing of professional learning and resources across Australia.

A set of *Leadership Profiles* has been developed to describe the five professional practices at gradually increasing levels of proficiency. The profiles are intended to provide a framework to support the growth and development of school leaders.

Importantly, the *Australian Professional Standard for Principals* and the *Leadership Profiles* do not describe school leadership as an administrative role. There is a significant focus on the role of the school leader in promoting, developing, and supporting teaching to impact student learning (AITSL, 2014a).

The standard is being widely used by professional associations as a framework for professional learning for current and aspiring school leaders, and is able to be used to support performance and development frameworks for school leaders.

Box 1.2 The Australian Professional Standard for Principals and Leadership Profiles

The standard sets out what principals are expected to know, understand and do to succeed in their work and to ensure their leadership has a positive impact. It takes full account of the crucial contribution made by principals in:

❑ raising student achievement at all levels and all stages

❑ promoting equity and excellence

❑ creating and sustaining the conditions under which quality teaching and learning thrive

❑ influencing, developing and delivering upon community expectations and government policy

❑ contributing to the development of a twenty-first century education system at local, national and international levels

Research and a substantial and evolving body of knowledge inform the leadership requirements and the professional practices that are at the core of the standard and show that:

❑ effective leaders understand their impact

❑ leadership must be contextualized, learning-centered, and responsive to the diverse nature of Australia's schools

❑ leadership is distributed and collaborative with teams led by the principal, working together to accomplish the vision and aims of the school

❑ the practices and capabilities of leaders evolve as leaders move through their careers

❑ almost all successful leaders draw on the same repertoire of basic leadership practices and behaviors, with some key personal qualities and capabilities explaining a significant amount of the variation in leadership effectiveness

(Source: Australian Professional Standard for Principals and Leadership Profiles, AITSL, 2014a)

Initial Teacher Education

Although teachers work in state-regulated education systems, initial teacher training (ITE) is predominantly a federal responsibility, a consequence of the Australian government's funding of higher education.

Teacher training is conducted primarily by universities (and a smaller number of other authorized providers). This has been the case for nearly 30 years, since the incorporation of the Advanced Colleges of Education into the university sector in 1987. Australia-wide, there are 406 ITE programs at 48 institutions (37 of which are universities) (AITSL, 2015). AITSL regulates the quality of ITE programs by establishing the national professional standards for teaching and the processes for accreditation of ITE programs.

Accreditation of Initial Teacher Education Programs

Nominally, universities have academic autonomy in determining the content of ITE programs. However, graduates are only eligible to register as teachers if they graduate from an accredited program, and this acts as a strong disincentive for providers to offer nonaccredited programs. Thus accreditation processes are contributing to shaping the curricular content of ITE programs.[5]

AITSL itself does not accredit ITE programs. Accreditation is conducted by the eight state and territory organizations, such as the Victorian Institute of Teaching, and NSW's Board of Studies, Teaching and Educational Standards. The main purpose of accreditation is to ensure that ITE programs prepare teacher candidates with the knowledge and skills expected of a graduate teacher as laid out by the national professional standards for teachers. The involves document review and site visits, and is informed by the principles of: continuous improvement; outcomes focus; flexibility, diversity, and innovation; partnerships; building on existing expertise; and evidence (AITSL, 2013).

Support for Teacher Education

The Australian government underwrites the majority of the cost of teacher education. Most universities are federally funded public universities, and private universities also receive some government funds. Some prospective teachers enrolling in ITE are eligible for Commonwealth Supported Places. This means that instead of charging students full tuition fees, the bulk of the full cost of program is funded by the Australian government, and teacher candidates pay a partial cost, known as the student contribution. This varies by university and program, but is typically around one-third of the full cost.

For example, at Deakin University in Victoria, the indicative annual fee for a Bachelor of Education (Primary) qualification is A$23,680. The student contribution for core curricular units is 31.3%, meaning that the expected student contribution is of the order of A$7,400 per annum.[6]

Teacher candidates may also receive grants, loans, and financial support from the Australian government through the combined Higher Education Contribution Scheme and Higher Education Loans Program (HECS-HELP). Under these programs, university students (including teacher candidates) receiving Commonwealth Supported Places may borrow the student contribution portion of the cost of their studies from the government, as a deferred, income-contingent, tax liability. Full–fee paying students may also be eligible for federal government loans to help with tuition fees. In each case, interest pegged to the consumer price index is charged on these loans at an average rate of 3% per annum, and graduates make automatic payments through income tax once they are employed and earning above a threshold amount (around A$47,000). Repayment rates vary from 4% to 8% depending on the salary level, but typically around 5% per annum for a beginning teacher.

The Australian government has moved to expand equity of access to higher education, including teacher education. It adopted recommendations to "uncap" the number of Commonwealth Supported Places in 2012. This was intended to lower financial barriers to particularly students from indigenous, remote, or lower socioeconomic communities (Bradley, Noonan, Nugent, & Scales, 2008).

However, this also means that universities are able to determine the number of places they can offer in undergraduate courses, incentivized to do so by federal funding. An unanticipated effect is that entry numbers into teacher training programs reflect only weakly the needs of the labor market, and can contribute to shortages in some areas, and excesses in others, as the University of Melbourne's Professor Dinham articulated in a 2013 article:

> Some universities have reacted to this "free for all" by greatly expanding their places and offers for teacher candidates, at a time when there is an oversupply of primary teachers and long waiting lists for employment more generally ... Put simply, we are training too many primary teachers and these resources would be better spent targeting areas of shortage.
>
> (Dinham, 2013)

Selection into Initial Teacher Education Programs

Teachers in Australia require a minimum of four years of tertiary education, which must include both discipline studies and teacher professional studies. Teacher candidates can choose to train at the undergraduate or graduate level. There are several different models of study:

- ○ A four-year undergraduate degree in education, such as the Bachelor of Education
- ○ A three- or four-year undergraduate degree followed by a teacher qualification. These may be a one-year Diploma of Teaching (being phased out), or a Master of Teaching (typically two years)
- ○ A combined or double-degree program, such as Bachelor of Teaching/Bachelor of Arts

Candidates may also incorporate specializations, such as indigenous education, into their programs (AITSL, 2014b). Applicants typically apply via state Universities Admissions Centers, organizations that function as intermediaries between applicants and the university sector, allowing potential students to submit applications to multiple universities and programs.

Entry to each ITE program is determined by each university or provider, although national guidelines stipulate the standard expected of teacher candidates by graduation. Previously, academic performance has typically been the main criteria, although some universities have also used written submission and interviews.[7] However, universities' entry ATAR scores (Australian Tertiary Admissions Rank)—a measure of relative rank among a high school cohort, used for entry to most undergraduate programs—showed considerable variation between universities, campuses, and even programs. Despite a recent trend towards graduate-entry courses (AITSL, 2015), analysis of ATAR data also showed that the average ATAR entry of undergraduates had declined (AITSL, 2014b), with concern from some quarters that this could challenge efforts to raise the status of teaching and recruit high-quality individuals into teaching (Dinham, 2013).

A second shift is efforts towards greater inclusion of personal qualities and attributes as part of selection into initial teacher education. (See also new reforms below.) This position was supported by union representatives we interviewed, who suggested that selection should combine both strong academic abilities as well as aptitude for teaching, such as strong communication skills. Some universities already incorporate these elements. For example, the University of Melbourne uses a Teacher Selector Tool to supplement its Master of Teaching admissions criteria for its Master of Teaching program. The tool asks candidates a series of questions that range from literacy and numeracy skills and spatial reasoning, to communication style, cultural sensitivity, and ethics. It gives a 0–6 rating on each of several dimensions, including conscientiousness, agreeability, openness, and persistence, allowing comparisons between candidates and population averages.

While accreditation processes serve an important quality check on the inputs to teacher education programs, the national government has begun to enact addition reforms to provide greater quality assurance of the outputs, launching the Teacher Education Ministerial Advisory Group in 2014.

Ongoing Developments—Initial Teacher Education Reform

A new and major policy plank of the federal government is the Students First approach to strengthening education, and highlighting the need to lift the quality, professionalization, and status of the teaching profession. A major initiative is in the area of teaching quality via the Teacher Education Ministerial Advisory Group (TEMAG). Comprised of members from the universities and schools sectors, TEMAG was established in February 2014 to provide evidence-informed advice to the federal government on how teacher education courses could be improved. Its report Action Now: Classroom Ready Teachers (Link 1-4) was released in early 2015, with 38 recommendations aimed at strengthening ITE programs and the accreditation processes, all but one of which was taken up by the federal government.

The key message emerging from the findings of TEMAG is that while Australia has a high quality teaching workforce, there is scope for establishing guidelines and regulatory systems to enhance both the quality and consistency of teacher education courses. Excellent practices exist where providers deliver evidence-backed programs that are constantly reviewed and improved, but reforms were needed to address considerable variation in the quality of the courses.

AITSL has been charged with leading these new reforms, which will have significant implications for ITE from 2016, and are grouped under the following eight areas:

- ○ *Accreditation:* the standards and procedures for guiding the accreditation of ITE programs by state-based authorities. There is an emphasis on providers being able to more clearly demonstrate the impact their ITE programs have on student learning.

- ○ *Selection:* transparent selection criteria will form part of ITE accreditation. Providers should use both academic and non-academic criteria—motivation to teacher, interpersonal and communication skills, conscientiousness—as part of selection, and evidence how their measures contribute to their effectiveness.

o *Primary specialization:* although primary teachers will continue to be trained and work as generalists, they will take a specialization in mathematics, science, or languages during their ITE. The intent is that deeper disciplinary knowledge will enable teachers to share expertise with colleagues, improve outcomes for students, and in turn increase student take-up of these priority subjects during senior schooling.

o *Professional experience:* AITSL will develop model university-school partnerships to increase communication, and provide greater consistency and transparency of professional experience during training. Partnerships will clarify the skills and activities pre-service teachers should experience during their professional placement, and the methods of assessment.

o *Literacy and numeracy tests:* Graduate teachers are expected to have literacy and numeracy skills equivalent to the top 30% of the population. All graduate teachers will be required to sit a personal literacy and numeracy test. Nationwide implementation will begin from July 2016.

o *Graduate assessment:* in addition to tests of knowledge, AITSL will develop new assessment tools for graduate teachers that reflects the skills in practice that teachers should possess before entering the classroom.

o *Induction:* although together the national professional standards and teacher registration processes shape induction practices, there is still much variability. AITSL will work with states to develop a nationally consistent approach to induction. Early AITSL research indicates longer (up to two-years), individualized but standards-based, peer- and mentor-supported induction is most effective (Deloitte, 2015).

AITSL has the key responsibility for the introduction of these initiatives, but will require the assistance of state-based regulatory bodies for their implementation.

In releasing the findings of the TEMAG report the federal Education Minister noted that he saw considerable scope in the practical nature of the reforms:

> Action Now: Classroom Ready Teachers is a landmark development in the quest to improve teaching quality in Australia. TEMAG's

recommendations are far reaching, but sensible, practical, and mainstream. They are entirely achievable and this Government is determined to have them implemented. Consequently, our response has avoided creating new institutions, but rather built on existing ones that are respected and have the expertise to implement the recommendations. We understand that improving teaching quality is a national issue needing a coordinated response that must use all the resources and advantages of our federal system. This is why we will work collaboratively with the states and territories and their respective accrediting bodies. It also requires the support from other stakeholders—deans of education, academics, primary and secondary principals, parents and the teaching profession itself. TEMAG may not be the last teacher inquiry in our lifetime, but it will be the one that will lead to real improvements in the quality of teaching in Australia. That is what we all want.

(Pyne, 2015)

Nontraditional Certification: Teach for Australia

A further move by the Commonwealth government has been to provide ongoing funding for the Teach for Australia movement increasing its investment by A$22 million to A$57 million by 2018. The program seeks to attract high-caliber individuals into teaching, and offer work-based training while placed in remote or difficult-to-fill teaching positions. Initially, teacher trainees received a six-week initial training course at the Melbourne Graduate School of Education (MGSE) followed by support from Clinical Specialists and Teaching and Leadership Advisors while on placement in schools, along with an in-school mentor. The program has since moved to Deakin University in Victoria.

Teach for Australia presently operates in Victoria, ACT, and the Northern Territory, but not all states have accepted the program. In NSW for example, senior government officials have firmly resisted the adoption of the program, expressing the view that children in the state, particularly those in high-need areas, should only be taught by teachers that have completed a four-year training program. The president of the NSW Board of Studies, Teaching, and Educational Standards has stated that all teachers should be fully prepared and as such they are yet to endorse the Teach for Australia model, a step that would be required for program participants to register to teach (Dodd, 2014).

The Teach for Australia program has drawn criticism from other universities as well as quarters such as the Australian Education Union (AEU), which argue that the program is more expensive than traditional teacher training pathways and incurs higher dropout rates. These assertions were supported by a government evaluation report into the program, although based on the early experiences of the first three program cohorts. However, the same report also highlighted that as an alternative pilot program, it may contribute to informing teacher education in Australia by highlighting the importance of rigorous selection processes, reduced teaching loads to retain beginning teachers, and the importance of ongoing support during the induction phase (Weldon et al., 2013).

Role of ACARA

A second prominent national education body is ACARA, the Australian Curriculum Assessment and Reporting Authority. ACARA was established in 2008 with a mandate to: "develop and administer a national school curriculum," "develop and administer national assessments," "collect manage and analyze student assessment data," and "publish information relating to school education, including information relating to comparative school performance" (Australian Government, 2008). In establishing a federal role for what is taught, and what is tested, ACARA's influence has already been pivotal in each of its two main responsibility areas.

Assessment

In the area of assessment, ACARA is responsible for the *National Assessment Program—Literacy and Numeracy*, known as NAPLAN. These are annual tests conducted for all Australian students in May of each year,[8] in grades 3, 5, 7, and 9, and in the areas of reading, writing, spelling, grammar and punctuation, and numeracy. NAPLAN does not test specific content of a state's curriculum, but is rather intended to assess skills in numeracy and literacy developed over time. Testing began in 2008, with responsibility passed to ACARA from 2010. Australia does not have a history of national testing (Mayer, Pecheone, & Merino, 2012), and thus the introduction of NAPLAN represented a significant shift in posture on this issue.

More controversial than the tests themselves however is how these data are used. ACARA hosts the MySchool website, which posts NAPLAN data for nearly every school in Australia. It is indicative of a broader trend nationally towards a focus on educational outcomes.

MySchool, first posted in 2010, shows annual scores on NAPLAN for each grade and year tested. The website allows for easy analysis of mean scores, of distributions across the six NAPLAN achievement bands, of student growth across a two-year period, and of school funding data. The website's built-in functionality also facilitates comparison either with all schools in Australia, or with 60 statistically similar schools, based on a community's comparative social and educational advantage (Gable & Lingard, 2013).

Early in its implementation, there were concerns that the data could be used to rank schools. For teachers, there was some concern that data could be used to reward or punish teachers based on performance. Mayer, Pecheone, and Merino (2012) noted that recommendations for teacher testing emerged following poor results in the first round of NAPLAN in 2008, although this plan was ultimately dropped in 2011. Vigorous opposition from the Australian Education Union saw an agreement reached with the federal government over the appropriate use of NAPLAN data.

NAPLAN is used nationally as a check on system performance. In states such as Victoria and NSW, growth in NAPLAN scores is also a common goal in school strategic plans. Teachers in Victoria are also appraised at the school level and in part based on their contribution to these strategic goals. Thus NAPLAN seems set to play an important ongoing role in the context of federal and state policy.

Curriculum

Process of Establishing the Australian Curriculum

Through ACARA, a national curriculum framework was developed and finalized in 2010, and is being phased in in each of the states, territories, and school systems. The establishment of the Australian Curriculum represents a significant political achievement, having been a recurring, and at times, contentious debate in Australian education since the early 1980s. The closest previous attempt came in the late 1980s, with education's contribution to economic productivity the driving rationale (Brennan, 2011; Gable & Lingard, 2013). While draft curricula were produced, consensus was not able to be reached among states. Australia is the only country in the OECD with a federal government structure to have a national curriculum (Drabsch, 2013, pp. 2–3).

Renewed impetus for a national curriculum began in 2001 with the election of a new national education minister and the enactment of the Schools Assistance Act, which included agreement for a national assessment plan (later NAPLAN) (Watt, 2009).

The Australian Curriculum drew on existing state curricula. It is an ongoing project, with the curriculum being evaluated, reviewed, and updated (most recently in 2015). Its implementation has been phased, beginning with English, Mathematics, and Science, and followed by other subject areas.

The development of the Australian Curriculum began with parallel efforts, and is connected to the study of history in Australian schools. The council of education ministers (MCEETYA) undertook a study of curricular content in states and territories in 2002, and later developed the Statements of Learning (2004–2006) for states to implement into curricula from 2008. Meanwhile, the Australian Council for Educational Research (ACER) was tasked with studying the consistency of states' curricular content. It found many commonalities in mathematics, English, and the sciences, but no such consistency in Australian history (Watt, 2009), with each states' curricula reflecting their own. This led to a national level summit on history education, which in turn opened a wider debate on the Australian Curriculum, ultimately leading to the establishment of ACARA in 2008 and the production of the Australian Curriculum.

The way in which curriculum is implemented is largely determined at the state level. While the Australian Curriculum establishes learning areas, general capabilities, and cross-curricular priorities, senior school qualifications is a state-level responsibility. Thus states retain the flexibility to design courses in order to meet content standards, and likewise retain authority over whether and how to report against the general capabilities (ACARA, 2012). States also retain responsibility for assessing and credentialing against the curriculum.

The development of the Australian Curriculum has emphasized a consensus-building approach among state and school systems. Some states have adopted the Australian Curriculum in its full form, while others have incorporated it into their own state curricula. In NSW for example, the Board of Studies, Teaching and Educational Standards (BOSTES) has developed syllabus documents from the NSW curriculum that incorporate the Australian Curriculum. In Victoria, the existing Victoria Essential Learning Standards (VELS) were incorporated into the Australian Curriculum framework to create "AusVELS," which has now developed into a new Victorian Curriculum to be taught from 2017. Moreover, each school in Australia develops its own curriculum programs and resources, to address the learning areas, standards, and priorities of Australian Curriculum.

The Australian Curriculum and Its Form

The Australian Curriculum reflects a combination of 21st-century learning competencies, with traditional subject disciplines and a set of priorities unique to Australia's context. Its aims are reflected in the Melbourne Declaration:

- o A solid foundation in knowledge, skills and understandings, and values on which further learning and adult life can be built
- o Deep knowledge, understanding, skills and values that will enable advanced learning and an ability to create new ideas and translate them into practical applications
- o General capabilities that underpin flexible and analytical thinking, a capacity to work with others and an ability to move across subject disciplines to develop new expertise.

(MCEETYA, 2008)

The Curriculum identifies three dimensions: "discipline-based learning areas, general capabilities as essential 21st-century skills and contemporary cross-curriculum priorities" (ACARA, 2012).

The general capabilities prioritized are literacy, numeracy, and abilities with information and communication technology (ICT), but also include ethical and intercultural understanding, personal and social abilities, and critical and creative thinking. The three cross-curriculum priorities—Aboriginal and Torres Strait Islander histories and culture, Asia and Australia's engagement with Asia, and sustainability—reflect areas regarded as of high importance and contemporary relevance to Australia. The capabilities and priorities are intended to be woven throughout the key learning areas to enrich the curriculum, although teachers have flexibility in how these are integrated.

There are eight discipline-based key learning areas: English, mathematics, science, humanities and social science, the arts, languages, health and physical education, and technologies (ACARA, 2012). Each of the learning areas is comprised of 10 levels, roughly corresponding to a year level. However, the Australian Curriculum encourages teaching to be flexible and move across learning areas and levels.

> The learning areas and the disciplines from which they are drawn
> provide a foundation of learning in schools because they reflect the

way in which knowledge has, and will continue to be, developed and codified. However, 21st century learning does not fit neatly into a curriculum solely organised by learning areas or subjects that reflect the disciplines.

(ACARA, 2012)

Full implementation of the curriculum to Year 10 in all states is anticipated by 2017. The Australian Curriculum has been developed for the senior years (11 and 12) in English, mathematics, science, history, and geography, although the nature of its implementation will depend on each state.

Implications for Teaching and Learning, and Teaching Quality

The Melbourne Declaration intends for the curriculum to be world-class, emphasizing both competency in the learning areas and in the capabilities of flexible thinking and communication skills. Although the Australian Curriculum is becoming firmly established—endorsed in all eight learning areas by the Education Council in 2015—it has nonetheless been the source of contestation. In particular, there remain challenges regarding how the curriculum meets the goals of the Melbourne Declaration, connects to NAPLAN, and segues with the implementation of teaching standards through AITSL.

One challenge relates to professional learning in states and school systems. States such as Victoria take a very decentralized and networked approach to professional development, while in NSW a significant proportion of professional development has been centrally coordinated with school networks, as well as through professional associations. Some education commentators have argued that the structure of the curriculum lends itself more easily to professional learning shaped along traditional disciplinary lines than those oriented to real-world tasks and interdisciplinary strategies (Atweh & Singh, 2011).

A second is the assessment of the Australian Curriculum in the context of NAPLAN. Some commentators contended that NAPLAN may serve as a de facto curriculum for underperforming schools, and influence educators to focus on curricular content at the expense of an emphasis on critical thinking skills (Aubusson, 2011; Brennan, 2011). Although NAPLAN began prior to the development of a national curriculum, it will be shaped by the Australian Curriculum from 2016 and delivered in an adaptive form from 2017. The adaptive form will mean that different students in a class or school would be taking a different form of the test. This is intended to make NAPLAN less predictable, and strengthen the case that the best preparation for NAPLAN is for students to experience a rich curriculum.

A third challenge is the degree to which consensus and accommodations in the formation of the Curriculum have led to an overcrowding of content, as it seeks to meet both national and state standards (BOSTES, 2014). A federal government review found that in some cases there was crowding of content, favoring breadth at the expense of depth. Implications for teaching included difficulties in linking content with cross-curricular priorities, and a curriculum that was unwieldly for teachers (Australian Government, 2014a). The report's recommendations to rebalance curricular content in each learning area, and benchmark pedagogical approaches against other top performing countries, were taken up by ACARA and are informing subsequent editions of the curriculum.

Education Funding in Australia and Gonski

Australia funds its education system at similar levels to other advanced economies. Total per student education spending was at around US\$7,700 at primary level and US\$10,000 at secondary level (in 2012 dollars at purchasing power parity), comparable with OECD averages (OECD, 2015, p. 211). This amount is a little below the average however, when considered as a proportion of GDP per capita. Nonetheless, education represents an important priority for Australian governments compared with other public services, accounting for 13.5% of all public expenditures (c.f. OECD average of 11.6%). Australia was also just one of a handful of OECD countries to significantly increase its public expenditures on education (by 19%) during the height of the global financial crisis from 2008 to 2012 (OECD, 2015, p. 260).

The federal government funds education in Australia in two important ways. Firstly, it provides funding (via state authorities) to schools, both government and the nongovernment Catholic and independent schools. Secondly, it provides funding to states for specific purposes and initiatives, for example, under national partnership agreements from 2009–2014. The rapid increase of federal funding, and dramatic political changes in 2014—specifically around the Gonski needs-based funding reforms—show both the efficacy and potential challenges of the cooperative federalism approach to national policy formation.

The significance of federal funding in Australian education is of interest in part due to its relative newness. In fact, there was almost no federal funding of education prior to 1964. Annual recurrent funding for schools was first introduced in the 1970s to address perceived deficiencies in school resourcing, with needs-based programmatic funds made available for "disadvantaged schools, special education, teacher professional development and innovation." (Harrington, 2013, p. 3) This established the basic funding pattern that existed until 2009, which saw changes to the funding formula, an increase in funding to states for specific initiatives, and the launching of the Gonski report focused on the more equitable distribution of resources.

Education Funding in Australia

Australia differs from many other countries in that it funds three different types of schools: government, Catholic, and independent. It thus provides significant funding to schools that would in many countries be considered private schools. Government schools typically receive around three-quarters of their funds from the state, and around 15–20% from the federal government. Catholic schools receive around three-quarters of their funds from public sources, with federal funds representing the largest proportion of this. Independent schools have greater flexibility to raise funds via private sources such as tuition fees, but on average around 40% of their funds come from public sources.

These funds to nongovernment (Catholic and independent) schools are divided into two major types: A base level of funding determined by the average cost of educating a student in a *government* school; and formula to provide additional funds based on the SES of the students' community.

Government schools are funded by states, but with significant differences between them. Victoria and South Australia have highly decentralized models with funds being distributed directly to government schools, while funding in NSW has until recent years been more centralized. Centralization relieves principals of many of the duties of budgeting and accounting, but also makes it difficult for schools attract needs-specific funding (Dowling, 2007).

Federal Funding and the Melbourne Declaration

The Melbourne Declaration brought a renewed focus on education funding—in particular issues of equity—and highlighted long-standing deficiencies with the system. Firstly, the SES rating of the community in which the student lives did not necessarily reflect that of the students attending the school. Secondly, the way the funds were indexed disproportionately funded the nongovernment sector relative to government schools. This meant that as costs increased, it had the effect of driving more students into nongovernment schools (Dowling, 2007).

Thirdly, different financial reporting and accounting systems, and even fiscal calendars, existed between state governments, between the Australian government and states, and between the different school sectors—a fiscal example of the rail gauge phenomenon. Even establishing accurate estimates of per-student funding at the school level was a complex and complicated process, with figures on educational spending often unavailable until two years later.

Following the Melbourne Declaration, COAG signed a National Education Agreement (NEA), which established a new framework for federal funding of education. It included Specific Purpose Payments to schools and National Partnerships funding for specific programs (Harrington, 2013).

The Specific Purpose Payments increased federal funding to government schools, but states retained control over how these funds were dispersed. Specific Purpose Payments for nongovernment schools consisted of a series of grants for capital funding. Additional SES were awarded using parental income, education, and occupation data. Each education system received the monies to disperse among schools according to their own method. However, as a result of "grandparenting" arrangements, around 40% of nongovernment schools still received a greater level of funding than they would be entitled to under the new system, a finding that prefigured the Gonski report (see below).

National Partnerships: Federal Funding to Improve Teaching Quality

National Partnerships (NPs) funding was provided to school systems for specific programs through federal-state agreements. The two most relevant to teaching quality were the Rewards for Great Teachers and the Smarter Schools National Partnership on Improving Teacher Quality.

The Rewards for Great Teachers program was developed to financially reward teachers of high quality, and to support uptake of the Australian Professional Standards for Teachers and the Teacher Performance and Development framework (COAG, 2012). Participating states were required to establish a system for certifying teachers against the standards, and for all teachers to have undertaken a performance and development cycle against the framework by 2015. Victoria, Queensland, and Tasmania, and the Catholic sector in Western Australia have yet to establish processes for certifying teachers at the higher levels.

The Smarter Schools National Partnerships were targeted specifically at raising teaching quality, and comprised agreements in literacy and numeracy, low SES school communities, and improving teacher quality. A quarter of Australian schools were eligible for the low SES school communities and literacy and numeracy funds, while the improving teacher quality plan was targeted at all teachers and school leaders in Australia.

The agreements focused on *"critical points in the teacher 'lifecycle' to attract, train, place, develop and retain quality teachers and leaders in our schools and classrooms"*(COAG, 2013). State governments were able to select reform areas and milestones from among the following six areas:

- ○ Improved pay dispersion to reward quality teaching.
- ○ Improved reward structures for teachers and leaders who work in disadvantaged, indigenous, rural/remote, and hard-to-staff schools.
- ○ Improved in-school support for teachers and school leaders, particularly in disadvantaged, rural/remote, and hard-to-staff schools.
- ○ Increased school-based decision making about recruitment, staffing mix, and budget.
- ○ Continual improvement program for all teachers.
- ○ Indigenous teachers' and school leaders' engagement with community members. (COAG, 2013)

The National Partnerships included "reward funding," paid to states that implemented plans and demonstrated improvements in literacy and numeracy against negotiated targets. The partnerships provided four years of funding to facilitate the implementation and evaluation of evidence-based strategies for improving student outcomes.

The Gonski Review

One of the most important developments in national level policy in Australia was the Review of Funding for Schooling, known as the Gonksi report (Link 1-5) after the chair of the review panel. Prior to the release of the report in 2011, there had not been a significant review into educational funding for over 40 years. Established by then-Prime Minister Julia Gillard in 2010, the review's purpose was to "provide recommendations directed towards achieving a funding system for the period beyond 2013 that would be transparent, fair, financially sustainable and effective in promoting excellent educational outcomes for all Australian students" (Gonski et al., 2012).

The report recommended comprehensive changes in the balance and alignment of funding between the Australian and state governments, and between government and nongovernment schools. The core principle was a movement to needs-based funding on a per-student basis, rather than on historical spending patterns (Australian Government, 2014b), as outlined in an explanatory report from the Australian Parliament:

> The Gonski Review's core recommendation was that the level of recurrent funding for all school students should be determined by a Schooling Resource Standard (SRS) that would include a per student amount (with different amounts for primary and secondary school students) and loadings for various student-based and school-based sources of disadvantage (SES background, disability, English language proficiency, Indigeneity, and school size and location).
>
> (Harrington, 2013, p. 36)

As the terms of the review required that no school receive less money as an outcome, it recommended a significant increase in funding in real terms of around 4.3%, or A\$5 billion, calculated to be less than 0.5% of the gross domestic product of Australia (Gonski et al., 2012; NCOA, 2014).

The Gonski funding model has a very strong equity focus. The six "factor loadings" are intended to provide greater resources to students who may require more support (Australian Department of Education, 2013). As the review panel Chair said in a speech to the Australian College of Educators:

> One of the easiest decisions we (the review panel) were able to take is what we as a review team believed "equity" should mean in determining a suitable funding system in Australia. We felt strongly and unanimously that a funding system must ensure that differences in education outcomes are not the result of differences in wealth, income, power, or possessions. Flowing from this, a funding system based on need was both obvious and important.
>
> (Gonski, 2014)

The Australian government committed to the review's core recommendations, in which states would increase funding by $1 for every $2 of federal funding over six years. State governments signed onto the plan, which was included in the Australian Education Act 2013, and took effect from 1 January 2014.

However, a newly-elected federal government eventually withdrew its commitment in 2014 to the final two years—those in which the majority of funding would have been provided—instead recommending handing responsibility for funding back to the states. "This means that while the Commonwealth has locked in funding increases over the next four years, there is no obligation for the States to increase, or even maintain, their own funding levels" (NCOA, 2014). This would also mean that the model of aspirational needs-based allocation would again be replaced by a resourcing model that is based on historical figures.

Several states have since implemented their own funding models based on the Gonksi recommendations. The issue remains part of ongoing political debate, and figured prominently in the 2016 federal elections (AEU, 2016).

The ongoing contestation around funding highlights the impetus that exists for addressing equity issues in Australian education under the Melbourne Declaration. It also underscores both that the movement towards national consistency in education is an incomplete and ongoing project, as well as the extent to which national education policies, although becoming more firmly entrenched, are still contingent upon political consensus.

Summary

States have constitutional responsibility for education, and historically, education policy formation has been conducted at the state level. The federal government manages significant funding including funds from taxation and is a significant provider of funding to the states, which has given it an influential voice in policy (Drabsch, 2013).

State-based education in Australia is being progressively transformed by national level education policies. These policies are aimed both at improving international educational and economic competitiveness, as well as improving educational outcomes for *all* Australians, including addressing equity concerns associated with remote communities, students from lower socioeconomic backgrounds, and those of indigenous Australians.

Teaching quality features prominently among these education reforms. Significant policies to date have included the development of nationally consistent standards to underpin teaching. This is being closely followed by efforts to draw processes for each of teacher registration, teacher performance and development, and professional learning into line with these standards.

There are also initiatives requiring accreditation of initial teacher education programs to align teacher training with the teaching standards. This has recently been joined by a suite of federal reforms that aim to significantly strengthen initial teacher education programs. Further initiatives in curriculum and assessment are helping to shape what gets taught, and the work of teachers in the classroom.

The federal government in Australia has played an important role in state-delivered education since the introduction of recurrent funding forty years ago. However, the process of achieving national consistency in education policy has mainly taken place in less than a decade. This has been possible through an approach that has emphasized consensus and harmonization. Thus although the federal role in education is well established, elements of the reforms, such as schools funding, remain contested.

This process has allowed for a degree of independence at the state level for education initiatives, as shown with the national partnerships agreements. Despite the national nature of the reforms, as state-based regulatory authorities maintain the primary role in their on-the-ground implementation, this will contribute to shaping the extent to which the reforms impact on teaching quality, and their effectiveness in achieving the twin goals of excellence and equitable education as set out in the Melbourne Declaration.

In the case studies that follow, we take a closer look at policy impacting teaching and learning in each of Victoria and NSW. We examine the different contexts for education policy, and look at how these influence teaching practices and the work of teachers.

NOTES

1. The federal government in Australia is known as the Commonwealth, but is now referred to as the Australian government in most contexts.
2. For much of Australia's early history, different states operated railway systems with different widths between tracks (gauges). With the development of interstate commerce, this often entailed the unloading and loading of goods from trains of one gauge to another, causing considerable inefficiency. The rail gauge phenomenon serves as a metaphor in present-day Australia for the parallel and independent development of initiatives in each state.
3. Previously known as the Ministerial Council on Education, Employment, Training and Youth Affairs (MCEETYA), and the Ministerial Council for Education, Early Childhood Development and Youth Affairs (MCEECDYA).
4. These system organizations serve as sector bodies for negotiation with state and federal governments, but are not directly involved in school management.
5. As with other university programs, initial teacher education is also subject to university internal accreditation processes, as well as external accreditation by the Australian Tertiary Education Quality and Standards Agency, the regulatory body for the university and higher education sector.
6. See http://www.deakin.edu.au/course/bachelor-of-education-primary-education-and-teaching#FEES-CHARGES

7. Applicants also require completion of a Working with Children Check (WWCC), an ongoing assessment of applicants' suitability for working with children made by each state's Department of Justice. It includes a national police check and determinations made by professional bodies such as VIT.
8. Although NAPLAN testing applies to all students, parents may choose to exclude their children from testing. Additional dispensation may be given for some students with disabilities, new immigrant students, and some students for whom English is not a first language.

FROM POLICY TO PRACTICE: TEACHER QUALITY IN NEW SOUTH WALES, AUSTRALIA

Ann McIntyre

IN NEW SOUTH WALES (NSW) there is a strong awareness that student outcomes are influenced by the systems that shape the work of teachers, the quality of teaching, the socioeconomic background of students, and the need for strategies that help mitigate the impact of a student's circumstances. At the heart of current NSW educational policy is a focus on both excellence and equity, underpinned by the fundamental democratic belief that all students are entitled to an education that will enable them to succeed and contribute to society.

The performance of NSW students in international testing programs reveals that while NSW performs well there remains a need to continue to focus on the relationship between student achievement and family background. Current educational policy in NSW outlines a coordinated web of actions that create reforms to build the capacity of the teaching workforce and increase local school decision making to address identified priorities. There is also increasingly strong whole of government policy coordination in order to address key educational challenges through a focus on the whole child.

There is a firm commitment to use both local and international research to inform educational policy decisions. Current educational policies seek to address:

o local authority within a state and national framework
o access to a broad curriculum within a national assessment framework

○ education funding to support equity

○ strategies to enable the development of teacher quality within a regulated system of professional standards

There is no silver bullet solution in education … our combined series of evidence-based reforms are the most comprehensive reforms to education in NSW in a century … and they are underpinned by our philosophy to put students at the centre of every decision we make about their education.

(Piccoli, 2014)

About New South Wales (NSW)

Demographics

New South Wales (NSW) is Australia's most populous state, with 7.5 million of the nation's 23.5 million people living in the state. Almost two-thirds of the state's population (4.84 million) live in the greater Sydney area (ABS, 2014), Australia's largest city, and 77% of the state's total growth in population has been in the greater Sydney area.

The state features a large immigrant population, with 31.4% of residents born overseas: 9.8% of these from Asia, and 8.7% from Europe. Around 22.5% of residents speak a language other than English at home (see Figure 2.1, ABS, 2014).

Figure 2.1 Population Density of Australia.

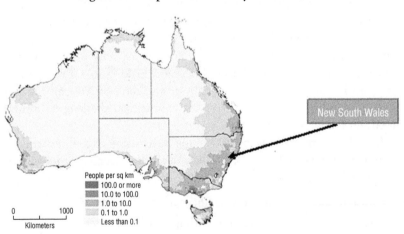

Reproduced from ABS, 2014b.

NSW has the highest number of people identifying as Aboriginal and Torres Strait Islander origin. The 2011 Census population estimates indicated that 208,364 Aboriginal people live in NSW, this being around 32% of the national total. Children under the age of 15 make up 36% of the Aboriginal and Torres Strait Islander population, as compared with 19% of the non-indigenous population (ABS, 2014). Unlike other parts of Australia, in NSW, 95% of Aboriginal people live in regional areas or major cities, and only 5% in remote or very remote locations (NSW Government, 2013).

Nonetheless, the census data highlight the disparities between Aboriginal people in NSW and the wider community; the unemployment rate for Aboriginal people aged 15–64 years in NSW was 17%, compared with 5.8% for their non-Aboriginal counterparts; the average income for Aboriginal adults was A$530 per week compared with a statewide average of A$801.

Addressing these disparities is an important part of the state's policy agenda. Professor Nicholas Biddle in his 2011 *Report on the Council of Australian Governments (COAG) Closing the Gap targets* found that without substantial improvements in Aboriginal employment outcomes, substantive improvements in areas such as life expectancy and education are unlikely to be achieved (Biddle, 2011).

NSW Economy and Government

NSW is a key hub of Australia's economy accounting for the largest proportion of the country's gross domestic product—around 31% of total GDP. The state economy is comprised of financial, professional, and health care services, tourism, manufacturing, and mining (NSW Government, 2014).

Sydney is regarded as the economic and business capital of Australia, with many national and Asia-Pacific regional corporations headquartered in the Sydney area. As such, NSW is linked to many international markets with greatest growth to markets in China, India, and Asian countries. Exports from NSW account for around 21% of those nationally. These are a combination of traditional primary exports, but more recently dominated by higher value-added services exports which now represent a third of all exports (NSW Department of Industry, 2015).

This combination of a knowledge intensive economy with an ethnically and linguistically diverse and internationally connected population helps inform the direction of NSW education policy.

The state government is administered through a premier and ministers, responsible for setting the policy direction of the state. The premier's office in NSW has since 1976 been dominated by the center-left Labor government. The movement back to a center-right Liberal government at the state level in 2011 has seen the release of a number of new education policies, focusing on devolvement of decision-making authority and some alignment with national policy developments.

Equity and Education in NSW

While NSW has a strong economy, the distribution of wealth is inequitable. Income inequality and rates of poverty sit above the national average (NCOSS, 2014). There is a considerable gap between the richest and poorest in the state with the top 20% of the population earning almost five times as much as the bottom 20% (ABS, 2016). Despite this inequity, education outcomes as measured by PISA are above the national mean, and although the average difference in results between students from the highest and lowest socioeconomic backgrounds is among the widest in Australia, it remains below that of the OECD average (Thomson, De Bortoli, & Buckley, 2014).

However when these results are disaggregated to population subgroups and regions, the difference becomes more apparent. As the NSW Minister for Education, Adrian Piccoli stated shortly after his appointment in April 2011, "The outcomes for students in some areas of the state are equal to the best in the world, while for some rural and remote towns the outcomes resemble those of an underdeveloped country" (Piccoli, 2011). Measures of child well-being also reflect these inequities, with child poverty levels higher for indigenous than non-indigenous children (ARACY, 2013).

The NSW State Plan, NSW 2021, has a significant focus on well-being through the provision of quality services including health care, family and community services, transport, policing, justice, and education. There is a strong focus in NSW that education has a role in breaking the cycle of generational education, health, and employment patterns of disadvantage. This includes the awareness that a child's background should not be the key factor in determining their future health, employment, and educational outcomes. NSW 2021 articulates the goal to "improve education and learning outcomes for all students." The rationale and focus for this goal is described as follows:

> Access to and participation in high quality education provides the foundations for long-term social and economic success. We will

support all students to reach their full potential at all stages of their education from early childhood to post-school learning and employment. To create an environment where students can continue to excel, and in turn lead productive lives and help build a strong NSW economy, we will ensure all children have access to quality early childhood education, recruit high quality teachers, and provide schools and their communities with a say in local decision making.

(NSW Government, 2011, Goal 15)

The NSW Education System

Overview of the New South Wales Education System

The New South Wales Department of Education and Communities oversees primary, secondary, and Technical and Further Education (TAFE) colleges in NSW. This authority is given under the NSW Education Act of 1990 No8. The Act outlines four principles:

(a) every child has the right to receive an education,

(b) the education of a child is primarily the responsibility of the child's parents,

(c) it is the duty of the State to ensure that every child receives an education of the highest quality,

(d) the principal responsibility of the State in the education of children is the provision of public education.

(NSW Education Act, 1990, sec. 4)

One interesting principle that stands out in this Act compared to education laws in other countries, particularly the United States, is Principle B, *"The education of a child is primarily the responsibility of the child's parents."* Although the state bears authority over schools and is tasked with providing education of the highest quality, parents are ultimately responsible for their child's education.

The NSW Department of Education and Communities (DEC) governs public schools in the state. NSW has a K–12 system, divided into K–6 primary schools, and grade 7–12 secondary schools. Schooling is compulsory from age 6 until age 17 (*NSW Education Act*, 1990, sec. 21B).

Table 2.1 Schools in New South Wales.

Number of schools in NSW by sector, 2012

School type	Government	Catholic	Independent	All schools
Primary	1623	417	73	2113
Secondary	370	129	16	515
Combined	66	32	205	303
Special Schools	110	7	34	151
Total	**2169**	**585**	**328**	**3082**

Source: ABS Schools Australia, Table 35a.

Each public school has a defined local enrollment area. Students are assigned to a school based on their permanent residential address. Parents have the option of applying to schools outside of their enrollment area, given staffing and classroom availability. In some areas, this has resulted in the segregation of students from different backgrounds and the marginalization of some schools.

As with many other parts of the country, the schools sector in NSW is divided into two broad groups: government and nongovernment schools (Table 2.1). Public schools are inclusive and enroll all local students while Catholic and independent schools are able to select students for enrollment. There is a broad socioeconomic gap between students from government and nongovernment systems, with students enrolled in nongovernment schools tending to come from higher socioeconomic backgrounds.

The Education Policy Context in NSW

The overall policy context in NSW is one of significant change, with present policies (2012–16) signifying closer alignment of state activities with national policies. These include alignment with the Australian Professional Standards for Teachers, and with the National Education Agreement, and National Partnerships agreements. The language in NSW policy reflects the 21st-century learning concepts and international competitiveness present in national level policy documents. Policy also reflects the movement towards a more devolved system consistent with the principles of the governing Liberal/National party.

The history of educational reform in NSW has four main reform areas that have evolved over time with incoming and outgoing policy tides. These key areas identified by Brock and Hughes (2008) are:

o Control of curriculum

o Centralization and devolution of administration, resources, and decision making

○ Growth of accountability

○ Changes to the conception of equity

Historically, the NSW Board of Studies has guided the actions of schools in the provision of curriculum and assessment practices. While there have been significant differences between government and non-government schools in governance and policy, the Board of Studies has provided and monitored school accreditation requirements, school registration, curriculum provision, and assessment across all systems. NSW has a tradition of strong curriculum and support material provided by the Board of Studies for all NSW schools. The degree of school discretion in the design of curriculum and the specification of required content has varied over time. The NSW Board of Studies, now the Board of Studies, Teaching and Educational Standards (BOSTES), has worked with the Australian government in the development of the Australian Curriculum, and is implementing the curriculum through new NSW syllabuses. Credentialing and related assessment practices remain the responsibility of the state.

The Australian Curriculum sets out "content descriptions" as the learning entitlements of students. Within this, there is significant local authority over teaching and learning. How teachers organize students' learning is a matter for schools, or for school systems where that system's curriculum authority provides guidelines. The nature of the content of the Australian Curriculum has been widely debated in NSW. A common theme in this debate has been the impact that this has on the professional judgment of teachers in the design of an engaging learning experiences for all students.

The current trend in state and school governance is moving away from centralization to increased devolution of policy decision making, resource allocation, and administration. This will have a significant impact on government schools in NSW as the DEC has traditionally been regarded as one of the most centrally controlled school jurisdictions in Australia. NSW has, for example, a more centralized system for teacher appointment that blends both school staff selection and a central teacher transfer system. The Professional Learning and Equity school funding programs have operated as devolved systems in which the schools decide on the expenditure of funds to address school priorities. The whole system of funding and school accountability has been changing under the current Local Schools, Local Decisions reforms and most program funding is now devolved to schools.

Changes in education and training in NSW are underpinned by a strong belief in the role of education in creating a more equitable society, as well as personal, social, and economic well-being. The key drivers for the new state education plan include current educational outcomes data and an educational evidence base that highlights the critical role of teachers and educational leaders in driving continuous improvement.

There are both national and state regulations that govern aspects of schooling for government, Catholic, and independent schools. Governance is in the area of school registration, curriculum, teacher registration, and accreditation. There is greater state control of government schools who are open to the enrollment of all students irrespective of their religion, culture, or socioeconomic background.

In highlighting the importance of teacher quality, the NSW state plan focuses on the capacity for teachers to improve student outcomes through teacher accreditation and standards. The NSW plan states that "Research provides evidence that a quality teacher is the most important factor in student success in learning. Improving teacher standards will position NSW as the Australian leader and improve our standing internationally" (NSW Government, 2011).

The NSW state plan identifies actions to influence school leadership through increasing the authority of public schools. "Providing schools with a greater level of decision making will better meet local needs and improve student learning. Increased local decision making in schools will align the NSW public education system with other high performing systems around the world." These references demonstrate the influence of international educational research on the NSW state plan (NSW Government, 2011).

NSW Five-year Strategic Plan 2012–2017 (Link 2-1)

The five-year strategic plan of the NSW Department of Education and Communities presents a vision for government schools that reflects economic and social outcomes, and identifies three strategic priorities and achievement goals at all levels of education. These strategic priorities are focused on improving teacher quality, closing educational gaps, and improved functioning of educational institutions (DEC, 2012).

Specific student and teacher achievement goals include:

○ Access measures and literacy/numeracy assessment standards for early childhood

○ Increased proportion of students meeting national standards, increased graduation rates, and closing gaps for Aboriginal and non-Aboriginal students

○ Increased accreditation of teachers at Accomplished and Leadership levels on the Australian Professional Standard for Teachers

○ Increased tertiary graduation rates with greater enrollments from low SES students

The policy approach that has developed under the strategic plan has been based on three main elements. The first has involved increasing the ability for schools to make decisions on how to address priorities specific to their school's need. Captured under the Local Schools, Local Decisions policy, this is a significant change and represents an accommodation of increasing decentralization in an otherwise centralized system. The second is a change in the funding model (Resource Allocation Model), aimed at greatly increasing funding equity for disadvantaged students, in line with principles of the Melbourne Declaration. These two policies are discussed below.

The third element—discussed later in this chapter—focuses on improving teaching quality. The Great Teaching, Inspired Learning policy takes a multipronged approach. It aims to recruit and retain the highest quality graduates, ensure rigorous teacher preparation, and recognize and reward high-quality teaching to promote student outcomes.

Additional priorities under the strategic plan aim to provide greater support beyond the K–12 system. These include implementing a national quality framework in the area of early childhood education and care, and promoting partnerships with Aboriginal communities including programs such as having Elders in classrooms to support learning (DEC, 2012).

Local Schools, Local Decisions

The Local Schools, Local Decisions (LSLD) policy shifts the balance of authority of decision making in government schools to school principals. Under the policy, principals have greater flexibility in the use of funds for public schools, including professional procurement and school maintenance and development. Principals also have some authority over selecting teachers to fill vacancies; following incentive transfers or Aboriginal teacher placements, vacancies will be filled on an alternating basis by "central appointment" (NSW Department of Education and Communities) or "local selection" (by the school).

The LSLD framework also provides funds for increased school collaboration. Sixty-five principals' networks have been created, each led by a Director of Public Schools NSW. The intention of the policy is to create professional communities for principals. Directors are responsible for forming close relationships with school principals (including facilitating sharing of best practice), and with service providers and government.

The other major tenets of the LSLD policy are increased resources made available for schools to engage diverse communities, and the development of a single budget plan for schools to replace the previous multiple budgets associated with various programmatic funds. As the leader of the NSW government school sector, Michele Bruniges, Secretary of the Department of Education and Communities, states:

> We're really moving from a highly centralized bureaucracy to a model where we have a notion of underpinning the work of schools as incredibly important, and so the policy formation is there ... in a model that underpins the work of schools, that gives community a voice no matter where they are, gives principals the autonomy to make those decisions away from the centralized system.

(interview with M. Bruniges, 2015 [Link 2-2])

Education Funding in NSW and the Gonski Review (Link 2-3)

As discussed in the first chapter, the Gonski review sought to create a more equitable resourcing model, acknowledging that performance gaps were strongly linked to indigenous students and those from lower socioeconomic backgrounds. The four key principles underlying the review—a single unified funding model, transparent and based on aspirational goals, an agreed formula for long-term planning, and a needs-based and equity-focused approach—are all strongly supported by the NSW government. There is a clear focus that the funding system should ensure that the differences in educational outcomes not be a result of differences in income.

The NSW government and Minister for Education were active supporters of the full implementation of the Gonski reforms, and NSW was the first state to sign on to the agreement with the federal government. This agreement required the state to contribute significant funding support to education, and although the full Gonski funding has yet to be implemented, the state has initiated the development and implementation of a new Resource Allocation Model. The student characteristics of the Gonski review informed the development of the RAM funding model in NSW public schools (Gonski et al., 2012).

Public criticism of the Gonski review has been primarily based on the assumption that increased funding to schools does not result in better student performance on standardized tests of literacy and numeracy.

Thus indicating improved student outcomes as a result of the Gonski funding is a key strategy to secure the continuance of the Gonski funding model. This strategy is shared by both the NSW Department of Education and Communities and the NSW Teachers Federation.

The Resource Allocation Model

Equity is a core tenet of education funding in NSW. Prior to 2013, funding to public schools occurred through a standard combination of per student funding with additional programmatic funds and utilities allocations. From 2014, funding was increasingly made according to the Resource Allocation Model (RAM) under the Local Schools, Local Decisions policy framework. This model added two new "equity loadings"—SES and indigenous status—and has doubled funding to over a thousand schools.

The introduction of the RAM was founded on the idea that in order to bridge the gap in student learning outcomes, resources need to be targeted to the students who are most in need. Michele Bruniges, Secretary of the Department of Education and Communities, highlights this in stating:

> There's no doubt that equity is one of those key principles at the heart of much of our reform, and probably the most significant thing that we've done is changed the way in which we fund schools through a new resource allocation model, that is fundamentally based on need, and it takes individual student data based on the needs of those students and builds up a model that funds schools as a needs-based funding model. And I think that's absolutely essential to recognize and to really step up to the plate on the fact that different students require a different level of support and need, and we've taken that big step to recognize and put in place a needs-based funding model.

The model's development was thus based on principles of equity, efficiency and transparency, and using evidence to align funding to evolving priorities. A core feature is that school funding is tagged to the *student*. This means that equity loading for SES is based on individual student data—including parent's education level and occupation—and thus if a student moves school, the funding moves with them.

There are three main components that make up the RAM. The first is targeted funding for students who face particularly high levels of need, such as significant adjustment due to disability or a newly arrived refugee. The second includes a loading for students with learning support needs, aboriginal students, those with English language proficiency needs, and a rate of funding for each student determined by their socioeconomic background. The third level of the RAM includes a loading that is determined by the school site and takes into account the school buildings and facilities, the school climate and the school location.

The design of the model underpins the Local Schools, Local Decisions strategy to enable schools to have greater control over resources to improve outcomes. Schools have increased flexibility to allocate funds according to the school priorities, with discretion over around 70% of the state funding for their school. The net effect is a move of resources from the state to the school and therefore a reduction in systemic intervention for schools.

Students in NSW Schools

The NSW Department of Education and Communities is the largest provider of education and training in Australia. In 2012, there were 748,234 students enrolled in government public schools. This included 438,681 students enrolled in primary schools, 304,632 in secondary schools, and 4,921 in schools for specific purposes. During this period there were also 390,756 students enrolled in nongovernment schools, making over 1.1 million students in total.

The public sector represents 77% of schools and 66% of all primary and secondary students in the state (Australian Bureau of Statistics, 2013). The percentage in government schools is lower for secondary than primary school students.

Class Sizes

The teacher staffing formulae for primary schools is based on class sizes of 20 for kindergarten, 22 in year one, 24 in year two, and 30 in years 3–6. In secondary schools the principal in consultation with staff is responsible for determining class sizes on the basis of the curriculum needs of the school, student needs, community expectations, and the expertise of the teachers. Staffing is based on the principle that no class need exceed 30 in the junior secondary school and 24 in the senior secondary school.

In 2014, there was an average class size of 24 students across kindergarten through to year 6, a reduction of 2.9 students per class since 1997. The decrease in class sizes has been most apparent in the early years of compulsory schooling, where average kindergarten classes have fallen from 22.1 to 19.3 over just the past decade (NSW CESE, 2015).

Diversity in NSW Public Schools

NSW has a very diverse student population. This great diversity informs the policy approach taken by the Department of Education and Communities. Of the more than 748,000 students in NSW public schools:

- ○ Around 220,000 or 29% are from a language background other than English
- ○ Around 90,000 or 12% have a disability and/or difficulties in learning or behavior
- ○ Around 75,000 or 10% are identified as gifted or talented
- ○ Around 48,000 or 6% are aboriginal
- ○ Around 12,000 or 2% are students from refugee backgrounds.

(DEC, 2015b, 2015c)

Language Backgrounds Other Than English

Students in NSW government schools are ethnically and linguistically diverse, in part due to the many immigrant, first generation students in its schools. Its students come from more than 240 languages backgrounds other than English (LBOTE), and represent over 31% of the school population statewide, including greater than 50% in the Sydney metropolitan area (NSW CESE, 2015). See Figure 2.2.

Figure 2.2 Language Diversity in NSW Government Schools 2014.

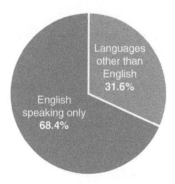

Source: NSW CESE (2015), Schools and Students: 2014 Statistical Bulletin

Of the total LBOTE students, Arabic is the most common single language background, comprising 13.2% of all LBOTE students. Mandarin (8.6%) and Cantonese (7.5%) are the next two most common languages, which together comprise the majority (95%) of Chinese language backgrounds. Vietnamese is the fourth largest single language background with 6.6% of all LBOTE students. Of the 232 single language background groups recorded across NSW government schools, 44 had more than 1,000 students.

The proportion of LBOTE students is also growing. Since 1998, the top three language backgrounds have grown significantly, with Chinese growing 48%, while Arabic and Vietnamese have grown 29% and 42% respectively over that period (NSW Department of Education and Communities, Centre for Education Statistics and Evaluation 2014). The needs of LBOTE students are recognized through an additional staffing allocation that enables greater teacher time to be provided to students learning English. The most prominent model for this allocation is an additional teacher working alongside the class teacher.

In addition to Australian LBOTE students, there is also a sizeable number of international students. The NSW education system is seen in Asia as providing high educational standards, and its Higher School Certificate is held in high regard internationally. There is thus strong demand for the placement of students from abroad. In 2012, there were 3,795 international students enrolled in 280 NSW government schools. The students came from more than 58 countries although seven countries provided 91% of these students: China (52%), Vietnam (15%), Korea (14%), Germany and Hong Kong (3% each), Thailand and Japan (2% each) (NSW CESE, 2013a).

Aboriginal Students

The Aboriginal student population in NSW is larger than in any other state. In 2014, 51,612 Aboriginal students attended government schools, equivalent to 6.8% of the public school population (NSW CESE, 2015). This proportion has grown from 5.3% since 2008, due in part to increased retention of Aboriginal students in upper secondary school (ABS, 2015), a goal of state education policy (DEC, 2012). The number of Aboriginal students completing school graduation and being awarded the Higher School Certificate grew from 528 to 1,139 over the decade 2004 to 2014 (NSW CESE, 2015).

Despite improving achievement and attendance for indigenous students, school engagement remains a challenge. Statewide, the academic performance of Aboriginal students still shows considerable disparities

Table 2.2 NAPLAN Achievement in NSW, 2012.

NSW NAPLAN data: proportion achieving at or above national minimum standard, 2013

	Reading			
	Yr 3	Yr 5	Yr 7	Yr 9
Male	95.1	95.8	93.5	92.5
Female	97.6	97.9	96.1	95.7
Aboriginal	88.6	91	81	80.4
LBOTE	95.9	96.4	94.1	93.6

Source: ACARA National Assessment Program Literacy
and Numeracy (NAPLAN Report, 2013)

with that of non-Aboriginal students, while that of LBOTE students is on par with their English-only counterparts. (See Table 2.2.)

Yet, as Professor John Hattie the Chair of AITSL stated in his address to the Australian Council of Educational Leaders, *Can Australian education become self-transforming?* We need to choose our metaphors carefully to ensure we focus on the growth of *all* students (see Figure 2.3):

Figure 2.3 Achievement Distributions for Indigenous and Non-indigenous Students.

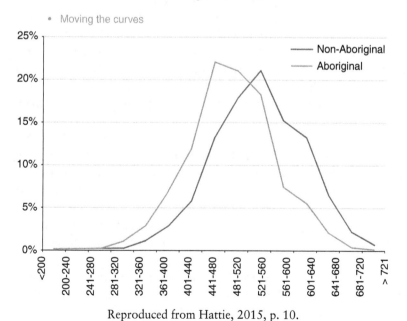

Reproduced from Hattie, 2015, p. 10.

We have had many years focused on "closing the gap", concerns about the tail, and the poor outcomes achieved for Aboriginal and Torres Strait Islander students. Such metaphors have led to high levels of resources being poured into reducing the gap, fixing the tail, etc. Let us look, for example, at the distribution for Indigenous and non-Indigenous students (based on NAPLAN reading). Where is the tail? Where is the gap? There is no tail, no gap; there are tails and gaps. Indeed we should be as concerned with those Aboriginal and Torres Strait Islander students (and there are many of them) who score above the average and demand that schools help these students realise and exceed what they are told is their potential. We should never use phrases such as "aboriginal underachievement" as it falsely implies all these students are in the bottom half of the distribution.

(Hattie, 2015)

The state strategy for enabling improved educational outcomes for Aboriginal students is illustrative of an holistic approach with a focus on the whole child. It involves both a stronger collaborative and consultative effort, together with targeted educational policies that include teacher professional learning in culturally responsive pedagogies. Firstly, as the difference in educational achievement is mirrored in other well-being indicators, the NSW Government has developed a whole-of-government strategy to coordinate support services, with a particular emphasis on education and employment. This is reflected in governance structures where the Secretary of the Department of Education reports to both Education and Aboriginal Affairs ministers. The key principles underlining this work are the following: partnerships over paternalism; opportunity over disadvantage; successes over shortfalls; "listening to" over "talking at"; local solutions over "one size fits all"; evidence over assumptions; participation over marginalization; and practice over theory (NSW Government, 2013).

Secondly, there has been more productive engagement with Aboriginal communities over the past fifteen years. In 1999, NSW government schools established a partnership agreement with the Aboriginal Education Consultative Group (AECG), aimed at ensuring Aboriginal people had a voice in establishing the directions and strategies for education by working through local communities. The agreement, now extended to 2020, establishes that priorities and focus areas be agreed with each leader of public education.

The partnership has enabled a genuine and practical approach to working together. At the heart of the agreement is valuing the cultural identity and heritage of Aboriginal students and ensuring that quality teaching practices and educational policies and strategies are conducive to enabling the success of Aboriginal students. There is still a great deal to achieve to realize this aim. Throughout the development of the strategy Aboriginal people repeatedly raised the need for healing to address the impact of transgenerational trauma as a result of the past policies and practices of successive governments.

Thirdly, at the policy level, the *Public Schools NSW Strategic Directions—Creating Futures Together 2015–2017* outlines the need for enhanced expectations for student achievement, teacher and leadership quality, and partnership pathways. The specific outcomes for Aboriginal students include establishing personalized learning pathways to ensure the achievement of Aboriginal students match or better the outcomes of all students.

Among the policy platforms, the Connected Communities strategy focuses on embedding high expectations and strategies to promote the achievement of all students:

> Connected Communities is a whole of government, long term commitment to working in partnership with school communities to create the generational change needed for students to achieve consistently better outcomes at school and also access stronger pathways from school into further learning and employment. The Connected Communities strategy is a reform where the education process is inclusive and involves the community, school staff, Government and Non-Government agencies, local Government and the business, TAFE and University sectors. The strategy is being implemented in 15 selected schools, mostly in rural and remote communities.
>
> (Aboriginal Affairs NSW, 2015)

Each *Connected Communities* school has an executive principal appointed for five years who reports to the director general of the Department of Education and Communities. These principals receive a salary that is significantly higher than the most senior principals in metropolitan areas. Each school has an additional executive position for a Community Engagement Leader. This leader is an Aboriginal person who provides cultural links to the community while also being a cultural mentor to the school leadership team.

The Connected Community Schools have a unique collaborative governance structure to ensure that the school is locally responsive to the students' needs and aspirations. Each school has a School Advisory Council to advise on the delivery of quality education. The local Aboriginal Education Consultative Group (AECG) also assists in planning each school's strategy. These partnerships are the key to achieving collaborative decision making between schools and Aboriginal parents, extended family, and the community. This strategy is designed to build strong cultural understandings. In their 2011 *Closing the School Completion Gap for Indigenous Students* for the Closing the Gap Clearinghouse, researchers Sue Helme and Stephen Lamb reported that school culture is a key factor in increasing engagement, achievement, and school completion (Helme & Lamb, 2011).

All staff in connected community schools participate in Aboriginal cultural education in partnership with their local Aboriginal community and undertake professional learning to increase their knowledge of Aboriginal students and how they learn. The professional learning is designed to support teachers to plan for and implement effective teaching, learning, and assessment for Aboriginal students.

Rural and Remote Students

Rural and remote schooling represents a challenge for education in NSW, with the achievement gaps similar to those of other states. Around 3% of schools and around 1% of students are regarded as being located in remote or very remote areas. The academic performance of students in rural and remote areas lags behind that of provincial and metropolitan students at all levels of education. However, this is also highly correlated with socioeconomic status (NSW CESE, 2013b).

Student achievement as measured on the common national assessment scale for students in Years 3, 5, 7, and 9 demonstrates the variation in outcomes between rural and metropolitan regions, with gaps as shown in Table 2.3. In addition, the percentage of students achieving the state minimum standard—basic skills in literacy and numeracy for each grade level—ranges from close to 99% in wealthier Northern Sydney, to around 85–90% in the more distant areas of Western NSW (DEC, 2011).

In NSW there is an increasing emphasis on the need to provide additional resources and use innovative strategies to improve the achievement of rural and remote students. Under the state's *Rural and Remote Education Blueprint for Action*, the NSW Government has allocated up to A\$80 million over four years to develop and implement actions to reduce the gap in educational achievement. These actions connect to those in the Local Schools, Local Decisions and Great Teaching, Inspired Learning reforms, and are focused in three main areas: increased access to curriculum opportunities; incentives to attract and retain quality teachers and school leaders; and specialist centers to coordinate interagency efforts in education, health, and well-being (DEC, 2013b).

Table 2.3   Enrollment and Performance of Schools by Remoteness.

Characteristics of school by remoteness

	Primary schools		Secondary schools	
	Metropolitan	Non-metropolitan	Metropolitan	Non-metropolitan
Average enrollment	381	260	832	519
% Aboriginal students	5%	14%	5%	15%
% LBOTE students	34%	7%	38%	4%
NAPLAN Yr 3 average score	411	386		
NAPLAN Yr 5 average score	494	474		
NAPLAN Yr 7 average score			522	510
NAPLAN Yr 9 average score			561	555

Source: Rural and remote education: Literature review,
NSW Centre for Education Statistics and Evaluation, 2013

Part of the strategy involves matching preservice teachers with rural and remote schools as part of their professional experience, in order to increase the attractiveness of teaching positions in these areas.

Additional curriculum strategies to bridge the opportunity gaps for talented students between metropolitan and rural schools also feature. Small country schools often did not have the subject variation that was sought by more able secondary students, and as a result they either left school or left town to pursue other interests—a major equity issue. As state Secretary of Education Michele Bruniges states:

> From the evidence that we have we know that the achievement gap between metropolitan students and rural and remote students is large, and therefore we've put a lot of thinking and research into a rural and remote strategy in which we have really tried to broaden the curriculum access that those students have. They're often very small school sites that don't have the same curriculum access as large

metropolitan schools, so we've made a deliberate strategy to look at rural and remote to increase the equity in our system and to reduce that achievement gap.

In response to this challenge, the directors of the western region of NSW explored a range of initiatives utilizing connected classroom technologies. In 2010 they established *xsel*, a virtual high school that offered selected subjects to students who remained based in their rural home town. The concept was to enable gifted and talented students in remote areas to access a broader curriculum taught by outstanding teachers.

The establishment of Aurora College in 2015 to enable gifted and talented students in rural and remote locations to access a broad and engaging curriculum is an example of the level of innovation that is being supported. Like xsel, Aurora College is a virtual high school of over 200 students. The college works in partnership with over 50 teachers in the 49 rural and remote NSW schools in the areas where the students live. The following quotes highlight the importance of this initiative for rural and remote communities:

> The provision of an equitable and high quality secondary selective curriculum for Western NSW students has long been a priority of the region. The nature of the Region, its unique needs and its distances necessitates a different model of curriculum design and delivery which offers the opportunity to capitalise upon current innovations in education, such as the technology of connected learning, and upon the strengths and interests of our young students. The executive positions and teaching staff have been selected on merit. Our teachers design learning frameworks to make full use of digital technology and peer to peer networking. In 2010 xsel had an enrolment of 30 Year 7 students. This 21st Century learning environment is innovative in design and mode of operation. We provided high quality support to our teachers, our students and our parents as we transformed the secondary learning environment.
>
> (Interview with C. McDiarmid, 2012)

Based on the values of equity, access and entitlement, xsel's mission is to bring a challenging curriculum to the selective school students of Western Region whilst they attend their local secondary school. xsel students can attend their local public secondary school and still access the selective strands of English, Maths and Science. They belong to their local community school yet are connected, via advanced technologies with other selective school students throughout this large region which spreads out over 385,000 square kilometres (the size of Germany). xsel parents no longer face the difficult decision to send their talented child away from home to access the selective schools which are concentrated in the metropolitan areas. Not only is this a financial burden, it is at an enormous emotional cost to the student, their family and their community. xsel teaching staff are selected from applicants across the region. They too can stay in their local rural community and participate in the xsel program.

(Interview with B. Adams, 2012)

Teachers in NSW Schools

The NSW Department of Education and communities is the employer of teachers in government schools in the state. It is the largest employer of teachers in the state, responsible for approximately 49,000 teachers. Employment opportunities for teachers in the nongovernment sector are coordinated through the relevant peak bodies: the Catholic Education Commission Offices (CEO) dioceses for Catholic schools; and Independent Schools of NSW for individual independent and other nongovernment systemic schools.

The majority of the permanent school teacher workforce in NSW is aged more than 45 years, including those of retirement age who choose to remain in the workforce. Over 47% of permanent school teachers are under 45 years of age, up from approximately 41% in 2005 (Table 2.4, DEC, 2015a). This requires effective planning processes by DEC to replenish the workforce with teachers in the younger age groups. Related strategies have included incentives to attract candidates to hard-to-fill positions, stronger teacher remuneration, and improved working conditions that include teacher time and class sizes.

Table 2.4 School Teacher Age Distribution: 2008, 2013, and 2018.

Age group	2010 (actual)	2015 (Actual)	2020 (projected)
Under 30	9.6%	9.6%	9.2%
30–44	33.8%	38.0%	39.5%
45 and over	56.6%	53.6%	51.3%
Total	100%	100%	100%

Source: NSW Department of Education and Communities, (2015) *2015 Teaching Workforce Supply and Demand.*

Teacher Remuneration

Salaries for teachers in government schools are set by the state, but in negotiation with the teachers union. In NSW, this includes the NSW Teachers Federation and other education stakeholders. At the beginning of their career, NSW teachers have high commencing salaries in comparison to graduates entering other professions. The starting salary for a graduate teacher in 2016 is A$63,621 (NSW Crown Employees (Teachers and Related Employees) Salaries and Conditions Award 2014).

NSW is one of several states that have recently moved to align salary structures with national professional teaching standards. Previously, teachers' salaries increased in 13 (typically annual) incremental steps, with the most experienced classroom teachers earning A$89,050. On reaching this level teacher's salary plateaued and was no longer strong compared to other professions. There was also typically little change in the teacher's role as they progressed through the salary scale.

The state has established a new performance and development framework for teachers, and from 2016 teachers will transition onto a new standards-based salary structure that certifies teachers at the three career path stages of Graduate, Proficient, and Highly Accomplished (Table 2.5). The new salary for teachers certified at the Highly Accomplished level of the national standards has been raised substantially, to over A$101,000, and almost a third higher than the average annual teacher salary. Teachers at this higher level will have greater responsibilities—including to support the development of high quality teaching practices in schools. Equivalent to the salary for an assistant principal, this higher certification provides a pathway for keeping experienced teachers in the classroom. (See also the Teacher Career Path and Leadership Development section below.)

Table 2.5 NSW Standards-Aligned Classroom Teacher Salary Rates, 2016.

Salary band	Standards-aligned level	Annual salary
Band 3	*Highly Accomplished*	A$101,614
Band 2	*Proficient Step 2.3*	A$95,466
	Proficient Step 2.2	A$87,096
	Proficient Step 2.1	A$83,793
		A$80,497

Band 2	*Proficient*	A$77,200
		A$73,903
		A$70,603
		A$67,300
Band 1	*Graduate*	A$64,008

Source: Australian Education Union (2015), Classroom teacher
salary/remuneration rates. (www.aeufederal.org).

Teacher Recruitment Incentives

Although competitive salaries for early career teachers contributes to
strong overall recruitment into teaching, the state government provides a
number of incentives to attract candidates in priority subjects and high-
need areas. DEC offers Teacher Education Scholarships for those interested in working in public schools in western and southwestern Sydney,
and noncoastal areas of NSW. Recipients receive a training allowance
during their studies (A$5000), relocation costs (A$3000), and loan assistance (up to A$1,700 annually), but must remain in their full-time teach-
ing positions for three years. Around 80 of the 300 scholarships provided
annually are made available exclusively for Aboriginal and Torres Strait
Islander candidates.

There are currently three additional opportunities for recruiting high
quality teachers in New South Wales. These opportunities include cadet-
ships, internships, and rural scholarships for student teachers. The Great
Teaching, Inspired Learning Cadetship and Internship programs offer student teachers the opportunity to work as an educational paraprofessional
during their initial or final year of teacher training respectively. In this
capacity, cadets experience the day-to-day life of a teacher while working
in a school, while interns assist, support, and work closely with teachers
to improve student learning outcomes. Each is paid for their work as
part-time educational paraprofessionals and are guaranteed a permanent
teaching position at completion of their teacher education program.

The third major recruitment opportunity is Teach.Rural. This opportunity is offered to high achieving students who are interested in experi-
encing living and teaching in a rural and remote community. The program
offers a way to fast track employment and promotional opportunities.
Teach.Rural scholars receive a A$6,000 annual training allowance while
studying full time for a teaching qualification. At completion of their
teacher education program they are guaranteed permanent employment

in an agreed rural and/or remote location and awarded an additional A\$5,000 to assist with expenses such as relocation costs.

Recruitment Incentives for Rural and Remote Areas

Incentives to teachers come in different forms. Teachers who accept positions in rural or remote sections of the state, typically in noncoastal areas receive a range of benefits. It is significant that 10% of NSW government schools are on the incentive program as they are in remote locations. The benefits vary from school to school and may include additional training days, rental subsidies, retention benefits for teachers in isolated schools, and additional summer vacations.

The Beyond the Line initiative is a pathway to teachers wishing to gain exposure in rural and remote schools. Successful applicants receive financial incentives towards accommodation and travel related to their placement. Individuals who are selected for this opportunity live in the community to learn more about the culture and gain insight on rural teaching. Students in their final year of teacher education participate in a week long exploratory mission placement. They observe teachers in their rural classrooms, ask questions, and make assessments based on what they experience before embarking on full-time professional experience.

Casual and Temporary Teachers

Many teachers in NSW schools start their careers as casual or temporary teachers. Casual teachers are employed on a day-to-day basis to replace permanent teachers who are absent from the classroom due to personal or professional reasons, while temporary teachers are employed full-time for four weeks to a year or part-time for two terms or more. Casual teachers earn between A\$323 and A\$370 a day, while the longer term arrangements of temporary teachers come with benefits similar to those of a permanent teacher, such as a prorated salary and leave entitlements.

DEC has a *Graduate Recruitment Program (GRP)* in place that allows students to apply for teaching positions while in their final two semesters of study. The GRP is the recruitment mechanism used for teacher education graduates seeking casual, temporary, or permanent employment in NSW public schools. Eligible applicants must be enrolled in an accredited initial teacher education program through a university in NSW or ACT, and a full-time or part-time student in their last two semesters of study. The graduate recruitment process is highly competitive and is a key strategy to enable the best graduates to enter schools immediately after graduation.

Portraits of School Practice

The increased opportunities for school decision making and the new resource allocation model under the Local Schools, Local Decision and the Great Teaching, Inspired Learning reforms are creating opportunities for schools to make changes to how teachers spend their time and create greater opportunities for teachers to work together to improve teacher practice.

Engadine High School: A Portrait of Practice

The School and Its Community

Engadine High School is located in the most southern area of Sydney and is adjacent to Sydney's Royal National Park. The school serves approximately 1,100 students representing a range of abilities and talents. This includes an integrated support unit with four classes supporting 52 students with intellectual disability. Together the school population provides a harmonious environment that is characterized by positive interactions between teachers and students. There is a genuine desire from teachers for students to make the most of opportunities to learn, as students are provided with a comprehensive cocurricular program to develop their abilities and talents. Of particular note is the outstanding work of student leaders in social justice, leadership programs, engineering, performing arts, and a wide range of sports.

Engadine High School is a popular choice of school by parents and their children. The community would be considered mostly middle class with a large proportion (34%) identified as working within the trade sector. However there is a wide variation in socioeconomic circumstances. Approximately 27% of parents have a tertiary education and many of the students will be the first in their family to attend university. In 2014, following school completion, 53% of students entered university and 27% enrolled in Technical and Further Education (TAFE) programs.

At graduation from school Engadine High School students perform well in the Higher School Certificate (HSC) state assessment program with a very high percentage of students attaining the top two bands of performance across most subjects. In 2014, 120 students sat the HSC exams. Among this group of graduates, three students achieved results that placed them in the top 10 in the state in a subject. The highest performing student achieved an Australian Tertiary Assessment Result (ATAR) of 98.7. Twelve students achieved ATARs over 90 and a very large number achieved in the 80s, enabling the majority of students the opportunity to enroll in a program of choice at university. The strength of student results is a reflection of the school's efforts to pursue a culture of learning with high expectations for achievement.

School Resources

The school receives a financial allocation that includes a resource allocation based on student needs. At Engadine High School the Resource Allocation Model (RAM) is calculated by data that indicates that in 2014, 126 students sit in the bottom quartile of the socioeconomic status range and 347 students sit in quartile 2. There are 8 Aboriginal students and 7% of the students are from non-English-speaking backgrounds (NESB). In 2015, the school was allocated A$106,000 to support the learning needs of students. In 2013, prior to the introduction of the equity based resource allocation model, the school was allocated A$4,000 to support the learning needs of students.

The school also receives a financial allocation based on the number of teaching staff and their career stage. The teacher funding allocation for staff salary is preserved for that use. Over the last year the school's annual teacher professional learning allocation for 75 teachers was A$48,000. The principal and teachers of Engadine High School highly value professional learning and over the last year the school allocated approximately A$68,000 to their learning.

In addition to the teacher professional learning funds, the school received A$13,127.38 for each of the six teachers in their first year of teaching. This funding is allocated to enable these teachers to have an additional two hours release from face to face teaching each week as well as one hour each week to release an experienced teacher to provide mentoring support. In their second year, these teachers each receive A$4020.05 for one hour release per week above the allocation of a more experienced teacher. The school uses a range of strategies to maximize the effective use of teacher collaboration which at times enables full days in which teachers work in collaborative teams or alongside their mentor.

Teaching Time and Teacher Professional Learning

The school is staffed with 75 permanent members of the teaching staff. Each classroom teacher teaches a total of 43, 52-minute periods plus 4 periods of sport per fortnightly cycle. On average, they would teach 21–22 periods a week, leaving 5–6 periods each week that are not involved in face-to-face teaching. With this allocation each teacher teaches a total of 18.6 hours per week plus 1.8 hours per week of sport. They have approximately 6.5 hours of non-face-to-face teaching per week. (This is the equivalent of one full day a week. In the local primary school teachers are allocated two hours each week nonteaching time.)

The teachers use non-face-to-face teaching time to prepare lessons, develop and review student assessment, and work together. Teachers at the school engage in a variety of collaborative professional learning strategies. These include, for example, working together on collaborative action learning projects, working alongside a more experienced teacher to implement new curriculum, sharing teaching strategies through professional learning meetings, and team teaching.

The school has established strategic direction teams, which contain representatives from all subject faculties. Each team has taken responsibility for the professional learning of staff and they collaborate in planning and sharing knowledge of best practice. These teams are allocated additional time to meet and a budget to support their initiatives.

Teachers have performance and development plans and are considering a range of ways in which collegial feedback can inform their further learning. This is common practice for teachers in their early years of teaching and is now being extended to involve more experienced staff.

Networking Schools

The principal has initiated collaborative professional learning for school leaders and teachers across a network of local primary and secondary schools. The aim is to build the strength of teaching practices and to work together to contribute to the success of each school in achieving common goals for student learning. Principal Joanne Jarvis is focused on the development of system leadership. She states, "I believe that by working in partnership with each other and our university partner; using evidence-based practices, sharing innovation, and developing the capacity of aspirational leaders across our schools, we will ensure that confidence in public education is maintained and our students learning will flourish."

Homebush West Public School: A Portrait of Practice

The School and Its Community

Homebush West Public School is located in Sydney's Western suburbs. The school provides education for approximately 500 children between the ages of five and twelve. Ninety-five percent of students at the school are from language backgrounds other than English and 21 languages and cultures are represented at the school. The student backgrounds are very diverse and this is reflected in the school's social indicators with the student population being spread evenly across each quartile of economic advantage. The school size and this level of complexity have a direct impact on the school's funding.

The school receives a funding allocation based on the number of teaching staff and their career stage. The school has 28 teachers including the principal. This includes two teachers to support students who have English as a Second Language, a community language teacher, and teachers who support students with specific learning difficulties. Ninety-five percent of the teachers at Homebush West PS are New Scheme Teachers and operate under the terms and conditions of the NSW Institute of Teachers Act.

The school has a strong emphasis on continual improvement to maximize both student learning and student well-being outcomes. Within the curriculum framework the school places an emphasis on creative thinking and collaborating both within and beyond the classroom and school. These elements of creative thinking and collaborative practice are key features of both student and teacher learning.

School Resources

The school receives a financial allocation that includes a resource allocation based on student needs. Since the introduction of the Resource Allocation Model (RAM) the school has received a significant increase in funding. This has been as a result of the needs-based funding model calculated on the basis of the school's student complexity data.

The school has successfully implemented the new reforms through a cohesive leadership strategy that has brought together utilization of the new needs-based funding RAM, the increase in the principal's capacity to make autonomous spending decisions based on the local context of the school (Local Schools, Local Decisions), and the increased alignment of policies within the Great Teaching Inspired Learning reforms. This has resulted in the development of new school systems to build teacher quality to maximize student learning outcomes.

Teaching Time and Teacher Professional Learning

As part of the government staffing formulae for primary schools each classroom teacher in the school is allocated two hours release from face-to-face teaching each week. On average, they teach for 5 hours a day, or 25 hours a week. In addition to this time teachers are allocated extra duties relating to student supervision. Primary school teachers are allocated two hours each week nonteaching time. The teachers who are in their first years in the profession receive additional funding to provide an additional two hours release from face-to-face teaching each week as well as one hour each week to release an experienced teacher to provide mentoring support. At Homebush West Public School these beginning teacher funds created a beginning teacher mentor coordinator position within the school. Teachers work with their mentors to develop individualized professional learning plans. Central to these plans are opportunities for lesson study based on classroom observations as well as access to instructional leaders who support data driven practice and provide feedback on classroom practice.

The school invests over A\$60,000 annually in teacher development, with an average expenditure of A\$2,500 per teacher. All teachers participate in extensive professional learning that is codesigned by teachers and the leadership team. The priorities for professional learning are determined in response to an analysis of quantitative and qualitative data regarding student and teacher learning needs. Professional learning is strongly embedded in a culture of collaboration and there is a strong emphasis throughout the school on observing the impact of teaching in classrooms and improving teaching through collaborative action learning.

The principal emphasizes the importance of a disciplined approach to professional learning to improve classroom practice. Principal Estelle Southhall noted:

> The lesson observations and clear learning goals were very powerful in changing classroom teaching practices. When you can see it in action you get a good sense about what you need to change to increase that learning environment for your students. Formative assessment has been an integral and key driver of change.

> The additional access to funds through the Resource Allocation Model and the additional flexibility through Local Schools, Local Decisions has enabled us to move our best teachers into instructional leadership roles within the school. We have a 2.5 teaching allocation totally focused on improving pedagogy through collaborative professional learning teams that operate both within and beyond the school's classrooms. This is a significant driver of increased teacher expertise and improved outcomes for our students.

Curriculum and Assessment in NSW Schools

The way that curriculum and assessment practices are arranged plays an important role in structuring the work of teachers in NSW schools. Curriculum and assessment are two of several matters managed by the NSW Board of Studies, Teaching and Educational Standards (BOSTES), established in 2014 from the merger of the NSW Board of Studies, and the NSW Institute of Teachers.

The Board of Studies was established in 1990 to serve government and nongovernment schools by providing leadership over curriculum development for K–12, managing the NSW Higher School Certificate (HSC) examination for grade 12, and providing advice on grading and assessment policies and procedures. It also had responsibility for the registration and accreditation of nongovernment schools, and establishing the high school qualifications: the Record of Achievement (year 10, formerly the School Certificate), and the HSC (year 12). The Institute for Teachers, established in 2004, was responsible for the registration and accreditation of all teachers at all levels, the approval of all teacher education courses, and the endorsement of teachers' professional learning and professional teaching standards.

Their merger was inspired by an analysis of high-performing OECD jurisdictions, including Finland, Singapore, and Hong Kong. This brought together into one governing body, the standards for school students as described in the curriculum and the professional standards for teachers. The strategy was designed to enhance the opportunity for research to inform improvements in teaching and learning, by bringing teacher training and accreditation into closer alignment with curricula, and linking teacher quality measures to student assessment.

Curriculum

The core principle underlying curriculum development in the state is that all students should have access to a broad curriculum that prepares them with 21st-century competencies. As with several other states, NSW has developed new state curricular syllabuses to align them with the Australian Curriculum. English, mathematics, and science were developed in 2011 and 2012, and geography was added in 2015. All government schools are required to deliver programs of study that comply with the requirements of Board of Studies syllabuses, but schools also have discretion to offer courses beyond the board's curriculum.

The NSW primary school curriculum includes six key learning areas: English; mathematics, science, and technology; human society and its environment; creative arts; personal development; health and physical education. The secondary curriculum adds technology and languages as two additional learning areas. A broad range of subjects, vocational education, and life skills subjects can be incorporated into these learning areas.

BOSTES provides indicative guidelines for the amount of time primary schools should allocate for each key learning area. It is envisaged that the syllabus requirements can be taught in 80% of the teaching time available each week, with English and mathematics making up about 50% of the school week (see Figure 2.4). Schools have some discretion for the use of the remaining teaching time. In NSW, there are clear policies that guide school practices to ensure the teacher focuses on the whole child. Thus primary schools may use this time for a variety of activities including school sport, child well-being projects, additional creative and performing arts programs, or community languages.

While *what* is taught in NSW is mandatory, *how* it is taught is the domain of the professional judgment of the teacher. As primary teachers teach all subjects, they will often integrate syllabus areas around a common question or theme. These may, for example, address cross-curricular priorities, or other units to deepen students' learning. BOSTES has developed a robust set of curriculum resources to support classroom implementation. BOSTES, DEC, and professional associations provide extensive quality teaching resources and professional learning to support the development of various teaching strategies.

**Figure 2.4 Indicative Guidelines for Time
Allocation to Learning Areas.**

Time allocated to primary learning areas

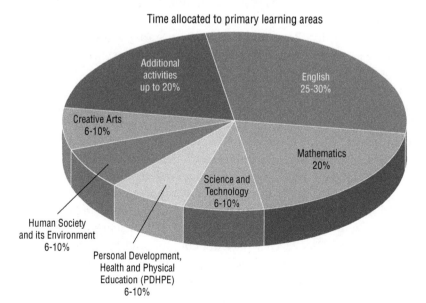

Reproduced from BOSTES, 2015.

One key resource is *Quality Teaching in NSW Public Schools,* developed by DEC in collaboration with the University of Newcastle (DET, 2003b). The resource provides teachers with an evidence-informed model that identifies three key dimensions of pedagogy linked to improved student outcomes:

- Pedagogy that is fundamentally based on promoting high levels of intellectual quality
- Pedagogy that is soundly based on promoting a quality learning environment
- Pedagogy that develops and makes explicit to students the significance of their work

The model and accompanying resources assist schools in implementing an evidence-based model of teacher professional learning. This is done through structured collaborative analysis of practice in the context of Professional Teaching Standards (DET, 2008). (See also Professional Learning below.)

Assessment in NSW Schools

NSW has a strong background in student assessment programs. A core principle for their use in NSW is that assessment information is primarily used formatively, providing information to guide school improvement and student learning. There are two major state assessments: the Basic Skills Testing Program, and the Best Start program. NAPLAN, now taken by students in all states and school systems, originated from NSW's Basic Skills tests.

The Basic Skills Testing Program NSW began full cohort testing of students in 1989, initially for students in grade six, the final year of primary school, and later applied to all students in grades 3 and 5. Individual student results were reported to parents and the school, but while extensive systemic data was gathered by the program, these were not used to compare schools locally. Throughout the development of the testing program, schools sought increased opportunity to use the test as a source of information regarding the impact of their programs. The emphasis within schools was on the provision of diagnostic assessment information to guide teacher programming for student learning. It was understood that the tests enabled only point-in-time information regarding literacy and numeracy, and were intended to be used in the context of the wide range of formal and informal assessments that schools used to assess student progress and future learning needs.

Basic Skills Test results were also communicated to government and the community through Annual School Reports. It is a mandatory requirement for NSW government schools to analyze and report on results from systemic testing, and to describe school improvement targets resulting from this analysis. Achievements against these targets form part of the next annual reporting cycle. As a result, the last decade has seen increased public accountability for educational outcomes largely driven by state and national assessment programs. This has resulted in increased public discourse about school improvement and teacher quality.

Assessment data from the Basic Skills program were also used for system improvement. Since the early 1990s, the NSW Department of Education initiated a range of strategies to promote the alignment of the program with school and system improvement. These included providing schools with increased information to enable the analysis and identification of diagnostic information, performance trends, and links to teaching strategies. By 2003, these additional resources were resulting in increased professional support for the testing programs (Eltis & Crump, 2003). Links to the NSW curriculum were added to the school testing data in 2005, and suggested teaching strategies by 2008. The NSW experience demonstrates that elements that enable a large scale testing program to contribute to improvement include links to a strong well-founded curriculum, extensive teacher professional learning, high quality support materials, and diagnostic tools to enable the analysis of student and school performance (Wasson, 2009).

NSW has since transitioned from Basic Skills to NAPLAN. With the publication of comparative testing and funding data on the MySchool website in 2010, a need to reestablish the balance between assessment for accountability and assessment for learning was identified. Teachers and school leaders have called for quicker turn around on the provision of results from the test, and a new strategy to enable the provision of diagnostic information. As a result, ACARA will begin implementation of online NAPLAN testing from 2017. It is intended that teachers will be able to receive information more quickly, and the tests will be more closely aligned to the Australian Curriculum.

The second major assessment program in NSW is Best Start, taken by children in the first term of their Kindergarten year. The program is designed to identify each student's literacy and numeracy skills on entry to school, and ensure that students are on track by Year 3. All children in NSW, including those with special needs, participate in the assessment, resulting in a profile that informs the development of teaching and learning programs that are aligned to each student's need. The profile is provided to parents and enables a shared platform for the discussion of student learning programs. The program is also designed to inform early learning programs, and is supported with teacher professional learning and a range of teaching resources.

The NSW commitment to provide frameworks to scaffold teacher assessment and guide learning is also evidenced in the further years of schooling. The Literacy continuum K–10 and the Numeracy continuum K–10, for example, provide an outline of the sequential development of key concepts in the key aspects of literacy and numeracy. Synthesizing extensive national and international research, these continua provide the framework for literacy and numeracy professional learning programs. They are designed to support teacher assessment of student learning, and to develop differential teaching programs based on current student achievement. The continua act as a mechanism for establishing learning targets and form a framework to guide professional discussions regarding teaching practices.

The systemic and school data obtained from Basic Skills, NAPLAN, and Best Start programs in NSW has over time been used to provide point-in-time information to identify successful school practices, allocate systemic resources, develop curriculum resources and professional learning programs, and to assist schools to determine key priorities and strategies for improvement.

When systemic assessment programs are strongly resourced and clearly aligned to teaching and learning, they are more likely to be well received by teachers and schools. In NSW, the provision of diagnostic information linked to curriculum resources and professional learning has enabled the assessment programs to be perceived as another source of credible data to guide the development of learning programs. When the balance is tipped towards assessment for the purpose of external judgment, school ranking, and marketing, professional trust in the assessment process is placed at risk.

Teacher Quality in NSW Schools

Great Teaching, Inspired Learning (NSW Policy) (Link 2-4)

The Great Teaching, Inspired Learning (GTIL) policy sets the present context for teacher education in NSW. It identifies teachers as the most important in-school factor related to student performance. The definition of *quality* is described in terms of 21st-century "knowledge, understanding, skills and values," including: deeper learning, creativity, interpersonal communication, problem-solving abilities, confidence, social connectedness, and lifelong learning (DEC, 2013a). Teacher attributes are articulated as a balance of content knowledge, the ability to assess student needs, and capability to employ multiple teaching strategies.

Great Teaching, Inspired Learning has been developed to provide an evidence informed, holistic strategy to guide the development of the teaching profession in all NSW schools. The strategy drew on international research, policy trends, and impact measures. The strategy also drew heavily on NSW student learning, teacher professional learning, and teacher recruitment and workforce planning data to inform the key areas for change.

The strategy was initially developed to shape teacher quality policy and practice within NSW government schools. Following the review of the initial draft, the Minister for Education requested that the reforms be expanded to focus on all teachers and all schools in NSW including Catholic and independent schools. This enabled the reforms to address the practices of the NSW Institute of Teachers, independent schools, schools within the eleven Catholic diocesan areas across NSW, as well as DEC schools.

The development of the reforms involved significant consultation between the Department of Education and Communities, the NSW Institute of Teachers, the NSW Board of Studies, the leaders of the Catholic Education Diocesan Offices, the Association for Independent Schools, the Tertiary Education Council representing the Deans of Education from the seventeen providers of teacher education, and the teacher education unions including the NSW Teachers Federation and the Independent Education Union.

The Great Teaching, Inspired Learning reform strategy focuses on the career stages of teachers with an explicit focus on initial teacher education (ITE); entry into the teaching profession; developing professional practice; and recognition and sharing of best practice. Each is discussed below.

Key aspects of the policy in initial teacher education include establishing literacy and numeracy standards for preservice teachers, raising the quality of ITE programs through greater involvement of the NSW Institute of Teachers with ITE providers, and placement of teacher candidates with Highly Accomplished or Lead teachers during their professional experience. These are accompanied by initiatives to strengthen the quality of, and access to, teacher induction and mentoring programs.

The GTIL policies also seek to strengthen teachers' professional practice by formally linking teacher performance processes and professional learning plans to the Australian Professional Standards for Teaching, and facilitating the removal of teachers unable to meet those standards. The policy suite also promotes the investigation of opportunities for professional collaboration and the sharing of effective teaching practices (DEC, 2013a).

Teacher Preparation in NSW

Under Great Teaching, Inspired Learning, NSW is implementing significant policy reforms to raise the status and ensure the quality of graduating teachers. These reforms include raising and mandating the minimum university entrance levels for education degrees to ensure that those who choose teaching as a career are high academic performers with strong personal attributes for teaching.

The reforms also continue the refinement of quality assurance processes to ensure teacher degrees produce high quality graduates. This includes strategies to ensure that all teacher education students receive high quality professional experience as part of their teacher education programs and that programs include a requirement for rigorous and continuous research. Thus the key themes in initial teacher education in NSW are:

o raised standards for entry into the profession

o consideration of personal attributes as well as academic outcomes for entry into teacher training programs

o increased emphasis on professional practice and close partnerships with schools

o a focus on the quality of graduates rather than auditing program content against the standards

Alignment of Australian Strategies to Improve Initial Teacher Education in NSW (Link 2-5)

As noted in the first chapter of this volume, the Australian government has federal responsibility for initial teacher education. Strategy at the national level for reform of initial teacher education was articulated in the 2015 *Action Now* report of the Teacher Education Ministerial Advisory Group (TEMAG), which specifically highlighted the need to lift the quality, professionalization, and status of the teaching profession. The implementation of the reform actions is being overseen by AITSL.

Yet the report also acknowledged the current work already under way in states and territories such as NSW, which is implementing strategies to quality assure teacher education courses. These actions are significant in that over a third of Australia's teacher training institutions are within NSW, and thus exercise influence on the shape of federal recommendations.

The future directions of the initial teacher education reforms outlined by NSW in Great Teaching, Inspired Learning are as follows:

- Entrants into teacher education will be high academic performers, have well-developed literacy and numeracy skills, and show an aptitude for teaching.

- Teaching will attract more of the brightest and motivated school leavers and career changers.

- NSW teacher education programs will produce high quality graduates with personal attributes suited to teaching.

- All teacher education students will receive high quality professional experience as part of their teacher education programs.

- The quality of the teaching workforce in NSW will be informed by a strong evidence base. (DEC, 2013a)

These actions mirror the five themes elaborated by the federal government in the area of initial teacher education reform—stronger quality assurance; more rigorous selection of candidates; improved and structured practical experience; robust assessment of graduates; and improved national research and workforce planning capabilities (TEMAG, 2015a).

In the media release in response to the release of national reforms, NSW Minister for Education Adrian Piccoli said the Australian government's response to the TEMAG review demonstrates a shared commitment with NSW to improve the quality of teaching:

"Great teaching leads to the best results for students so I welcome the Commonwealth Government's focus on the quality of teacher education," Mr. Piccoli said. "This review and the Commonwealth's response endorses the approach taken by NSW through our Great Teaching, Inspired Learning (GTIL) reforms which have focussed on improving the quality of teaching." Mr. Piccoli said that in some areas NSW has already introduced higher standards than those suggested by the review. "For example, from next year, school leavers entering teaching degrees in NSW will need to have a mark of 80 or higher in three of their HSC subjects, including in English," he said. "I make no apology for setting high standards—it is what the community expects—and NSW will continue with its new requirements. Quality teaching is the single largest in-school influence on student results, which is why the NSW submission to the review was coordinated by the Board of Studies, Teaching and Educational Standards (BOSTES) and endorsed by all school sectors, presenting a united NSW position. Over the next few months BOSTES will go back to schools and universities to consult with [the Australian Government] on the [TEMAG] review's specific recommendations and opportunities to build on the successes of GTIL."

(DEC, 2015e)

Entry Standards

Traditionally, there has been significant variation in the entry levels of people entering teacher preparation programs. In 2013, the ATAR scores of entrants into ITE programs ranged from 58.80 to 94.30 (DEC, 2013a, p. 7), indicating that entrants ranked above at least 58.8% of students from that year. In 2012, more than 20% of entrants to undergraduate initial teacher education courses had ATAR scores below 60, and education was the least popular course for students with ATAR scores of 90 or above.

While ATAR scores are very high in some teacher education institutions and have remained steady in others, some institutions admit a much larger proportion of their cohorts with ATAR scores lower than 60. There has not been a formal study in NSW to determine which educational programs are most highly regarded, however principals frequently cite the high quality of students from specific institutions. These students tend to be from universities who have placed an emphasis on the value of teacher professional experience and the connection of this experience to the program content and they have strong systems of support for the school placements.

Raising the entry standards is an important platform of the NSW GTIL reforms. Reflecting on the raising of entry standards DEC Secretary for Education, Michele Bruniges, stated that:

> [It has]caused a great deal of discussion and debate, healthy discussion and debate here in New South Wales and indeed in Australia, but I think importantly we've come on a landing on some of the things, and we're working with the tertiary sector to get a better alignment between what we believe should be there and what they believe from their research to make sure that we get high-quality applicants coming in but also acknowledging the work that the tertiary sector does through the teaching profession. You can't ever put enough emphasis on a love of learning, the passion for teaching and the capacity to really support students on their lifelong journey.

(Bruniges, 2015)

NSW has recently introduced a range of strategies and incentives to attract more high performing academic school leavers into teaching. These strategies include increasing the number and range of scholarships for students who achieve very strong school results in subjects where there is a need for more teachers such as mathematics and science, and for students who wish to teach in rural and remote communities. Another strategy involves the identification of high performing students with an aptitude for teaching early in their secondary schooling and supporting them on graduation in a pathway into a teaching career.

Entry standards into Initial Teacher Education in NSW reflect both the movement toward national policies in education as well as a significant drive to enhance the professional status of teacher education. This is leading to a strengthening of requirements for admission into initial teacher education programs. At both the state and federal levels, NSW and AITSL have three interrelated policy initiatives: the development of national selection guidelines—focusing on both academic achievement and personal qualities such as communication, social, emotional, and interpersonal skills—and the development of both national literacy and numeracy, and professional experience, assessments.

NSW standards are higher than those at the national level. There is a requirement that applicants for an education degree should be in the top 30% of the population in literacy and numeracy (AITSL, 2011a). NSW formerly required all entrants to undergraduate initial teacher education programs to have at least a Higher School Certificate (HSC) level of Band 4 in each of English and General Mathematics for primary teaching, and in English for secondary teaching. Under the Great Teaching, Inspired Learning reforms, these have been raised to a minimum of three HSC Band 5 scores, one of which must be English. An additional literacy and numeracy assessment is being developed by BOSTES in consultation with initial teacher education providers to ensure that their graduates meet the 30% requirement (DEC, 2013a, p. 8).

The new entry standard also includes a framework to identify personal attributes for teaching that are aligned with the Graduate Teaching Standards, and are a component of the final professional experience assessment. The framework underpins the development of instruments and strategies for assessment of candidates for teaching at different points, such as prior to entry into Initial Teacher Education programs, at strategic points during teacher education programs, and prior to graduation and employment. It also supports school principals in identifying and encouraging promising school students to consider a career in teaching.

Accreditation of Initial Teacher Education Programs in NSW

There are seventeen different providers of Initial Teacher Education in NSW. Traditionally, the NSW Department of Education managed the approval of initial teacher education programs. Quality assurance of these programs became a role of the NSW Institute of Teachers in 2004 when it was formed in 2004. The NSW Institute of Teachers policies for the accreditation of initial teacher education programs were approved in 2006, and updated in November 2012 to conform to the Australian Professional Teaching Standards. A new guide to the accreditation of initial teacher education programs was subsequently released by AITSL in 2013, and was again updated to reflect new initiatives promulgated in 2016.

The accreditation process requires that initial teacher education program providers collect evidence for training teachers against each of the descriptors for each of the standards on the Australian Professional Teaching Standards. Approved providers in NSW are primarily the universities, although there are approved courses from a small number of smaller colleges and institutes.

Under the Great Teaching, Inspired Learning reforms, annual assessments of the quality of Initial Teacher Education programs have been introduced (DEC, 2013a, p. 9). This phraseology suggests that NSW is approaching the reforms from a state-centered perspective, while aligning to and being ahead of, coming federal policy reforms.

It is clear that the systems introduced by the NSW Institute of Teachers (now BOSTES) have increased the rigor of the review of teacher education programs. The professional teaching standards have increased clarity regarding the required content of the programs, including the requirements for professional experience. Current discourse between providers, employers, and AITSL is now focused on the quality of the audit of course content compared to a focus on the quality of program graduates.

It is also clear that the systems that have operated in NSW have provided guidance for AITSL in the implementation of a national approach to the assessment of teacher preparation programs. Patrick Lee, the former CEO of the NSW Institute of Teachers, described the previous "chaotic way we do education policy in Australia" when he refers to the fact that prior to 2012 "more than half of the jurisdictions had never really ever assessed teacher education courses" (Lee, 2014).

Teacher Education Curricula

The introduction of the NSW Professional Teaching Standards in 2004 created a framework for the review of teacher preparation programs.

Since 2007, to help strengthen teacher preparation, all teacher education programs delivered in NSW have undergone a rigorous assessment process designed to improve the quality of graduate teachers and ensure they have met professional teaching standards. The first cohort of students from programs based on these standards entered the profession in 2012.

In 2012, NSW Initial Teacher Education requirements were further revised to incorporate the nationally agreed *Accreditation of Initial Teacher Education Programs in Australia: Standards and Procedures* (AITSL, 2013). Under the GTIL reforms, the impact of changes to teacher preparation programs will be assessed.

The requirements for teacher preparation are designed to support the Graduate Teaching Standards and include a rigorous intellectual preparation with strong subject discipline knowledge, as well as knowledge and skill in the key elements of teaching practice. All teacher education degrees must also include detailed instruction in areas that have been identified as a priority, including classroom and behavior management, literacy, technology, Aboriginal education, special education, and education for students with diverse linguistic and cultural backgrounds. There is a strong focus on developing teacher expertise to interpret student assessment data, evaluate student learning, and modify teaching practice.

Applicants for graduate entry programs must have completed an undergraduate degree that includes discipline-specific content relevant to the curriculum area or areas in which they intend to teach. Explicit subject content requirements must be met during undergraduate teacher education programs or by graduates, who undertake postgraduate Initial Teacher Education. Primary teaching programs address subject curriculum subject content and related pedagogy. Secondary programs must provide for a major in the first teaching method and a minor in additional methods. Entrants into postgraduate programs must meet these discipline requirements in their initial undergraduate degree.

The NSW and Australian Standards and procedures include requirements for entry, subject content, discipline specific pedagogy and curriculum knowledge, nationally agreed priority areas of study, and professional experience.

Professional Experience in Initial Teacher Preparation Programs

As part of any education qualification all student teachers must spend some time in a school working as a teacher in professional placements, developing and demonstrating their knowledge and skills. These placements must be at least sixty days in two-year graduate courses and eighty days in four-year undergraduate courses. Each year more than 18,000 professional experience places are provided in NSW government schools. The quality of the professional practice is considered to be a significant factor in the development of teacher quality. Under the NSW Institute of Teachers Act (2004), evidence of clinical practice is a requirement for the accreditation of teacher education programs.

Undergraduate and postgraduate initial teacher education programs incorporate professional experiences (a teaching practicum) into their curricula. For example, the Bachelor of Arts (Primary) program at the University of Sydney is a four-year program that combines education theory, pedagogy, subject knowledge, and indigenous education with professional practice placements. The placements are in the second semester of each of the second, third, and fourth years, and are fifteen, twenty, and thirty days in duration respectively. The University's two-year Master of Teaching program involves twenty days placements for the second semester of year one, the first semester of year two, and a semester-long internship throughout the second semester of year two.

NSW has introduced a range of strategies with the aim to ensure that all teacher education students receive high quality professional experience as part of their teacher education programs. The features of successful placement include clear partnership protocols between the university and the school, professional learning support for teacher supervisors, transparent and agreed guidelines for the assessment of students, and agreed funding arrangements to support the placement. Successful professional experience includes a whole school commitment to the collective examination of teaching.

Under the Great Teaching, Inspired Learning reform strategy, greater emphasis is being placed upon professional practice as a core component of initial teacher education programs. The intent of the policy is that professional placements of students in these programs be supervised by teachers accredited to Highly Accomplished or Lead Teacher levels, and that these teachers have undergone specific professional learning in order to supervise students. A second arm of the policy sets out expectations for providers for the outcomes of professional placements, and develops evaluation tools to provide consistent assessment of professional experience by students in initial teacher education programs across providers in NSW (DEC, 2013a, pp. 9–10).

Paul Brock, Director of Learning and Development Research in the Department of Education and Communities, highlights the important of collaborative practice between initial teacher education and schools when he states:

[T]here are some things that a student can learn in pre-service teacher education at a university that the university is the best place, most appropriate place and context to learn. There are other things in a pre-service teacher education program that can only be learned in practicum, out there in the classroom, in schools ... and it's a mistake to blame or expect one to provide the learning experience that can be provided really only by the other ... the trick is to make sure ... they reinforce each other.

Innovations in Initial Teacher Education

Under recent policy changes, postgraduate programs in initial teacher education are required to be a minimum of two years, although several universities have been developing their programs in terms of length and rigor in advance of policy.

The national leader in this process has been the University of Sydney, who made significant changes to the quality of teacher preservice education well before this was mandated. In 1996 the University of Sydney established Australia's first Master of Teaching (M.Teach) program. The two-year, full-time program of study was developed in recognition of the importance of a high-level, inquiry-oriented professional study to enable teachers to meet the needs of both the rapidly changing society and the profession. The highly competitive program, catering to 2,050 students annually, was underpinned by a strong commitment to enable teachers to focus on their own ongoing learning as well as that of their students. This focus entailed a strong commitment to social justice.

The program provides ongoing case-based inquiry through school experience, including a final ten-week internship that is designed to provide a bridge between study and full-time teaching. During the internship, the teaching load is about two thirds that of a teacher. This strategy supports teacher inquiry to implement a final action research study during the internship. The preservice teacher's learning is supported by a mentor who assists them to develop new and explicit professional understandings. The preservice teachers graduating from this program are highly valued by school and system leaders.

Teach for Australia in NSW

In contrast with some states that have provided greater space for alternative entry programs, NSW has resisted the Australian federal government's strategy to implement the Teach for Australia program. This program enables graduates from other professions to enter teaching after an introductory six-week program that is then supplemented with further learning over two years. The NSW Board of Studies, Teaching and Educational Standards (BOSTES) has not approved the course as it was not deemed to adequately prepare a person to meet the requirements of the professional teaching standards and therefore could potentially compromise the learning of school students. Tom Alegounarias, president of the BOSTES, stated, "It is imperative learning opportunities for students are not compromised for the convenience of short-term packaged approaches. All students deserve teachers that have been fully prepared" (Dodd, 2014).

There is a strong belief underpinning the policy decisions in NSW—that all students should have a teacher who is well prepared and that the development of the professional teaching standards requires a rigorous focus over time. This view is also shared by academics at the University of Sydney, school leaders, and teacher unions in NSW who consider that the program does not support the Australian government agenda of increasing the quality of teaching. Professor Robyn Ewing, the acting pro-dean from the Faculty of Education and Social Work at the University of Sydney highlights the importance of a rigorous approach to teacher education when she states:

> [P]rograms like Teach for Australia that give such a small amount of time to actually engage in the issues and to look at things from a lot of different perspectives don't necessarily give pre-service teachers enough reflection and time to really think about what they're doing. If we don't do that we are just in danger of repeating the way that we were taught, because after all we've all had 16,000 plus hours being at school, and we will just do what Michael Apple says and repeat what is part of our saturated consciousness. We wanted to intervene. We wanted people to reflect very consciously about their own education and about what they needed to do to interrupt that, if they were going to be truly innovative in terms of what's needed to be learners in the 21st century.

This view is also shared by the NSW Teachers Federation, the union for government school teachers. The vice president of the NSW Teachers Federation, Denis Fitzgerald, notes his concern regarding attempts to deregulate aspects of the teaching profession:

> This may be the biggest wave of threat to education, because of the attraction for some in politics to embrace the metaphor of deregulation

and to apply it to education. What we've seen is the coming of both training and educational delivery which almost embraces the concept of the lack of standards and prerequisites. We've seen it in Teach for Australia, which, of course, is merely a pinch from Teach for America, where people can be teachers without any substantial education background, with six week and ten week training courses. Therefore, we need to corral and embrace our standards, if only for this pragmatic reason ... it's not the only reason, but it is time that we do it: that teaching is a profession ... it takes a long time to get to know the first underpinnings of it; that we need substantial undergraduate and postgraduate training. We need standards which are explicit, observable, and occasionally measurable, every year of performance. And that's the complete antithesis to the deregulatory model that has been entertained by policymakers in certain Western countries, and that would be the single most dangerous threat to mass, quality public education. An elite may do well out of it, but the great bulk of people will be left behind, and those kids and communities in greatest need will be the ones that suffer a grievous disservice if that deregulatory model is embraced.

These stakeholder views highlight both some of the resistance along teaching quality grounds to alternative entry programs, as well as the support for quality professional standards to underpin the teacher profession in NSW. However, while the Teach for Australia program is not being implemented in NSW, it is being implemented in four of the seven states and territories, including Victoria.

Teacher Accreditation in NSW

All NSW teachers who began teaching on October 1, 2004 (new scheme teachers), or who have been away from teaching for five or more years, are required to be accredited. This is known as Professional Competence accreditation—or if first employed after 1 October 2012, Proficient Teacher accreditation. Professional competence is accredited against the NSW Professional Teaching Standards (PTS), while Proficient Teacher accreditation is benchmarked against the Australian Professional Standards for Teachers. The Australian standards are similarly structured and map closely to the NSW standards. NSW was the first state to introduce professional teaching standards. The standards were introduced to apply to all teachers employed after the passing of the NSW Institute of Teachers Act in October 2004.

The Act requires teachers employed on a full-time basis to gain accreditation at Proficient Teacher (Professional Competence) within three years. Currently teachers who are offered permanent employment in NSW government schools must be accredited at Proficient in their first year of teaching. Teachers in NSW nongovernment schools employed on a permanent basis generally have up to three years to meet this requirement, with most completing the requirements within 18 months to two years.

NSW is presently amid a reform process combining federal and state initiatives which is shaping teacher accreditation processes. The Great Teaching, Inspired Learning policy reforms will require all teachers to be accredited (DEC, 2013a). By 2018, all teachers in NSW will be required to meet the requirements for, and maintain, accreditation and against the Australian Professional Standards for Teachers.

New graduate teachers are granted either a provisional or conditional accreditation when they are initially employed. A provisional accreditation is granted if the teacher has completed an approved initial teacher education program such as a graduate diploma in education, bachelor of teaching, and master of teaching after completing a bachelor's program or a bachelor of education. Programs are approved by the Institute of Teachers, at a university or other approved higher education institution. A conditional accreditation is granted if the teacher has not completed an approved program but has a bachelor's degree in the content area in which they teach and will enroll in a teacher education program, or has completed a substantial part (3 or 4 years) of an approved teacher education program. In mid-2013, a total of 58,500 teachers were accredited with the NSW Institute of Teachers. Of these, some 26,000 have been accredited as proficient and 32,500 are provisionally or conditionally accredited.

Moving from Provision to Full Accreditation

Achieving full accreditation requires meeting both the employer's accreditation policy, and the criteria set by the NSW Institute of Teachers/ BOSTES. The process for proficient/professional competence involves the following steps:

1. A supervising teacher is assigned and a schedule of observations of teaching practice is established

2. Samples of evidence of teaching practice are collected that reflect the standards is required for each element of the Professional Teaching Standard

3. An accreditation report is sent to the Teaching Accreditation Authority (TAA):

   - in government schools, this may be the Director of Public Schools or the principal
   - in Catholic schools, this may be the Director of Schools for the Diocese
   - in independent schools, this may be the principal or other delegate

4. The Teacher Accreditation Authority will send the evidence and a determination report to the NSW Institute of Teachers, who will contact the teacher to confirm the result.

Maintenance of Accreditation

All teachers must maintain accreditation to at least the proficient/ professional competence level every five years (or seven years for part-time/casual teachers). Maintenance of accreditation (known as teacher registration in some states) requires both demonstration of competence in teaching practices and undertaking professional development, as well as payment of an annual fee (A$100).

Demonstration of professional competence begins with a self-assessment report. Teachers are asked to reflect on their practices and give examples of how their work meets the elements of the NSW Professional Teaching Standards or the standards of the Australian Professional Teaching Standards as applicable. A separate narrative must be submitted for each of seven elements (or standards). The report is then submitted to the designated Teacher Accreditation Authority.

The professional development portion of the accreditation requires that teachers conduct 100 hours of training, at least 50 of which must be through a provider or organization approved by the NSW Institute of Teachers; the remaining 50 hours may be selected by the teacher. All recognized teacher professional learning is classified as registered (quality assured against the professional teaching standards) or teacher identified (identified as addressing the professional teaching standards).

Once the designated Teacher Accreditation Authority has received the accreditation report and verified the number of hours of professional development and the articulated learning that has occurred, a determination of accreditation is made and sent to the NSW Institute of Teachers.

NSW *Professional Teaching Standards (Link 2-6)*

The NSW Institute of Teachers Act (2004) created the opportunity for the creation of a set of teaching standards, a process for accrediting teachers against those standards and a process for maintaining accreditation through professional development. The NSW Professional Teaching Standards were in operation for eight years prior to the introduction of the Australian Professional Teaching Standards. The Australian Standards were strongly influenced by the NSW standards, which were formed through an extensive collaborative process through which the profession tested their validity and efficacy. As a result of this process, the application of the standards have been readily accepted by the profession.

> I think that the standards really put us at a level where we are respected just like other professions are respected out there that have associations and have standards. It also helps to have that common drive or vision or understanding ... we're working towards a common level of profession.

(interview with A. Albini, 2014)

DEC Secretary for Education, Michele Bruniges, highlights the importance of ensuring the standards underpin all aspects of teacher policy when she states, "I think at the heart of the profession a lot of energy, effort and research went into the development of those standards, and not to use them in the most productive way would be educationally negligent"(Bruniges, 2015).

The guiding framework of what teachers should know, understand, and be able to do is outlined within the NSW Professional Teaching Standards. This framework provides direction and structure for the preparation and development of teachers. The four key stages—Graduate, Professional Competence, Professional Accomplishment, and Professional Leadership—map closely to the Australian professional teaching standards. While it is a requirement of all new teachers to be accredited at the Proficient level, certification at Highly Accomplished and Lead is voluntary, although teachers at all levels must maintain accreditation to teach throughout their careers through professional learning and competent teaching practice. The transition to the implementation of the Australian Standards in NSW occurred during 2012–14 (Link 2-7).

Within each of the four stages, the standards describe the nature or depth of the teachers' work in three specific domains: professional knowledge, professional practice, and professional commitment. As with the Australian professional standards, the NSW standards emphasized teachers' knowledge of their subject areas, students and how they learn, effective pedagogies and learning environments, communication with students, ongoing professional learning, and a commitment to the teaching profession and wider community.

Teacher Induction

In NSW, there is a strong evidence base that guides the development of effective induction policies, but matching that knowledge with effective practice in schools requires systems to enable teachers to plan, teach, and assess student learning together. Approaches to induction practices in the state were shaped by the release of *Quality Matters: Revitalising Teaching: Critical Times, Critical Choices* in 2000. This paper provided a critical review of teacher quality in NSW and created a foundation for the establishment of professional teaching standards and related policies and practices. The review highlighted induction as a key point of leverage in the development of teachers:

> The quality of induction following appointment to a teaching position is one of the most important determiners of the self-perceptions which beginning teachers will hold as professional practitioners. What happens in induction is critical to shaping the quality of the teacher's future performance. The induction period is a major test of the extent to which employers, school leaders and the profession are interested in and committed to the quality of teaching in schools.
>
> (Ramsey, 2000)

There are three main strategies to support early career teachers in NSW. The first is the provision of an induction program that enables new teachers to have a reduced teaching load. This facilitates more in-school time for lesson preparation, evaluation, and collaborative work with more experienced teachers. The second strategy is support from a trained mentor teacher. The third is the provision of structured personalized professional learning aligned to the needs of early career teachers and the professional teaching standards.

During the first years of a teaching career, induction programs play a critical role in supporting the development of capable and confident professional teachers. The quality of induction into the profession for beginning teachers is greatly enhanced when teachers have reduced teaching loads and support from trained mentors.

The implementation of a comprehensive induction program for beginning teachers in each school has also been enhanced through the provision of online professional learning for teachers, mentors, and school leaders with the responsibility of supervising the development of teachers. NSW has a significant rural and remote teaching population, and there is a disproportionate number of early career teachers in these locations. The provision of equitable access to quality professional learning has been a strong stimulus for the creation of online professional learning. The NSW Department of Education and Communities online Classroom Teacher Program has provided over 100 hours of registered professional learning for school-based implementation. The program creates an individualized professional learning pathway for teachers that is based on the core practices of successful teaching. The program units have been very popular with teachers across the state and have an average evaluation response of 4.4 on a five-point Likert scale. The professional support for mentors and school leaders is integrated into the program design to support their role in both professional learning and teacher accreditation.

Teacher mentors play a pivotal role in the implementation of induction programs, providing advice and feedback for beginning teachers to develop their skills and compile evidence of their attainment of the professional teaching standards for accreditation. NSW Department of Education and Communities has provided a teacher mentor program since 2003. The program employed 50 teacher mentors who worked across 90 to 100 schools that had a significant numbers of new teachers. These mentors were appointed to schools and annually supported about 60% of the total number of newly appointed teachers in government schools. An evaluation of the teacher mentor program indicates that it has provided benefit in terms of both teacher quality as well as teacher retention.

The impact of the introduction of NSW professional teaching standards in 2005 was clearly seen in the change of focus in the teacher mentor program. The 2004 program evaluation sought information regarding the characteristics of the mentor that were most valued by early career teachers. The most valued characteristics were interpersonal qualities such as empathy and communication. These qualities remained highly valued in the 2006 evaluation but they were ranked alongside evidence of successful teaching practice. The process of teacher accreditation had created a sharper focus on performance and evidence of practice. The standards had in effect created an outcomes framework for teacher professional learning.

Time for mentoring and collaboration is an important factor. All teachers in NSW government schools receive an allocation of two hours each week to enable collaborative planning, lesson preparation, and assessment. Since 2007, beginning teachers in NSW government schools have received an additional allocation of one hour per week. Under the Great Teaching, Inspired Learning reforms, the responsibilities and teaching loads for beginning teachers have been restructured to create greater opportunities for mentoring and collaborative practices that include classroom observation and structured feedback. Teachers in their first year now receive a total allocation of four hours each week. As Michele Bruniges states:

> The collaboration within the profession is absolutely fundamental to teacher development and continuing learning. At a great cost to government and supported by government we put in the release time for the first two years for our beginning teachers, and we wanted certain conditions to be met within the schools for that to happen, so having a mentor in place where that would be consistent over a period of time, that we have ongoing support, that we link to the teacher professional standards so they have a roadmap there for their own professional learning and growth and how their professional learning needed to be linked to that roadmap is incredibly important. So one of the ways in which I see it, that's just the entry to the profession of support for beginning teachers, but every teacher in every classroom deserves the right to be supported, and it's very, very critical that we support teacher collaboration and teacher professional learning right throughout the cycle.

> (Bruniges, 2015)

There are numerous factors that impact the development of teachers in the early phase of their career. Research in teacher quality and retention was undertaken by the NSW Department of Education and Communities in partnership with the University of Technology Sydney between 2005 and 2009. This research sought to identify the key factors that contribute to the retention of teachers during their early years of teaching. This research highlighted the importance of professional learning and collegial support for early career teachers.

A cohort of final-year preservice teacher education students was tracked through their first four years of teaching. When asked to identify the factors that had the greatest impact on their teaching and their desire to stay in the profession nine key factors were seen to be significant. It is interesting to note that the top two factors—student engagement and professional challenge—relate to the capacity to engage students and find satisfaction in teaching. The next seven factors—collegial support, professional collaboration, supervision and mentoring, executive support, staff culture, school climate, and pedagogical support—all relate to professional learning and within school collegial support.

The study revealed that one of the most significant factors contributing to teacher expertise is the provision of feedback on teaching practices and collegial, collaborative professional learning. It is clear that the school must become not only a place for students to learn, but also for teachers to learn. This research now underpins both the policies and practices for teacher professional learning and the new policies for teacher performance and development (McIntyre, 2012).

All teachers returning to the profession are required to refresh and update their knowledge of curriculum, pedagogy, and educational expectations. Returning teacher courses are designed to ensure the currency of teachers returning to the profession after an absence of five years or more. These teachers are also required to undertake accreditation at the level of Proficient Teacher.

Professional Learning and Accreditation

As noted above, teacher professional development is required as a part of teachers maintaining their accreditation to teach. The NSW Institute of Teachers (BOSTES) conceptually separates professional development and learning. Professional development refers to courses or training intended to improve teacher capabilities, while professional learning refers to the demonstration of those capabilities exhibited through teaching practices. Evidence both of participation in teacher professional development and of competent teaching practices is required for accreditation.

Teacher professional development can take the form of courses registered with the NSW Institute of Teachers (BOSTES), or they may be teacher-identified professional development courses, workshops, or other experiences. The proportion of institute-registered versus teacher-identified professional development that may be counted towards accreditation varies depending on the accreditation status of the teacher. Highly Accomplished and Lead Teachers may elect a greater proportion of teacher-identified professional development activities.

Providers of teacher professional development must be registered with the NSW Institute of Teachers (BOSTES) to be able to offer courses for teacher reaccreditation. This involves application to the Institute's Professional Learning Endorsement and Advisory Committee. If the committee endorses the application, it is referred to the Institute's Quality Teaching Council for their decision on registration with the Institute. The Quality Teaching Council is comprised of a chair, 10 elected members who are practicing teachers and principals, and 10 appointed members representing other educational stakeholders.

The institute's processes for endorsing potential professional development providers is guided by consideration of five principles: continuous improvement; Professional Teaching Standards–focused professional development; relevance; flexibility; diversity and innovation; evidence and expertise (NSW Institute of Teachers, 2013). As such, providers seeking registration must demonstrate the Australian Professional Teaching Standards descriptors met by their courses, the research basis for the course, assessment criteria, as well as a range of quality assurance processes to which the provider adheres.

Effectiveness of Teacher Professional Learning

The NSW Department of Education and Communities is the largest endorsed provider of registered professional learning in NSW. As such, the department is required by the institute to keep records of the content and standards addressed in all registered professional development. Records of the delivery date, site, and participants in the program are also required. In order to manage and retain this data, DEC established an online program development, enrollment, and evaluation system.

The online professional learning system, MyPL@Edu enables teachers, schools, and DEC to have records of teacher engagement in, and evaluation of, professional learning. It also enabled a study of the professional learning design attributes that were associated with an improvement in teaching and student learning. The programs that appeared to have the greatest impact on teacher learning were those that had a clear focus on quality teaching, involved active learning over a semester, and engaged teachers and leaders in shared learning. It was also found that the greatest impact occurred when there was a clear link between student learning needs and teacher and school leadership professional learning.

The introduction of professional learning based on the achievement of professional standards created an outcome focus for teacher learning. As awareness increased, more professional learning programs were aligned to the standards, were quality assured in terms of content and learning processes, and were registered. The quality assurance and evaluation systems provided the capacity for program redesign and feedback regarding practices that were most likely to enhance teacher learning. Between 2011 and 2013, the increase in quality assured programs that were registered to the professional teaching standards was over 30%.

MyPL@Edu currently contains data for over 1.2 million enrollments and for over 12,000 courses. The key themes of teacher professional learning are quality teaching and curriculum. There is high engagement in classroom focused professional learning and programs to support school leadership and teacher quality. In 2013, there were over 400,000 enrollments in professional learning programs in MyPL@Edu.

Teacher feedback regarding the benefit of engagement in quality-assured professional learning is strong with an average of between 4.1 and 4.6 on a five-point Likert Scale. This high satisfaction rate is considered to be an indication of the success of the quality assurance process and the professional learning for program designers.

Professional Learning Continuum

The NSW Department of Education and Communities introduced a professional learning and leadership development strategy to build the capacity of teachers and school leaders at each stage of their career. In 2005, the strategy was articulated in a professional learning continuum that mapped professional learning requirements from teacher preparation to school and system leadership. Each career stage was articulated in terms of the impact of the role for students, such as "making a difference in your classroom," "making a difference in your school," and "making a difference in the school next door." The professional learning at each career stage was framed by the Professional Standards for teachers and the NSW School Leadership Capability Framework, and in 2011, the Australian Professional Standard for Principals (Figure 2.5).

Since 2005, the NSW Department of Education and Communities has provided a fully devolved system of professional learning and leadership development. Each year the full professional learning budget of A$36 million has been distributed to all 2,220 schools. The allocation was calculated on the basis of the number of teachers in the school and the distance of the school from large regional centers. In general figures, this funding amounted to an average allocation of A$700 for each teacher in the school or A$1,000 for teachers in rural areas. Additional funding was allocated to support teachers in their first year.

The Annual Teacher Professional Learning survey drew information regarding professional learning priorities from each school's professional learning team. An analysis of this information and consultation with representatives of teachers and school leaders within reference groups enabled the department's Professional Learning and Leadership Development team to design professional learning programs for teachers and school leaders. The programs operated on a cost recovery model with schools selecting which programs or providers to address their priorities. The NSW Department of Education and Communities programs were the most popular with schools.

Figure 2.5 Professional Learning Aligned to Professional Standards in NSW DEC.

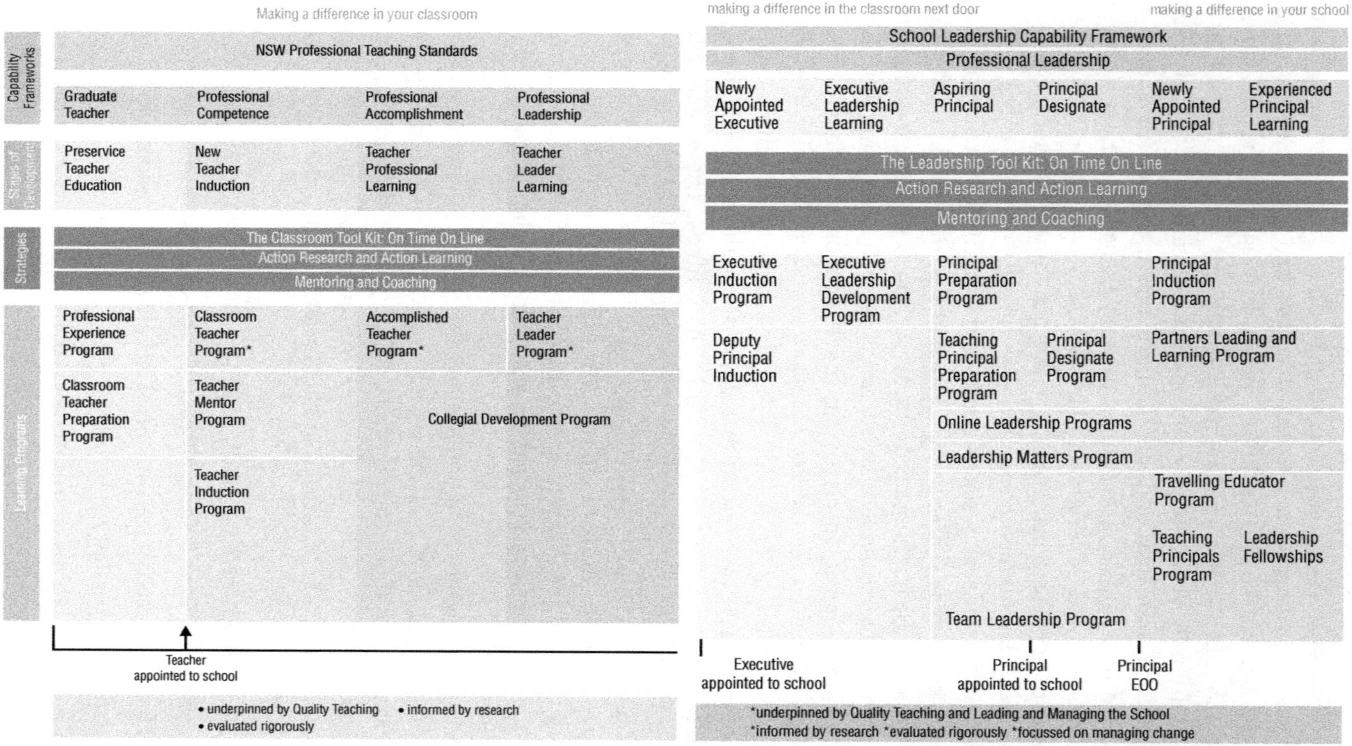

Source: NSW Department of Education and Training, (2005) Professional Learning and Leadership Development Professional Learning Continuum.

Evidence-informed Professional Learning Policy

The NSW professional learning strategy drew on the growing body of evidence regarding what it is that teachers and school leaders do and can do that has the greatest impact on student learning. In NSW government schools, teacher professional learning was the key strategy articulated within the school improvement plan and was linked to both teacher professional standards and school improvement targets. All teachers are required to complete professional learning aligned to their performance management and development plan. Teachers are responsible for determining their professional learning within the context of their professional and career development needs and the priorities of their school.

The devolved school-based professional learning system was driven by two key beliefs. These were, firstly that schools were in the best position to align the learning needs of their teachers with the learning needs of students, and secondly that the professional learning that would have the greatest impact on classroom practices would be that which was closely aligned to the day to day work of teachers within the school. The devolution of professional learning funding to schools required the development of a system to account for both the allocation and the impact of the teacher professional learning funds. This system enabled the gathering of substantial evidence from teachers and school leaders regarding the professional learning strategies that had the greatest impact on the learning of students, teachers, and school leaders. It also paved the way for longitudinal research to establish what teachers find has the greatest impact on their learning and their capacity to teach (McIntyre, 2013).

When approximately 6,000 teachers contributed to research regarding the factors that have had the greatest impact on their learning and the development of their teaching skills they highlighted the relative impact of six key elements of collaborative within school actions. The six key elements that had the greatest impact for primary teachers were, in order of influence:

1. The collaborative preparation of lessons and teaching resources
2. Lesson observation and observing each other's lessons
3. The collaborative assessment and evaluation of student work
4. Structured feedback meetings
5. Developing evidence to demonstrate the achievement of professional teaching standards
6. Team teaching

The six key elements that had the greatest impact for secondary teachers were, in order of influence:

1. Lesson observation and observing each other's lessons
2. Structured feedback meetings
3. The collaborative preparation of lessons and teaching resources
4. Developing evidence to demonstrate the achievement of professional teaching standards
5. The collaborative assessment and evaluation of student work
6. Team teaching (McIntyre, 2013)

The allocation of the system's professional learning budget directly to schools enabled teachers and school leaders to structure time within schools to enable lesson observation and feedback and the collaborative development and evaluation of lessons. This provided a significant source of professional learning for teachers. Each year an average of 60% of teacher professional learning funding was spent on additional teaching time. The benefit of teachers working together highlights the importance of reframing activities within schools to ensure that schools are not only places for students to learn but also places for teachers to learn.

In 2012, the NSW DEC Professional Learning and Leadership Development team completed a further study with an emphasis on teachers who were described by their principals as being accomplished and of high quality. In this study, 750 teachers responded to the question: what are the most effective ways to develop your teaching practice? It is of interest that they also noted the positive impact of collaborative professional learning on the development of their capacity to teach well. These teachers cited the impact of:

o The collaborative preparation of lessons and teaching resources
o The collaborative assessment and evaluation of student work
o Lesson observation and observing each other's lessons, and
o Structured feedback meetings

They also cited two additional influences. The first was their capacity to critically reflect on their teaching practice and its impact on student learning. They also cited as an influence on their own learning the act of leading the professional learning of other teachers. These two factors combine to provide a powerful reason for enabling collaborative teacher-led inquiry to strengthen the link between teaching and student learning.

Figure 2.6 Feedback Informing Teaching Practice.

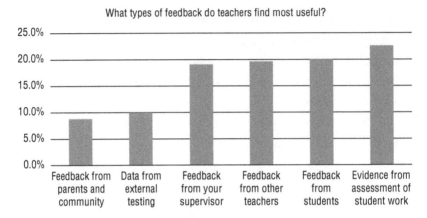

Source: McIntyre (2013), Teacher Quality: Evidence for Action, Australian College of Educators Conference, Sydney, 2013.

Investigation into the most significant sources of feedback to improve teaching has highlighted the importance of within classroom and within school feedback. When 750 highly experienced teachers were asked to describe the type of feedback they found most useful they highlighted the importance of evidence of assessment from student work and feedback from their students. The second most useful source of feedback was feedback from other teachers and their supervisors. (See Figure 2.6.) Data from external testing were rated as having less than half the impact of in-class assessment of student work. It is evident that the key driver of teacher learning is formative assessment conducted during the teaching process. This assessment is most closely connected to the classroom and creates a cycle of continuous feedback for teachers to monitor the impact of their teaching as well as for students to chart the progress of their learning. The highly accomplished teachers were constantly evaluating the difference they make and how they made it (McIntyre, 2013).

In the same study the teachers were asked what types of feedback they sought more often. They identified feedback from other teachers. It is clear that in NSW collaborative inquiry between teachers that is focused on the connection between teaching practices and student learning is a significant, powerful, and sought after opportunity for professional learning. When these teachers were asked to identify the most valuable way of acknowledging teaching excellence they described the value of within school acknowledgment and the significance of the recognition of student achievement.

While teachers were not seeking public recognition it is important that as a profession we identify, share, and learn from the practices of excellent teachers.

In NSW there has been a growing awareness of the impact of collaborative inquiry for teachers and schools to work together to find solutions to shared concerns. This is highlighted in the new teacher quality reform, Great Teaching, Inspired Learning. The final reform is to identify and share excellence in teaching and professional learning through collaboration and learning and to provide teachers with increased opportunity to learn through observing the practices of others and to identify and share evidence of professional learning that improves teacher practice and student outcomes.

Teachers who were interviewed for this study frequently highlighted the value of collaborative professional learning and practice.

> We've talked about our school being a community of learners, seeing everyone as a learner and that we can learn off each other. Teachers learning off teachers and students off students. Teachers off students and vice versa. We thought it's a great way for teachers to learn. They're not just sitting in the classroom by themselves or going to a one-off professional learning and then coming back and trialling something or not trialling something in the classroom. Just having that support with each other. We've looked at changing our professional learning in our school so that teachers are learning as we want the students to learn. Obviously we want students in the classroom working with each other—group work, supporting each other. Reflecting and being critical of each other. That's what we want our teachers to be in their own teaching profession.
>
> (interview with D. McKay, 2014 [Link 2-8])

> The other thing that works with schools is I think just the ability and the willingness of teachers across schools and across areas to share information, to work together, recognizing that we are all part of a profession: the profession of teaching. We don't just lock ourselves away and say, "Well, this is our school. This is our thing. We're going to do well. We're not going to help anyone else." Building up those relationships are so important. That's something that certainly public education really fosters. There's a sense of egalitarianism in those who are involved in public education, who support public education. That's a big thing. That's certainly what makes me and keeps me passionate about what I do.
>
> (interview with S. Holz, 2014 [Link 2-9])

I feel this recently more than ever because we're a larger community. No longer are we in the age where you used to go to a course and you'd bring back something and it would benefit your classroom, your program, but it would stay within those four walls. Those four walls are not there anymore. Working in this manner, collaboratively, you're part of a team. You feel that it's benefiting not only the school but the community as a whole, not just your program.

(Albini, 2014)

In NSW, the evidence of the impact of professional learning on school improvement has demonstrated that effective change in schools requires the alignment of teacher and school leader professional learning. From 2008–2011, NSW designed and implemented an evidence-based professional learning strategy with the aim of providing a cohesive strategy for school improvement in literacy. The strategy involved the implementation of the Team Leadership for School Improvement Program, The NSW DET Analytical Framework for Effective Leadership and School Improvement in Literacy and Numeracy©, and the Focus on Reading 3–6 program in 30 schools. The study provides an overview of school improvement through professional learning that resulted in significant sustained improvement in student learning outcomes in literacy. It incorporates the findings of the *Evaluation of the Take-Up and Sustainability of New Literacy and Numeracy Practices in NSW Schools* (Erebus International, 2012).

The NSW professional learning research has found that the effectiveness of professional learning upon student learning is enhanced when there is:

o An aligned evidence-based collaborative professional learning program for teachers and school leaders

o An explicit framework to guide and chart school and classroom improvement

o A system of data analysis to guide teacher and school leaders actions over time

(McIntyre, 2011)

There has been a strong focus on investigating the types of professional learning that have the greatest impact on teacher and school leader quality and student learning outcomes. This research has been used to inform the development, implementation, and evaluation of teacher professional learning to improve student learning outcomes. NSW research indicates that teaching excellence is enhanced through building the collective understanding of what works best in improving student learning outcomes.

Teacher Appraisal, Performance, and Development

In NSW, professional teaching standards are playing an increasingly significant role in the evaluation of teacher performance. All NSW government teachers, school executive, and principals are involved in an annual performance and development process that is aligned to their role. The evidence of teaching quality that is required for accreditation aligns to the teacher's annual performance management and development process.

Prior to 2015, the performance management policy and procedures for teachers in government schools has been the Teacher Assessment and Review Schedule (TARS) and for executive it has been the Executive Assessment and Review Schedule (EARS). These two policies are implemented within schools by the principal. There has been significant variation regarding the process of implementation both within and across schools. The systems implemented for early career teachers have had a more detailed evidence framework than those for more experienced teachers. This is a direct result of the application of the policies resulting from the implementation of the NSW Institute of Teachers Act. The principals' performance management system is the Principals Assessment and Review Schedule (PARS) and this is implemented by the director.

The Great Teaching, Inspired Learning strategy highlighted the need to reform policies and processes that relate to the development and maintenance of professional practices. The reform areas included amending legislation and policy to bring all NSW teachers within the scope of the Institute of Teachers Act 2004. This will enable all teachers in NSW to be accredited and engage in professional learning and develop their practice in alignment with the Australian Professional Standards for Teachers. The reform also highlighted the need for all teachers to be supported by high quality performance and development processes that align to the standards and the Australian Teacher Performance and Development Framework.

The performance management and development process have been enhanced to strengthen the setting of professional learning goals and the development and implementation of professional learning plans. These plans are linked to the teacher's professional needs, based on an assessment of their performance and school priorities. There is an increasing emphasis on the use of feedback to inform the next stages of professional learning and career development. There is also a strong focus on the provision of professional learning to enable teachers to identify and develop strategies that best support student learning within their school context. Feedback on teacher performance is informed by evidence from student performance data, feedback from direct observations of their teaching practice, and evidence of collaborative practice with colleagues.

All teachers, principals, and executive staff are now required to receive both formal and informal ongoing feedback on their performance and development through the annual review cycle.

In March 2015, the NSW Department of Education and Communities released the policy *Performance and Development Framework for Principals, Executives and Teachers in NSW Public Schools (Link 2-10)*. The purpose of the new framework in the context of effective teaching is evidenced in the following introduction.

> The NSW Department of Education and Communities is committed to attracting, inducting, developing and recognising a high performing workforce. Effective performance and development requires a collaborative and supportive workplace committed to a positive culture of ongoing learning by individuals and teams.
>
> All teachers have a right to be supported in their professional learning as well as a responsibility to be involved in performance and development processes that facilitate their professional growth for the provision of quality teaching and learning. The overarching purpose of the performance and development process is to support the ongoing improvement of student outcomes through continuous development of a skilled and effective teaching workforce.
>
> (DEC, 2015d, p. 1)

The release of this document was forecast in Great Teaching, Inspired Learning and the agreement for its development was referenced in the terms of settlement for the teacher's Salaries and Conditions Award (DEC, 2013c, sec. 5.2). As such, this performance and development process is an agreed framework that has been negotiated from the terms of the award between the NSW Department of Education and Communities and the NSW Teachers Federation. The framework builds upon and replaces the existing TARS, EARS, and PARS processes. The framework also expands the application of the Australian Professional Standards for Teachers as the basis for guiding the development and assessing the performance of all teachers.

The Australian Teacher Performance and Development Framework

The Australian federal government has released the Australian Teacher Performance and Development Framework, which outlines what is required to build a comprehensive and effective approach to high performance and development. The guiding principles include:

- ○ A focus on student outcomes
- ○ A clear effective understanding of effective teaching

o Leadership

o Coherence

o Flexibility

The cycle begins with the teacher and principal working together to set agreed upon goals that are based on the school's shared view of effective teaching derived from the Australian Professional Standards of Teachers. The goals must be documented, regularly reviewed, and measurable. Teachers must receive support toward working on these goals. Teacher performance review must include evidence showing an impact on student outcomes. Teachers must receive regular formal and informal feedback on their performance and development goals. Each state must determine how to operationalize this framework within their system.

In NSW, the teacher's award of 2014 established the industrial framework for the establishment of a new performance and development system for teachers and school leaders (Figure 2.7). It will be important to lead this system to build capacity rather than merely compliance. One key to achieving this is the development of a culture of feedback with an emphasis on professional learning, growth, and shared responsibility rather than on judgment for the purpose of control and external accountability.

Figure 2.7 Australian Teacher Performance and Development Framework.

Source: AITSL (2012) Australian Teacher Performance and Development Framework p. 3

The NSW Teacher Appraisal Cycle

The new performance and development process is based on an annual cycle to guide the planning, implementation, and review of practice. Within the cycle, teachers, school executive, and principals are required to develop a performance and development plan that documents a concise set of three to five professional goals that are explicitly linked to their performance and development needs and the professional standards. There is an expectation that the goals should align to the school plan and systemic strategic directions. There is also an expectation that the goals establish a personalized pathway for each teacher through the alignment to standards by recognizing existing expertise while also identify areas for professional growth.

Teachers and school leaders are then required to work with colleagues and their supervisor to document appropriate strategies and professional learning to support the achievement of their goals. Throughout the implementation of the plan, teachers are required to collect evidence, sourced from their everyday work, that when considered holistically, will demonstrate their progress towards their goals. The evidence that is required must include data on student learning and outcomes, feedback from peer observations of teaching practice, and the results of collaborative practice with colleagues.

The new framework mandates that all teachers, executive, and principals receive ongoing formal and informal feedback on their performance and development throughout the annual cycle. Within this process, they are required to engage in professional discussions with their supervisors to facilitate the provision of a review of their progress towards the goals. The formal written feedback that results from this process is expected to inform the next annual cycle of development.

There are two main formal reviews in the annual cycle. The first is a self-assessment review that should be conducted midway through the cycle and the second is the formal annual review at the end of the cycle. As the Australian Professional Standards for Teachers form the basis of the performance and development process, the annual written feedback can also be used as evidence for maintenance of accreditation.

The aim of the process is to improve individual and collective effectiveness. The plan is to be collaboratively developed and while it is designed to operate on an annual cycle, it is to be responsive to ongoing professional learning needs identified through reflective practice and feedback (Figure 2.8).

Figure 2.8 NSW Teacher Performance and Development Cycle.

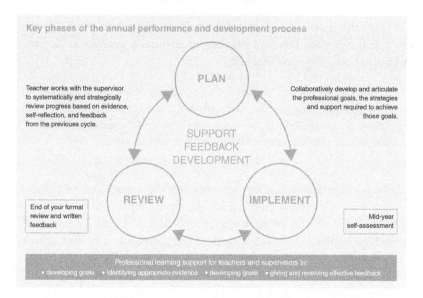

Source: DEC (2015), Performance and Development Framework.

The performance and development system has an emphasis on classroom observations, assessment practices, and curriculum design, and supporting the growth of teacher expertise through action learning, professional reflection, and feedback. Direct observation of classroom practice is an important component of the process and is an essential element of the NSW teacher performance and development framework. There is also a requirement that documented observations by the supervisor of leadership practices of executives and principals are to be conducted.

The framework requires that each teacher receives regular, appropriate, and constructive feedback on their performance, and is supported to identify areas for development and to engage in professional learning to further develop their practice. DEC Secretary for Education Michele Bruniges highlights the importance of high-quality feedback:

> Really teachers have the right for that feedback, and all of our own research tells us that they seek good, constructive feedback. They want to know what they can do better. They want to know what other teachers are doing. They need to construct a means of comparison for

their own learning, and I think through a really healthy collaboration approach and looking at constructive feedback loops, we'll help teachers grow. Now, that is integral to me as part of their performance.

Within the performance and development systems in NSW, there is an expectation that teachers observe each other's practice to improve practice, as noted by one teacher:

> I think the benefits of teachers opening up is that we are able to be sincere in working together to improve those student outcomes and learning experiences. If we're not seeing what's happening in the classroom, then we can't really address the problem of practice.
>
> (interview with A. Albini, 2014)

Lesson observation is a key strategy for the assessment of teaching practice for both teacher training and in-service teacher accreditation at each level of graduate, proficient, accomplished, and lead. Lesson observation and feedback has also been increasingly used as a key strategy for teacher professional learning.

The Australian Professional Standards for Teachers and Quality Teaching in NSW Public Schools frameworks underpin much of the professional learning for teachers, including approaches such as lesson study and instructional rounds. Professional learning programs and resources that have been provided by the Department of Education and Communities to support teachers have focused on reflection and goal setting, classroom observation, collecting and annotating evidence, and using feedback to improve performance.

Over the last 10 years, school leaders have engaged in professional learning and leadership development programs that focus on understanding and developing the skills to implement successful performance management processes. These programs include, for example, giving, receiving, and utilizing feedback and managing professional feedback conversations.

Underperforming teachers who fail to meet the requirements for accreditation and performance management and development are removed from the profession. Currently school authorities, in partnership with principals' organizations and teaching unions, are streamlining existing teacher development and performance policies and practices, including related industrial processes, to ensure that underperformance as assessed against the Professional Teaching Standards and is expeditiously, effectively, and fairly addressed to minimize adverse impacts on the learning of students.

Teaching and learning results are an important component of school strategic plans, and the student learning outcomes of teachers are visible to colleagues within the school. Student learning outcomes and the analysis of teaching are also a key components of both professional learning and performance and development. Thus the teacher's contribution to school goal priorities is an important element of the performance and development process.

Career Paths and Leadership Development

In NSW there is a desire to keep teachers who demonstrate excellent performance in classrooms so they can provide the leadership and modeling of best practice from which other teachers can learn. Traditionally, in order to achieve higher wages or higher levels of professional recognition and responsibility in schools, teachers have sought promotional positions in schools and local consultancy positions that were responsible for the provision of professional learning for large networks of schools or the development of professional learning materials at a state level.

To encourage these teachers to stay in schools a new career path has been established to enable them to remain teaching and support the development of other teachers. These teachers are rewarded financially and professionally and have the responsibility at the school level of providing leadership and collaborative professional learning for other teachers. These teachers engage in collaborative lesson preparation, evaluation, and teaching and are well positioned to observe practice and its effect and to provide feedback to enable teacher professional learning both within and between schools.

In NSW, the teachers who achieve higher levels of professional accreditation are those who are recognized and rewarded with higher salary. Traditionally, the salary of NSW teachers' increased annually with each completed year of service over the first eight years of a teacher's career. After eight years teachers attained the top level of the salary scale. There was no financial incentive for teachers to seek to demonstrate higher professional standards. After reaching the top of the scale the only way to access higher salaries required teachers to be selected on the basis of merit to be appointed into the role of a school executive. School executives in NSW schools have both a teaching role and a role in leading a faculty or grade.

The new professional standards–based salary structure enables teachers to receive higher salary when they achieve higher levels of professional accreditation. Under this award, teachers receive significant increases in pay when they are accredited at the Proficient Standard and are paid a salary in excess of A$100,000 when they achieve the Highly Accomplished and Lead Standard.

NSW has also introduced a school classification structure that recognizes the complexities of school context such as the number of students, student backgrounds, and community isolation. The principals who work in more complex schools receive the highest salaries. The industrial award structure negotiated in 2014 uses the amount of funding allocated to a school under the Resource Allocation Model (RAM) as the means to determine the level of school complexity. This funding model consists of a base student allocation as well as an equity loading based on the socioeconomic background of the students and targeted individual student funding based on background and learning needs. Previously teachers had identified that effective teaching was recognized locally within schools, but that high-performing teachers were not receiving recognition or reward within the system. It was also evident that the system could benefit by identifying, rewarding and learning from excellent practice.

Teachers in NSW schools identify that the most valid forms of recognition of outstanding teaching practice are centered on the classroom and include lesson observation and the assessment of student progress. It was considered by professional associations, teaching unions, and employers that the Professional Teaching Standards provided a valid and professionally robust framework for teacher remuneration based on demonstrated highly accomplished and lead teaching. While excellent teaching practice linked to evidence of student progress is identified, analyzed, and shared it was clear that neither teachers nor system leaders believed that it was appropriate to use external student assessment data as the indicator of teacher quality.

Teachers identify that feedback from other teachers is a significant source of professional learning. They also find that collaboration through planning lessons, teaching, and analyzing student achievement together provides them with the opportunity to reflect on, refine, and recalibrate their teaching practice (McIntyre, 2013).

School and system leadership roles provide another career pathway. In NSW, school and system leadership is seen as a key driver of increased school performance. NSW has provided a comprehensive suite of professional learning and leadership development programs to build the capacity of aspiring, newly appointed, and experienced school leaders. These programs were based on educational research and focused on leading improvement within the context of the key accountabilities of each school leadership role. The programs formed a leadership continuum and were designed to support each stage of career progression and included for example, Executive Induction, Executive Leadership Development, Deputy Principal Induction, Principal Preparation, Principal Induction, and Team Leadership for School Improvement. Each of these programs emphasized the importance of the leader's role in the professional learning of teachers to build their capacity to support the learning of all students. While the teacher professional learning programs had the focus of "making a difference in your classroom," the first stage of the leadership programs had the focus of "making a difference in the classroom next door." The principal level programs were described as "making a difference in your school" and the programs for senior officers and directors were focused on "making a difference in the school next door."

Currently the NSW DEC has moved away from the provision of professional learning and this role is increasingly being assumed by professional associations such as the principal associations and cross sectoral associations such as the Australian Council for Educational Leaders.

The Australian Professional Standard for Principals provides a clear framework for principal development and credentialing as it describes what principals need to know, understand, value, and do to effectively lead the continuous development of a school. The credential will be developed as a higher education degree. School authorities will be considering strategies to use the credential as a requirement in applications for principal positions. In the future it is envisioned that teachers who aspire to the position of principal will have achieved the higher levels of teacher accreditation and undertaken the required professional learning principals' credential to prepare them to be leaders of a school.

The NSW, Primary Principals Association provides a Principals Credential Program that is founded on the Australian Professional Standard for Principals and is closely aligned to the key professional accountabilities of school leaders. These accountabilities exist within the context of increased local school leadership authority, increased transparency of education processes and outcomes, and the increasing need to personalize learning to ensure all students irrespective of their circumstances are enabled to succeed. The program has two pathways. One pathway is for excellent teachers and school executive who aspire to school leadership. Another pathway provides professional learning and credentialing for current principals who seek to review their leadership practices and drive improvement innovation and change. This program is aligned to a masters of educational leadership degree and it is envisioned that the program will inform future credentialing in NSW.

In NSW systemic approaches have been implemented that foster excellent leadership practices through collaborative leadership learning across schools and systems. This includes support for teachers and school leaders to share successful practices across schools and systems and develop the leadership skills of current and aspiring school leaders.

The collaborative identification, recognition, and sharing of excellence in teaching and professional learning in NSW is creating greater opportunities for teachers to learn from each other within and across schools and school sectors.

NSW Principals' Credential: A Portrait of Practice

In 2014 the NSW Primary Principals Association (NSW PPA) developed a credible, accessible credential for school leadership that focused on learning excellence for students, teachers and school leaders.

Prior to 2014, the entry pathway for teachers to become principals of government schools was through merit selection and the demonstration of leadership capacity in teaching or executive leadership positions. This entry pathway was supported by a continuum of professional learning programs that included executive induction, executive leadership development, and team leadership programs. There was a strong correlation between teachers who had completed the executive development program and team leadership program and the teachers who were appointed to the position of principal. The strategies articulated in the final career stage of the Great Teaching, Inspired Learning reforms included the development of new school leadership credentials to provide pathways to employment as a school leader.

New School Leadership Credentials Will Be Developed to Provide Pathways to Employment as a School Leader.

> School leadership credentials will be developed to support the preparation of high quality teachers for the role of principal. The credentials will be based on the Principal Standard and could be developed as higher education degrees or allow articulation into appropriate degrees. The credentials could be used to access school leadership roles or provide leadership renewal programs for current principals. School authorities should work with universities and other relevant organisations to have the credentials available from 2014. School authorities could consider using the leadership credential as a requirement in applications for principal positions.
>
> (Great Teaching, Inspired Learning 15.3 NSW March 2013)

The NSW PPA Principal Credential is designed for both current and aspiring school leaders. It aligns to the key accountabilities of school leaders as they lead improvement, innovation, and change within the context of increased local school leadership authority and increased transparency of educational processes and outcomes. The credential has been developed with two pathways. One pathway is for excellent teachers and school executive who aspire to school leadership. Another pathway provides professional learning and credentialing for current principals who seek to review their leadership practices and drive improvement, innovation, and change.

The Credential:

- is based on the Australian Professional Standard for Principals
- is driven by the key accountabilities of the principal's role
- is aligned to the core work of principals in schools
- is aligned to the individual learning needs of participants
- provides structured conferences and personalized learning
- incorporates explicit and systematic coaching with highly credible principal facilitators
- is accredited to half of the master degree in education leadership
- strategically addresses a key priority area 15.3 in the Great Teaching, Inspired Learning strategy

The program commenced early in 2014 and the first cohort completed their assessment validation phase and graduated in October 2015. The NSW Primary Principal's Credential is an 18-month professional learning program that involves the formal assessment of evidence of performance through a professional portfolio, executive summary of learning, and referee reports of the participants leadership impact.

The credential has provided principals and aspiring principals with a new and innovative leadership learning program involving national and international educational researchers. As a key component of the program participants are required to drive innovative change within their school and to map the evidence of their impact through their e-portfolio.

Formal learning is provided through three residential seminars that enable access to international best practice educational research and thinking. The seminars also provide scaffolding for the development of a personalized professional learning plan and a school research and learning plan. Participants work in collegial, collaborative groups in the implementation of individual action projects and their professional learning plan. Participants are supported through the program by a selected group of highly competent, practicing principals who have strong expertise in professional learning.

Completion of the program, the assessment of the portfolio evidence, the presentation of an executive summary seminar, and refereed validation leads to recognition of leadership capacity and the award of the NSW PPA Credential.

The evaluation of outcomes for the first cohort graduating from the program highlights the benefit of a program that is aligned to the key accountabilities of the principal's role through an emphasis on instructional leadership. As Jodi Bennett the assistant principal of Oxley Park School stated in her validation review panel:

> I have learnt to stop and think, what is the data that is helping us to understand what we need to do and why, what is the evidence that informs me of the best next steps to take, and how can we work together in collaboration to ensure that in the end we are able to make a real difference for our students. I understand that our context matters greatly and that we need to establish a model for our team and work out how we can align our resources to achieve what we need to achieve.

> We have been breaking down those classroom walls to see teachers as leaders of learning working together to make a difference with our children. We are now able to work together and study our work use our learning continuum and we now provide each other with feedback. We needed to develop trust and focus on our learning together. The teachers can now clearly state what they are learning from their collaborative examination of their teaching. For teachers to go beyond their school gate and learn from other teachers in other schools is a great source of professional learning. I have had this opportunity to connect with other teachers in other schools through this program and the power of these professional networks for my learning has been great and I want other teachers to have this opportunity.

> One of the key elements of this program has been the leadership challenge. The challenge has provided a focus that I needed to see through and through implementing the challenge I have needed to focus on my growth as a leader. If you want to grow if you want to be accountable and if you want to be forced to examine your practice this is the program for you. This program that been connected to action and to seeing things through it has been different to being accredited at

highly accomplished as this program has been connected to action rather than placing individual evidence against standards.

(Statement from Jodi Bennett Oxley Park School made within her presentation to the NSW PPA Credential Validation panel on August 24, 2015, by Video Conference at Australian Technology Park)

Policy Principles and Design and the Teachers Union

In describing comparative processes for negotiating policy change, Patrick Lee, the former Chief Education Officer of the NSW Institute of Teachers, stated that "One of the industrially hardest, toughest jurisdictions in Australia is New South Wales ... the union is very powerful" (Lee, 2014). He was referring to the NSW Teachers Federation which is the union that represents NSW government teachers, and appears with the NSW Department of Education and Communities before the NSW Industrial Relations Commission every three years. The Industrial Relations Commission determines matters relating to teaching conditions and salaries through the development of industrial awards for teachers.

Yet despite the rigor of the industrial landscape, in many ways NSW has been at the national forefront of policy development and implementation to impact teacher quality. There appears to be two key aspects contributing to this outcome. The first relates to the emerging professional purpose of the teachers union and the second relates to the educational policy development process in NSW.

The NSW Teachers Federation has an articulated focus that links to and also goes beyond the working conditions of teachers to include the quality of educational provision for all public school students.

> The NSW Teachers Federation looks after a multiplicity of issues on behalf of teachers. It also regards public education as a strong foundation for a sure future. Thus, it campaigns for betterments for all students who attend public schools so that they will receive a quality education.

("NSW Teachers Federation," 2016)

The six Principles of Public Education are displayed on the NSW Teachers Federation website and provide clear insight into the key values and principles of operation of the union. There is strong congruence between these principles and the purpose of public education that is evidenced in many policy positions held by the Department of Education and Communities but there are also key differences in ideas about how these principles should be operationalized in practice.

Principle One

The public system must deliver equal opportunity for all children to develop their abilities to the fullest, regardless of where those children attend school. This will be achieved through:

- ⊃ Strong core curriculum
- ⊃ The recognition and addressing of disadvantage
- ⊃ An equitable distribution of adequate numbers of qualified and skilled teachers

Principle Two

The public school system is primarily concerned with the education and welfare of its students. School and system administration must reflect the primacy of teaching and learning. The central relationship in schooling is that between student, teacher, and parent. This relationship should be reflected in decision making throughout the system.

Principle Three

A successful public education system is one which provides a service to the community and attracts students because of the availability of that service. To see this service in market place terms is totally inappropriate. Governments must be held accountable for public education and not allowed to privatize this vital public service, or to separate themselves from responsibility for resourcing schools adequately by transferring those responsibilities onto local administration.

Principle Four

A strong public education system with a well-qualified and supported teaching profession, free from political interference, is among our greatest safeguards of democracy.

This profession must have:

- ○ Appropriate preservice teacher training
- ○ Substantial opportunities to enhance professional expertise
- ○ Assessment and promotions systems which enhance professionalism

No system of education can flourish unless it develops and supports the profession of teaching.

Principle Five

Public schools must be able to continually attract new teachers and retain the experienced teachers. Not only should teachers receive public support in their work, but they should also receive working and employment conditions which are competitive and attractive. Among the major benefits of teaching in the public education system are security, tenure, and a statewide transfer and promotions system.

Principle Six

A public education system flourishes with active parent and community involvement. To ensure this, opportunities must be created to strengthen parent and community participation.

Maurie Mulheron, the president of the NSW Teacher Federation, described the need for system support for the outcomes of schooling when he stated:

> Our belief is that the entire public education system has to lift student achievement. That we don't measure it on the success of some individual schools. We've got to measure in terms of what the entire system and system priorities and case strategies and directions are. So we want to have within New South Wales and have the government through its department, articulate very clear directions and strategies. Not straitjackets, but set quite clear strategies and directions and a whole performance and development framework for teachers, school planning processes that support that.

In relation to the NSW government commitment to the Gonski funding model, Maurie Mulheron describes his focus on results for students when he says, "In a very simple way, there's money that can be spent wisely and money that can be spent unwisely ... having fought so hard to get the money, we now want it spent wisely" (Mulheron, 2014).

Angelo Gavrielatos, the president of the Australian Teachers Union, and previous president of the NSW Teachers Federation, concurred:

> We're talking about a developmental strategy, a formative strategy, where schools together with communities and systems and governments set the report against targets, showing the money is being used for the purpose by which it was intended, and showing the growth that was achieved as a result of it.

> (interview with Mulheron, Hopgood,
& Gavrielatos, 2014 [Link 2-11])

DEC Secretary for Education, Michele Bruniges, highlights the value of ensuring that consultative processes underpinned the design of the Great Teaching, Inspired Learning directions, when she states:

> We've had a very close working relationship with our principals and our teaching workforce ... and right from the development of

the evidence base looking at the literature review and the evidence base we're very transparent. We shared the literature review with the general public. We went along the way with taking constructive criticism jointly. There's nearly a sense of co-design and co-delivered reform. I think that's been really at the heart of all that we've done. We haven't come out and gone "From a government's point of view this is the government policy, and this is the first time you've seen it." We worked in really synchronized fashion and all the best ambition in the world in the policy formation step is one thing, but at a certain time once that policy is crafted and written the baton hands over to every classroom and every teacher. And unless that policy ambition is translated in a coherent form at a classroom level then not much will change. You could have the best policy statement in the world but very little change, so I think the hardest bit is actually the translation of that policy position into practice within every classroom and an ownership. And I'd say ownership is incredibly important, and that's why the co-design principle and the collaborative spirit in which you develop it. You do the evidence base, you develop the policy statement, it's owned by the profession, and then the delivery becomes easier. You don't have to overcome the barrier of saying designed here and delivered here and there's a big transitional gap in between. So for me the co-designing of that policy and feedback is one of the key drivers that will help us bring the ambition and the practice together and, ... the closer we will get to policy ambition, to putting things in place that really makes a difference for children that we take responsibility for.

Common Platforms for Government, Catholic, and Independent Schools

While there are substantial differences in policies and operational practices across the NSW government, Catholic, and independent schools sectors there is also a strong history of shared policy platforms. These platforms relate to the NSW school curriculum and assessment programs that have been traditionally overseen by the NSW Board of Studies. The shared curriculum framework and the school graduation measures of the School Certificate and Higher School Certificate provides the state with a coherent platform for the provision and assessment of student learning. This provision has also been supported by the NSW Board of Studies through the registration of schools process that determines the right of a school to operate following an assessment of the schools capacity to meet a clear framework of quality assurance measures.

The introduction of the NSW Institute of Teachers Act (2004) with the introduction of professional teaching standards, processes for teacher accreditation, and requirements for the maintenance of accreditation provided a shared platform for the creation of new policies and procedures to guide teacher employment, development, and career progression.

All teachers employed in NSW since the passing of the Act are required to be accredited with the NSW Institute of Teachers and now the Board of Studies Teaching and Educational Standards (BOSTES). This means that those in the Catholic and independent sectors, like their government counterparts, have to meet graduation requirements from an accredited university, demonstrated proficiency through evidence of practice against the standards, and be engaged in the maintenance of professional practice through professional learning. The processes that support teacher accreditation, ongoing professional learning, and evidence-informed career progression vary between government, catholic and independent schools. These variations are shaped by local contexts, system policies, and industrial award agreements.

The operation of Catholic and independent sectors in NSW is strongly supported by federal government funding and is also supplemented by NSW state funds. As a result of this funding and the nationally agreed policies, Catholic and independent schools are required to meet similar regulations to government schools. There are eleven Catholic dioceses in NSW. Each has local authority to design policy within the guiding support frameworks of the Catholic Education Commission NSW.

Catholic schools work within a regulatory environment that Ross Fox, executive director of the National Catholic Education Commission, describes as:

> [Applying] predominantly through our funding agreement with the commonwealth government and our obligations that arise there. So there are strict regulatory and legislative requirements. But I would say that the professional commitment to actually the development of teachers are governed more by the environment of professional expectations that are set within a state and territory jurisdiction and also within dioceses and a school environment where there is a commitment to school improvement and recognizing that quality teaching is essential to that. So there is lots of shared commitment. The other obvious reference is the industrial environment which does vary state to state and particularly the extent to which the AITSL

standards for example are being adopted as relevant references for pay progression and other issues. So summing that all up I would say that locally Catholic education in a school or dioceses has a very similar commitment to the teacher standards and professional development of teachers consistent with AITSL's frameworks as our government school colleagues although there will be variations because of our unique funding arrangements particularly with the federal government and the commitment that we have got to the subsidiarity of the systems and the school approaches and their response to context.

Ross Fox describes the role of the National Catholic Education Commission in relation to policy design and development. He states:

> Our responsibility on behalf of the Australian Catholic Bishops, who are the ultimate owners of catholic education, is to maintain the relationship with the commonwealth government and in the last decade that has become increasingly prominent on matters other than funding in school policy. So there is a need for us to have a national interaction and a national relationship that is also with the national education institutions of AITSL and ACARA. Now we are not a school authority. So every state and territory has a Catholic Education Commission which is the school authority meaning it receives funds and in most instances is the responsible compliance authority to a school registration body, and also to the funders being the state and territory governments and the federal government.... There is still a significant autonomy invested in some dioceses particularly in NSW and somewhat in Victoria but also at a school level and it varies. It is sort of a rich diversity of governance arrangements depending on the history and tradition but it is reflective of the sophistication of conical governance in the church and that commitment to local engagement and local authority.

The introduction of the Great Teaching, Inspired Learning reforms in NSW involved strong consultation across the government, Catholic, and Independent school sectors and the NSW Institute of Teachers and the NSW Board of Studies (now BOSTES). As a result the shared aspirations that are contained within the recommendations of Great Teaching, Inspired Learning provide a comprehensive platform for the further development of aligned context specific policies to improve the quality of teaching and learning in NSW schools.

Conclusion

The impact of the recent reform agenda leading to systemic and school based policies and practices to support teacher quality in NSW will be evidenced over time. It is critical that the core emphasis on the role of the teacher in enabling student learning and the role of the school leader in supporting teacher learning and school improvement remains at the forefront of educational reforms in NSW.

The congruence between state and federal policy reforms to enable quality teaching and learning is a key strength of education in Australia and NSW. The federal framework provides a quality benchmark for all states and territories and while many of the federal reforms mirror previously developed policies and actions in NSW they provide the impetus for ongoing review and refinement.

A strength of the current systems in NSW is the congruence of policies and practices within the Great Teaching, Inspired Learning reforms. The continuum of standards-based reforms in preparing and selecting future teachers, developing, recognizing, sharing, and learning about outstanding practice within the profession provides a strong evidence informed framework for NSW.

While the Australian constitution provides states with the authority over education, there is a strong rationale for the federal government to invest in education in a way that builds both excellence and equity.

Future success will be dependent on both state and federal government support of a collaborative profession that is committed to continuous improvement through evidence-informed innovation that places students at the heart of all decisions and quality teaching at the center of all reforms.

3

BUILDING TEACHER CAPACITY AND COLLABORATIVE CULTURES: TEACHING AND TEACHER QUALITY IN VICTORIA

Dion Burns

AS INTRODUCED IN THE earlier chapters, the signing of the Melbourne Declaration in 2008 by Ministers of all Australian states led to a raft of nationally agreed education reforms across the country. These included a renewed focus on teachers and teaching quality as key policy levers in raising student outcomes. In particular, the national professional standards for teachers and concomitant policies characterize a collaborative and professionally engaged teaching workforce, and seek to promote standards-based professional learning at all phases of the teaching career.

Victoria has been well-positioned to adapt to these changes. Conscious policy effort at the state level has been part of a transformation of the discourse of teaching over the past decade from teaching as an individual exercise in imparting content, to a collective responsibility aimed at lifting student outcomes, in line with the domains articulated in the standards.

More generally, Victoria's education system also provides insight into navigating some of the education policy challenges presently experienced globally: finding balance between capacity-building, resourcing, and accountability; developing teaching collective capacity while providing for school autonomy; balancing progressive education goals with increasing attention to literacy and numeracy outcomes; and incorporating growing national-level education policy influence into a state-based system.

In this chapter, we outline the key policies and policy developments that have helped shape teaching practice in Victoria and are aimed at producing strong and equitable outcomes for its students, in keeping with the goals of the Melbourne Declaration. We also provide examples from school-level interviews and observations that provide a snapshot of how these policies manifest in practice.

Characterizing the Victorian System

Victoria's approach to education is characterized by several factors. Firstly, it has adopted a policy framework of school-based decision making. Since its inception and despite political tensions, this system has been adapted, but not overhauled, with successive changes in government. Political debates tend to be centered on the balance of government resourcing and direct provision of services, rather than on the architecture of the system itself. This movement towards this framework has occurred simultaneously with political contestation at the federal level around the development of national education policies, particularly in areas such as school funding and curricula.

Secondly, policy reform has, at key junctures, been accompanied by investments in capacity-building. This has helped develop a culture of schooling in which induction and mentoring, feedback on practice, and ongoing teacher professional development are regarded as strategies central to school improvement and raising learning outcomes for students.

Thirdly, policy development in Victoria and nationally is typically grounded in evidence from educational research, and largely made through consultation with principals, teachers, and the community. This process has helped to craft policy that can attract a measure of consensus within the education community, and become educator-led, rather than simply imposed.

Fourthly, the government has helped form strategic networks and relationships between schools to support the sharing of good practice across schools, rather than just from the center outward. Together with other factors, such as compulsory teacher registration supported by evidence of teacher learning, and strong unionization, this has helped to support a growing professionalization of teaching even while framed within a school system that also incorporates market-like principles.

Together, these factors have resulted in a teaching workforce increasingly characterized by professional collaboration and the use of evidence to inform teaching practices focused on student learning.

Overview and Context

Demography and Economy

A brief look at Victoria's demography and economy helps inform some of the differing challenges from those of other Australian states, and the context for education policy in the state. Located on the south coast of the Australian mainland, Victoria is the second most populous of Australia's eight states and territories. Of its 5.8 million residents, the majority—around 4.25 million—are concentrated in the Melbourne metropolitan area (ABS, 2014a). Less than 0.1% of the Victorian population lives in areas described as remote or very remote (ABS, 2014b). (See Figure 3.1.)

Victoria is Australia's fastest growing state due to a combination of both overseas and interstate migration (ABS, 2014a; Victorian Government, 2014). Melbourne in particular has grown by over 600,000 in the past decade. The city is anticipating even greater growth in its outer suburbs over the next twenty years, and this is expected to challenge a host of public services, including education (MPA, 2014).

Victoria has a diverse, predominantly services-sector economy, accounting for around 22% of Australia's total economic output. Financial services, healthcare and social services, international education services, construction, and information and communications services are among the highest contributors to economic growth. Melbourne also serves as a hub for international trade, particularly with the Asia-Pacific

---

Figure 3.1 Map of Victoria.

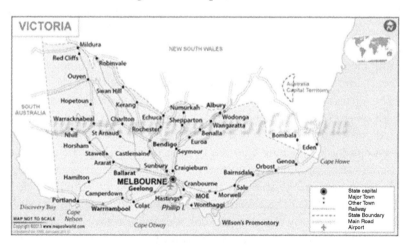

Source: www.mapsofworld.com

region; China, Japan, Korea, Thailand, New Zealand, and the United States are the state's top trading partners (DFAT, 2013). There is significant migration to and from these countries, and the state is home to a large number of internationally connected companies.

As a consequence, Victoria has a diverse, multicultural, and multilingual population. Around 37% of the population was born overseas, and 58% have a parent who was born abroad. Among the more than one hundred languages other than English that are spoken by the state's residents, Mandarin, Cantonese, Vietnamese, Greek, and Italian are the most common (Darling-Hammond, 2013).

These factors inform thinking on education policy in the state. The goals of education policy are commonly framed in terms of increasing productivity and international competitiveness, individual success, as well as the formation of a strong and diverse society (DEECD, 2012c). Victoria also places considerable emphasis not just on English as an additional language for newer residents, but more recently on second language learning for all students at all levels of compulsory education.

Education policy in Victoria is situated in a larger vision of child health and well-being. Learning, development, and skills are regarded as one of five dimensions of well-being that contribute to development of the "whole child" (see Figure 3.2). The principles underpinning this approach include cultural competence and taking a holistic approach to well-being. State government policy places education in this broader context: "Health and well-being is an important outcome in its own right, but it is also a precondition for learning and employment, and is an indicator of successful education" (DEECD, 2014b [Link 3-1]). The state takes a multiagency approach, measuring 20 indicators of well-being across the five dimensions. Priority areas for schools include the following: healthy eating, physical activity, sun protection, mental health, alcohol and tobacco control, sexual health, and promoting positive relationships and bullying prevention (DEECD, 2014a).

The Victorian government also provides a range of educational and health services at the preschool level to support well-being and learning ahead of formal schooling. These include 10 free health and development screenings for very young children leading up to their participation in preschool. Participation in preschool in the state is nearly universal, with 97% of four-year-old students using state-funded preschool services (Harrington, 2008). The Department of Education is moving towards funding 15 hours a week of preschool education in the year preceding school entry for all students, and provides fee subsidies for some students, including those from indigenous backgrounds.

Figure 3.2 Dimensions of Well-Being.

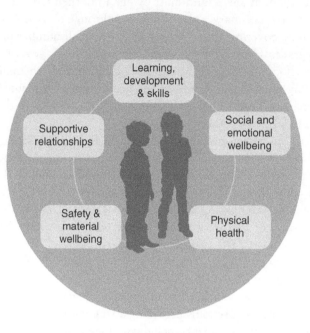

Learning, development & skills

Supportive relationships

Social and emotional wellbeing

Safety & material wellbeing

Physical health

Reproduced from DEECD, 2014b.

Recent policy initiatives are aimed at raising the quality of provision in the early childhood sector, including the development of an early years learning and development framework (Link 3-2) linking learning from birth through age eight, a requirement that all facilities have a teacher with university training to the level of a bachelor's degree, and the registration of all early childhood teachers with the Victorian Institute of Teaching (VIT) from 2015 (DEECD, 2014c; DEECD & VCAA, 2011; Kent, 2014).

School System

As with other states in Australia, schools in Victoria are classified as either government or nongovernment schools, with the latter divided into Catholic and independent school sectors. Around 63% of all students in the state attend government schools, 23% in Catholics schools, and 14% in the independent schools (DEECD, 2014f). Although this chapter focuses mainly on policies that impact government schools, it also provides some background to the governance and policies of Catholic and independent schools.

The state has a 13-year, Prep–12 schooling structure. Students typically start school at age 5 (and must by age 6) in the Preparatory grade (Prep), and attend primary school from Prep through to Year 6, with secondary school covering Years 7 through 12. A small number of schools cover all grades from Prep–12. Although students 17 years of age or older may choose to leave school at the end of Year 10, the majority of students stay on to finish Year 12. The proportion of students successfully completing Year 12 has increased from 76% to 83% in the period 2002–2011 (DEECD, 2014f).

Victoria's student population is ethnically and linguistically diverse. Of the 565,000 full-time equivalent students in government schools, over a quarter are from a language background other than English (LBOTE). The most common non-English languages spoken in the home are Vietnamese, Arabic, Mandarin, and Cantonese (DEECD, 2014f). A significant proportion of Victorian teachers also speak a language other than English at home—10.9% of primary teachers and 13.1% of secondary teachers—although this is a lower proportion than that of the student body (McKenzie et al., 2014).

As a consequence, Victoria has initiated a languages policy, seeking to have all government schools providing a languages program by 2025, and at least 25% of all students including a language other than English (LOTE) in their secondary study by the same date (DEECD, 2013f). There are also efforts to increase the level of second language training taken during initial teacher education.

Indigenous Students in Victoria

Victoria has a smaller indigenous population than that of other Australian states. Although indigenous students comprise just under 2% of the student population, this number has grown by 27% since 2009. This increase has been aided by a nearly 50% growth in the number of indigenous students staying in secondary school through to Years 11 and 12 since 2009 (DEECD, 2014f). Apparent retention rates from Year 7/8 to Year 12 of indigenous students have risen to over 60%, although this still trails that of the overall student population (ABS, 2015). (See Figure 3.3.)

With the increased national focus on raising outcomes for indigenous learners, arising in part from the Melbourne Declaration, an ongoing challenge is the recruitment of Aboriginal and Torres Strait Islanders into teaching. Although having grown since 2010, a nationwide survey

Figure 3.3 Retention Rates for Indigenous and Non-indigenous Students to Year 12.

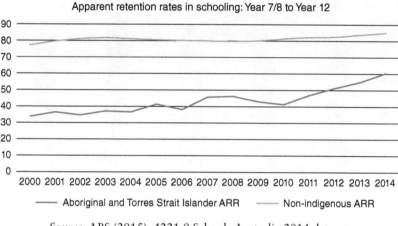

Apparent retention rates in schooling: Year 7/8 to Year 12

———— Aboriginal and Torres Strait Islander ARR ——— Non-indigenous ARR

Source: ABS (2015), 4221.0 Schools Australia 2014 dataset

of teaching showed that in 2013 just 1.1% of Australian teachers and school leaders identify as Aboriginal (McKenzie et al., 2014).

As with other Australian states, there exist large gaps between indigenous and non-indigenous students in school participation and in achievement in reading and mathematics. Though significant, these gaps tend to be less pronounced in Victoria than in other states. On NAPLAN 2013, the reading achievement gap between indigenous and non-indigenous students was the lower than all states other than Tasmania for each of the years measured (ACARA, 2013a). The smaller geographic area of Victoria, and lower proportion of indigenous students living in remote areas compared with other states contribute to explaining these lower gaps.

Victoria has also seen a significant rise in the proportion of indigenous students enrolled in early childhood education, increasing from below 60% to over 70% since 2007. (See Figure 3.4.) The retention rate of indigenous students in school from Year 10 to Year 12 has also increased somewhat from 51% to 57% over the period 2008 to 2012. Yet gaps in participation and retention remain, with overall attendance in early childhood education in Victoria standing above 95%, and Year 10–12 retention at 82%, in 2012.

Figure 3.4 Proportion of Indigenous Students
Enrolled in Early Childhood Education in Victoria.

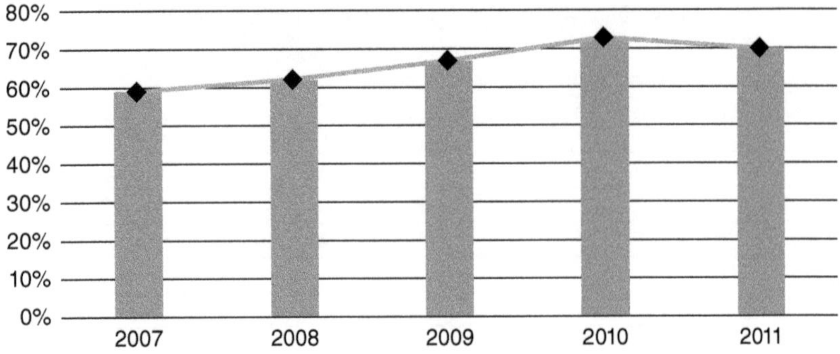

Source: Victoria State Government (2014), www.data.vic.gov.au/

Curriculum

Victoria has been in the process of transitioning to the "AusVELS" curriculum, created by integrating the Victorian Essential Learning Standards (VELS), the state curriculum in place since 2006, into the framework of the Australian Curriculum for each of English, mathematics, science, and history. An updated Victorian Curriculum will be introduced in 2017 to reflect new state priorities.

AusVELS has 11 levels, each roughly corresponding to the 11 years of compulsory schooling from Preparatory to Year 10. However, the Victorian Curriculum and Assessment Authority stresses that these levels do not represent bodies of knowledge for each school grade, but rather are intended to be used flexibly to personalize learning to the range of student abilities that exist within classes.

The AusVELS curriculum incorporated the learning domains from the Australian Curriculum, which represent the main bodies of knowledge, into the three interconnected learning strands of the former VELS:

o Physical, personal, and social learning: Learning about oneself and ones place in society, taking responsibility for learning, and understanding global citizenship

o Discipline-based learning: The arts, English, humanities, mathematics, science, and other languages

o Interdisciplinary learning: Thinking, problem-solving, communication, creativity, and design principles (VCAA, 2013b).[1]

Each of these learning domains is further separated into eleven learning levels from Foundation Level through to Level 10, with each level consisting of content descriptors of learning goals.

The integrated national and state curriculum structures the work of teachers in two important ways. Firstly, the curriculum is not prescriptive; schools have almost complete flexibility on questions of pedagogy, so long as they can demonstrate through their strategic and implementation plans that they have planned and are implementing a school-based curriculum that meets curricular standards, and that all students have the opportunity to achieve the goals as set out in the curriculum (DEECD, 2013d). Each school can establish its own curriculum by adapting and shaping it to fit their school's particular context. Thus teachers can, through school leadership and grade-level teams, have input into deciding how learning will be arranged, and which resources will be used to teach that curriculum.

Secondly, the curriculum sets out both achievement standards and progression points towards meeting those curricular standards. The progression points are intended as examples to inform teachers' planning, rather than mandated mid-year assessments. Schools can adapt these progression points and map them onto their own school curricula, and teachers periodically collect student assessment data, which can also be mapped against these points. Such resources help teachers plot student progress and provide a ready mechanism for seeing that they are meeting the goals of the curriculum. The progression points also assist schools in biannual reporting to DET on student progress.[2]

Education Policy Context

Three Waves of Reform

The teaching policy context in Victoria has been shaped by three waves of reform since the 1990s, representing something of a political pendulum swing in terms of a lesser or greater role for government in decision making and assistance to schools. The reforms focused firstly on the decentralization of authority to schools, then on increased state resourcing for capacity-building, and later on reducing the role of government in school management and the direct provision of materials and services. Together these waves have maintained a system of autonomous schools, and sought to increase the sharing of knowledge and capabilities within the system, while balancing this with accountability measures from the center. We outline key elements of each of the reform phases, and look briefly at new state initiatives going forward.

First Wave of Reform: Schools of the Future

The first wave of reforms represented a dramatic change in Victorian education, and instantiated many of the organizational and resourcing systems that characterize the system today. It involved a radical restructuring and decentralization of the administration of schooling, commensurate with broader economic changes and restructuring of public services occurring Australia and other countries in the late 1980s and early 1990s. Motivations for the change were both economic and organizational. Economically, the decentralization of schooling was part of a broader push towards the privatization of state assets to reduce government debt, and more closely tying the functions and goals of government organizations to global competitiveness and economic growth.

Organizationally, there was a sense that a central government bureaucracy was inefficient and inflexible in management and resource distribution. A movement towards market-like efficiencies, shifting decision making closer to those impacted, and assuming control over outcomes rather than inputs were seen as solutions (Blackmore et al., 1996). Thus the Schools of the Future reforms created a system of autonomous, self-managing government schools. This involved the decentralization of school administration, but with a simultaneous centralization of accountability processes.

The most significant changes were in the areas of school funding and management. Under the new system, schools received all their funding as an annual allocation called the School Global Budget. Rather than funding based on the number of teachers and an assumed student-teacher ratio, the School Global Budget was a weighted per-student funding formula, based on perceived student needs. Schools were then responsible for determining their own spending priorities within this financial package. This was a significant change for principals, who were required to strategically allocate expenses, balance budgets, and become quasi accountants for their schools (DEECD, 2013e). The shifting (and increasingly complex) role of the principal was a notable feature of the reforms (Blackmore, 2004).

The second major change was that schools were required to set their own strategic priorities, through the use of school charters, essentially a strategic planning and accountability document from schools to the state government developed in discussion with school councils.[3] The aim was greater flexibility and autonomy for schools over their strategic goals in order to more closely meet the needs of their students. It was also intended to provide opportunity for local communities to have greater input into school goals than could be accommodated in a centralized system (Townsend, 1995).

However, there were also concerns that decentralization could lead to greater inequality. Critics noted the following: smaller schools with fewer students, and therefore funding, may have more constrained choices in curricular offerings than larger schools; parent and community involvement in school councils may be greater in middle-class communities; and shifting strategic goals to schools while centralizing accountability would not, on its own, necessarily result in the change in professional culture in schools that may be needed to achieve those goals (Blackmore et al., 1996). Thus the second wave of reforms sought to address these concerns.

Second Wave of Reform: Blueprint for Government Schools

The second wave of reforms began in 2003 under a center-left Labor government. The reforms were characterized by significant government investment in leadership, infrastructure, and especially teacher capacity-building. This wave of reforms was transformative in developing many of the teaching practices, and shaping the culture of schooling in Victoria today.

Findings of a research inquiry into government schools in Victoria showed that there were high concentrations of poor outcomes in some schools and some regions, frequently high variations in outcomes between classes in the same school, and variations in outcomes between schools with similar student populations (DET, 2003a). The response by the Victorian Department of Education and Training (DET) was the Blueprint for Government Schools (Link 3-3), which set out three goals:

o "Recognizing and responding to diverse student needs
o Building the skills of the education workforce to enhance the teaching–learning relationship
o Continuously improving schools" (DET, 2003a)

There were two factors that were key to the shape of the Blueprint strategy. Firstly, there was a recognition of the tension between system-wide improvement and greater equity in a system characterized by self-managing schools. Secondly, there was an understanding of the limitations of market-like principles in the provision of education. The Blueprint strategy document acknowledged the benefits of competition that encourages innovation and improves student outcomes, but was explicit in its criticism of the negative consequences of unfettered competition:

> Unfettered competition between schools may not be conducive to meeting the needs of all students and all communities, nor to the

provision of a full range of programs for the more diverse range of students now staying on at school.

Schools which are competing against each other for mainstream enrolments and that are focused on high achievement data often do not pay due attention to those students requiring additional support. Unfettered competition is also counterproductive to the development of a learning and sharing culture between schools.

(DET, 2003a, p. 11)

The Blueprint strategy also provides insight into how policy development has been approached in Victoria. Firstly, it was research-based, drawing on evidence from education research such as Elmore's Effective Schools in informing professional development (Elmore, 2002), and Sergiovanni's Model of Transformational Leadership to inform the role of school leadership (Sergiovanni, 1984b). Secondly, the policy framework was formed after broad sectoral consultation. This included leadership groups comprised of teachers, principals, and researchers, as well as parent forums, and the creation of a Better Schools website for student and parent feedback.

The resulting strategy situated principles of equity and the role of government as central:

○ Every child is entitled to a quality education

○ Government's responsibility is to establish a framework that will deliver this

○ Government has an obligation to respond to the diverse learning needs of students (DET, 2003a)

The policy was structured around seven flagship strategies (DET, 2003a). Key among these for shaping practices in Victorian government schools and raising teaching quality were the following:

○ *Performance and Development Culture framework*: a program to which almost all schools were accredited, and which sought to shift the culture of schooling towards one of teacher collaboration and continual improvement

○ *Teacher professional development and teaching coaches:* which helped open classroom doors and directly model new teaching practices

○ *Leadership development*: which helped increase the role of principals as guiding professional development in the context of school improvement

Also important was the use of school networks and clusters to share good practices among schools. These policies signaled not only a shift of focus for teachers from content delivery to student learning outcomes, but also communicated that government, schools, and the teaching profession together held a shared responsibility for educating students.

Third Wave: Towards Victoria as a Learning Community

Victoria's third wave of reforms began under a center-right government in 2011. Although only in power until late 2014, several of the initiated reforms that sought to significantly shift from a department-led, towards a school-led, education system have continued. The case for change behind the reforms was concern with education as a policy lever for lifting economic growth and global competitiveness (DEECD, 2012c). Despite the investments of the second wave, these efforts had not materialized in higher educational achievement, and Victoria still trailed the international jurisdictions against which it benchmarked.

The key aspects of the third wave thus involved a reduction in the direct government provision of some services, shifting greater responsibility directly to schools. An example is school networks, which were to function under the direction of schools rather than being government-led. This move was controversial among educators, with many we interviewed expressing concern that the state was abandoning areas seen as of great importance to school improvement.

The state set a 10-year goal of raising its international educational performance to be competitive with high-achieving jurisdictions such as Finland, Canada, and Hong Kong, drawing on their experiences, but adapting them to the local context. The department's four-year strategic plan (Link 3-4) focused on narrowing gaps between Victoria and these jurisdictions in the areas of early childhood education, development, and wellness; and in student achievement on international assessments such as PISA. Domestically, the strategy focused on closing gaps in student performance between rural and metropolitan areas, and raising the education and health outcomes for lower socioeconomic groups and for Aboriginal communities (DEECD, 2013a).

The strategic plan also evidenced a tension between marketization and professionalization to effect change. The then-named Department of Education and Early Childhood Development (DEECD) viewed itself as an "owner" of schools and education providers, a "system architect" that designs incentive and regulations, and a "manager of system performance" (DEECD, 2013a, p. 6). Among the approaches outlined in the strategic plan, of interest are the shift of balance "from a focus on inputs to accountability for outcomes," and "from central direction to the use of markets and guidelines." However, it simultaneously highlights the values of "collaboration and knowledge sharing," and "respect and diversity" (DEECD, 2013a).

Each of these flags the department's role as one of setting the policy environment, and providing services primarily in areas where it can achieve economies of scale. It also involved the state stepping back from previously large work areas—such as the direct provision of professional development—and drawing upon teachers and principals to create a "self-improving system."

Teaching Quality and a Self-improving System   Policy efforts in the realm of teaching quality under these reforms were framed by the *Towards Victoria as a Learning Community* (Link 3-5) vision for school improvement, and the *From New Directions to Action* vision for the teaching profession. The policy reforms are built along the following four axes: professional trust, autonomy, accountability, and support (DEECD, 2012c). Among the accountability measures were controversial proposed initiatives in the area of teacher performance and evaluation, discussed later in this report.

A key facet of the policy vision was a focus on moving towards a "self-improving system," drawing on elements of similar models trialed in the United Kingdom. Under this model, schools become the lead organizations of system improvement (Hargreaves, 2010, 2012); the primary role of government as system architect is facilitating change through the establishment of favorable accountability and other policy frameworks. Such a system utilizes school clusters to develop and communicate good practices.

Raising teacher quality was at the core of these reforms, as the *New Directions* document notes: "A self-improving system is the key to success—and requires a strong culture of self-improvement in the leaders and staff of our schools" (DEECD, 2013b). DET Executive Director of Priority Policy Ian Burrage underscored the shift of the state's policy role towards that of leading increased workforce quality:

> Fifteen years ago we were probably talking more about governance and management arrangements rather than what is an overwhelming acceptance of the importance of the teacher and getting into the classroom as being the issue that we'll see systems move... [I]t's only by your workforce that you'll make the move that you want, [and] it's only by our quality leadership of that workforce. That narrative is much more embedded in our system now.

More specifically, the *From New Directions to Action* (Link 3-6) policy set out the Victorian government's strategy for supporting higher teaching quality with the following three key elements:

- *Attract great people into teaching:* increased flexibility of entry into teaching for high-quality individuals, including Teach for Australia; the establishment of Teaching Academies of Professional Practice to raise the quality of preservice teacher education
- *Create a high performance profession:* strengthening principals' capabilities to assess teacher performance, and raising teacher capacity to conduct peer observation, evaluation, and feedback to colleagues
- *Provide strong direction and support:* supporting training and coaching in leadership development at all levels of the system from aspiring and middle leaders through to experienced principals (DEECD, 2013b)

In contrast with the second wave, which was focused on the direct provision of teacher capacity-building, the third wave of reforms sought to capitalize on and sustain the capabilities already generated within the teaching workforce. Examples include the use of school networks to facilitate knowledge-sharing within the teaching profession, greater accountability to school principals for teacher performance, and investment in developing potential school leaders earlier in their careers.

The strategy also attracted some criticism, particularly in the area of evaluation of teacher performance. For example, some commentators have contended that despite efforts to facilitate knowledge-sharing networks, the policy approach leans towards a bureaucratic approach to teacher performance that runs counter to a broader movement towards greater teacher professionalization, as noted by education researcher Lawrence Ingvarson:

> Professions are delegated major responsibilities, such as defining standards for advanced careers stages, promoting developing toward those standards and providing valued recognition for those who reach them. This is what professions do to lift quality.
>
> Rather, the Paper puts its faith in greater managerial surveillance and control over teachers' work, ignoring the repeated findings from Auditor-General reports and other research, that performance management schemes match poorly the nature of professional work and have little effect on professional development.

> (Ingvarson, 2012, pp. 2–3)

Others argued that the policy lacks a clear focus on addressing equity concerns (ACE, 2012), which may become exacerbated in the absence of direct provision of capacity-building. Similarly, there has been criticism that the third wave policies lacked the depth of consultation with the teaching profession that characterized earlier reforms and that the withdrawal of key supports could result in the unequal distribution of learning opportunities among schools.

Despite these reservations, and as we discuss later in this chapter, there is also some evidence to suggest that many of the teacher professionalization practices that emerged as a result of the second wave of reforms—such as teacher professional development centered on student learning needs and schools goals, and the transmission of good practice via teacher collaboration and school networks—continued, at least to some extent, in the leaner support environment.

Indeed, this appears to be an intention of the policy. As noted by one DET senior policymaker:

> Collaboration is at the heart of this. We're really trying to push the boundaries of a self-improving system … We started off at the leadership collaborative level and we've not moved beyond that, recognizing that teacher collaboration is probably the wisest investment you can make. We want the schools to see that themselves.

To the Present: Victoria as the "Education State"

In a sign that the pendulum is swinging back towards increased direct government support for education, a center-left government was elected in late 2014, campaigning on a platform of transforming Victoria into the "Education State." Consultation processes with both the public and the education sector took place throughout 2015, and focused on the following themes: excellence, equity, lifelong engagement in learning, valuing expertise, partnerships with communities, and increased integrity, accountability, and transparency (DET, 2015c). These consultations led to the launch of significant funding increases and new initiatives relating to teaching quality (Link 3-7).

The key findings echoed the values of the earlier reforms, with a focus on quality teaching, student well-being, and increased equity:

- ⊙ improving the quality of teaching is the single biggest thing we can do to improve outcomes for children and young people
- ⊙ the need to ensure the overall wellbeing of children and young people is as high a priority as numeracy and literacy, and that the

characteristics of a good educator are broader than the capacity to teach literacy and numeracy in a mainstream setting

o the need for all students to have access to quality education regardless of their location, learning needs or backgrounds. (DET, 2015a)

The new initiatives provide an indication of additional direct support for teachers. The strategy includes funds for training specialists in mathematics and science to work in disadvantaged primary schools, and new monies for the developing school leadership. It also includes support and professional development funds for teachers in delivering an updated Victorian Curriculum (Link 3-8) from 2017, "including mandatory new subjects like digital coding and respectful relationships," and will implement a new "insight" assessment system to help teachers track student progress against the curriculum. The strategy also includes a new needs-based school funding system, with additional funds to help reengage students who have dropped out of school (DET, 2015a).

In contrast with the previous emphasis on increasing the independence of school networks from government, the new administration has indicated funds to employ 150 new staff for regional offices to support principals and "play a key role in facilitating collaboration between schools" (DET, 2015a).

Understanding the Reforms

The waves of reform in Victoria have largely reflected the differing philosophies of governance between the major political parties in the state, moving between periods of increased direct government support to schools, and periods of leaner government and the greater use of market-like principles aimed at increased efficiency. Aided by a stable education bureaucracy, many of the initiatives from one wave have endured into the next, with electoral changes not leading to significant discontinuities in reforms.

Victoria has maintained the basic structure of self-managing schools and the global funding model throughout each wave. Across the reform efforts has also emerged a greater consensus of teaching quality and developing teacher capability as key elements of school improvement. This has been supported by a growing understanding that expanding from school- to system-wide improvement requires taking advantage of expertise within schools and among educators, and establishing mechanisms for sharing that across schools and regions. An emphasis of the reforms has thus involved a focus on principal and school networks, and on ongoing leadership development, as former AITSL Chair Tony Mackay explains:

> I expect quite frankly the leadership of schools to be part of network leadership, of cluster leadership, and therefore to become system leaders. Because in the end, if we're not thinking about this in system terms, a whole learning system, I do not see that we'll get beyond pockets of great excellence, but not a great system.

Education Governance in Victoria

Education in Victoria is governed by three sets of organizations. Governmental departments, which establish the policy framework, regulate schools, and administer qualifications and assessments; a teaching regulatory agency, assuring compliance with standards in teaching and teacher education; and educators' unions, involved in bargaining for salaries and working conditions.

Governmental Organizations

The major policymaking and implementation organization in Victoria is the Department of Education and Training (formerly the Department of Education and Early Childhood Development),[4] and its policies and their impact form the majority of this report. Leadership of the department is controlled by three ministers appointed by the political party that holds office.

DET implements policies and administers schools through its four regional offices (reduced from nine regions in 2013). These offices played a critically important role in the implementation of the Performance and Development Culture framework, deploying coaches, developing region-specific school improvement policies, and facilitating professional development among schools in the networks. The offices serve as an important link between department and school, negotiating, reviewing, and approving school strategic plans, and reviewing the appointments of school principals.

State education governance is supported by two further governmental organizations. The Victorian Registration and Qualifications Authority registers government and nongovernment schools and vocational education providers, assuring compliance with quality standards relating to school governance, infrastructure, staffing, curriculum and learning, and student welfare as set out in the Education and Training Reform Act (2006) (VRQA, 2014)—the legislation that governs schools.

The Victorian Curriculum and Assessment Authority is the organization responsible for curriculum, assessment, and reporting activities in Victoria. Its chief executive officer is also a senior official in the Department of Education and Training, and its board members are comprised of teachers, principals, and academics, facilitating input from the education community.

The Authority develops and implements the AusVELS curriculum for schools, the Victorian Early Years Learning and Development Framework, and administers the NAPLAN assessments on behalf of ACARA. It also administers assessments for the two state senior secondary qualifications: the Victorian Certification of Education, marking the successful completion of secondary education for the majority of students, including those moving on to university; and the Victorian Certification of Applied Learning, an industry-focused qualification for students intending to progress on to study or work in a trade or apprenticeship.

The Victorian Institute of Teaching

A body of particular importance in shaping the work of both teachers and providers of initial teacher education is the Victorian Institute of Teaching (VIT). Established in 2001, VIT is a statutory body with regulatory responsibilities for the quality of teaching and of teacher education. Although the Institute reports to the minister of education, it is positioned more as a professional authority than a bureaucratic body. VIT is no longer government-funded, and its council is primarily comprised of practicing teachers. As VIT's Director of Special Projects, Fran Cosgrove explains, this gives them a high degree of professional independence:

> We're self-funding through teacher fees, so teachers' view is: We're paying our fee—what are we getting for this? Really, what they're getting is the right to call themselves a professional, to be protected in their professionalism.

VIT's two major areas of responsibility are the registration of teachers, and the accreditation of initial teacher education programs. Accreditation involves VIT reviewing evidence from providers that their programs equip graduates with knowledge and skills equivalent to that of the

Graduate Teacher level of the standards. All teachers in Victoria, whether in government and nongovernment schools, must also be registered with VIT in order to be permitted to teach. Registration requires evidence that teachers have undertaken mentoring and professional learning sufficient to meet the Proficient Teacher level of the national teaching standards. As discussed in more detail later in this chapter, VIT's dual role in registration and accreditation gives coherence to policy efforts to raise teaching quality in Victoria.

Teacher Unions and Professional Organizations

The Australian Education Union's Victoria branch (AEU Vic) plays an important role in establishing salaries and working conditions for teachers, principals, and teaching support staff in the state. The union, with a membership over 50,000, negotiates with DET to produce the Victoria Government Schools Agreement. The most recent agreement, in 2013, addressed salary competitiveness, and the use of short-term teaching contracts (and is discussed in more detail in the salaries section).

Teachers and principals are represented by the same union, which creates an interesting dynamic. On the one hand, principals are required to act on behalf of the employer—the department—assuming responsibilities for the selection and hiring of teachers, salary negotiations, teacher performance assessments, and raises; and on the other, teachers and principals are colleagues involved in supporting collective bargaining and better working conditions. Principals may also belong to other state or national professional and advocacy organizations, such as the Victoria Principals' Association, the Australian Principals' Federation, the Australian Primary Principals' Association, and the Australian Secondary Principals' Association.

Of significance is that AEU plays both an industrial advocacy role as well as a teacher professionalization body. The union is a cofounder of the Teacher Learning Network, a provider of teacher professional learning programs. On policy matters, AEU has advocated for reduced workloads for beginning teachers to provide time for mentor-mentee conversations. It also conducts annual beginning teacher surveys to assess issues of attraction and retention among early career teachers, and has advocated for greater government resourcing for professional development, as noted by AEU Victorian Deputy President Justin Mullaly:

> It all comes down to resources. If you are in front of the students
> in a classroom day in, day out and you don't really have access to

decent professional development and collaborative development with your colleagues in a way that you can genuinely reflect with a bit of distance at times, then we're actually not serving our students the best way we can, and that is having highly energized and continually energized educators.

Governance of Catholic and Independent Schools

Although the majority of this chapter focuses on policy and practices in the government school sector, a look at nongovernment schools—accommodating around one-third of all students in the state—helps illustrates the balance of national and state policies that shapes the work of educators. Although private schools in the Catholic and independent sectors receive a significant proportion of their funding from public sources, and are also subject to many of the same regulations as government schools, particularly in the wake of nationally agreed education policies.

For example, all teachers in Catholic and independent schools are required to be registered with VIT and to have graduated from an accredited, four-year program. This means that teachers in nongovernment schools are trained to meet the same standards—those of the Australian Professional Standards for Teachers—as well as take part in mentoring and professional learning against the standards, as their government school counterparts.

Catholic and independent schools must also show that their school curricula provide students with learning opportunities to meet the achievement standards of the Australian Curriculum, including the eight learning areas specified in the Melbourne Declaration. Some independent schools have chosen to adopt the same AusVELS curriculum as used by government schools, although they are not constrained to do so.

In the case of Catholic schools in Victoria, the sector has adopted the state's curriculum, with the addition of religious education as core curricular element. Catholic schools are likewise free to tailor the curriculum framework in a way that meets the needs of the students, teachers, and community. For example, the Catholic Education Office Melbourne, the office representing largest of the four Catholic dioceses in Victoria, has developed Learning Centered Schools, a framework to assist in planning learning and teaching programs in Catholic schools.

There are also commonalities with government schools in external assessments. Students in senior secondary school in both the Catholic and independent sectors sit exams towards one of the two state-offered school qualifications, and in Years 3, 5, 7, and 9 are also required to sit the NAPLAN assessments.

Regulation of schooling also works similarly. Institutional registration and compliance and quality assurance for the nongovernment sector are formally responsibilities of the Victorian Registration and Qualifications Authority. In the case of the Catholic sector, the Authority approves the Catholic Education Commission of Victoria as the review body on its behalf; for independent schools, the Authority conducts these reviews directly. The review process, which takes place at least every five years, assures that all schools can provide evidence to demonstrate they meet minimum standards in the following key areas:

○ *School governance:* schools must be nonprofit organizations, support democratic principles, have a clear philosophy of learning, and be led by a capable principal

○ *School infrastructure:* buildings must meet standards of occupational safety and health, and be suitable for educational purposes

○ *Curriculum and student learning:* there must be a framework and implementation plan for a whole-school curriculum, and processes to plan for and achieve improvement in student learning outcomes

○ *Student welfare:* schools must demonstrate a safe environment, including plans to deal with issues ranging from bullying to bushfire risk management (VRQA, 2014)

The review process also assures that all teachers are registered and have permission to teach from VIT.

Policymaking in the Catholic schools sector is organized through a central organization—the Catholic Education Commission of Victoria, which sets policy in areas such as teacher accreditation, school funding, and leadership development. Policy is implemented in schools via the Catholic Education Office Melbourne, representing schools within the four dioceses of Melbourne, Ballarat, Sale, and Sandhurst.

Policymaking in the independent sector is more diffuse. However, Independent Schools Victoria, representing many of the independent schools in the state, serves as a peak body for the sector. The organization acts an advocacy body, as well as a provider of services related to teaching and learning, and supporting compliance and reporting requirements for its member schools.

Teacher Employment, Salaries, and Working Conditions in Nongovernment Schools

Finding a teaching position in the Catholic and independent sectors functions in a similar manner to the government sector (described later in this chapter), with prospective teachers submitting an application directly to the principal of the relevant school. Independent schools may advertise on their school websites or online job boards. In the case of the Catholic sector, a comprehensive job list is also posted on the website of the Catholic Education Commission of Victoria.

Teachers beginning employment in Catholics schools are required to work towards one of two additional accreditations: a two-year, part-time program in teaching religious education for all primary teachers and those teaching the subject at secondary level; or a 50-hour, nonassessed credential for those not teaching religious education. In each case, teachers have up to five years to complete this accreditation.

A large number of teachers in the Catholic and independent sectors belong to the combined Victoria and Tasmania branches of the Independent Education Union. Teacher salaries and working conditions in the nongovernment sector are specified in negotiated contracts. For example, salaries and working conditions for teachers in all Catholic schools in the state are addressed in the Victorian Catholic Education Multi-Enterprise Agreement.

The conditions in this agreement, such as working hours and a reduced load for beginning teachers, closely parallel those for teachers in the government sector schools. It also includes an identical salary schedule and teacher levels establishing direct pay parity between teachers in the government and Catholic sectors. Catholic and government sector teacher salaries were also at parity under previous enterprise agreements in 2007, and the negotiated agreements for each sector followed a period of joint industrial action including teacher strikes from both sectors in late 2012 (Gosper & Karvelas, 2012; Topsfield, 2012). The tying of salaries and working conditions between each union and the teacher employers provides for ease of movement of teachers between the Catholic and government sectors.

A large number of schools in the independent sector also have enterprise bargaining agreements with the Independent Education Union, but the working conditions and salaries may vary from school to school. Teachers in Independent schools for which there is no agreement with the Independent Education Union are covered by the federal Educational Services (Teachers) Award 2010.

Teachers in the nongovernment sector are, like government school teachers, required to undertake professional learning to maintain their registration through the Victorian Institute of Teaching, and to be able to continue teaching in schools (discussed later in this chapter). In some cases, teachers in nongovernment schools may also participate in the same externally delivered professional development as their government sector counterparts. These may be courses run by universities or private providers, teacher professional associations, or those provided by the Teacher Learning Network, which receives support from the Australian Education Union and the Independent Education Union.

In other cases, these may be professional learning developed by the sector or individual school. Some of this has been supported in recent years through federal funding. Although discontinued in 2013, the Australian Government Quality Teacher Program (AGQTP) provided significant funding for both government and nongovernment sectors in a range of areas connected to school improvement. These included school-based professional learning, such as action research (Darling-Hammond, 2013).

School Management and Funding

A feature of Victoria's system of autonomous schools is that much of the decision making that shapes the daily work of teachers is made at the school level, including strategic planning and goals, school timetabling, curriculum and resource decisions, and funding allocation for professional learning. At the policy level, DET views its role as one of setting frameworks to manage system performance, developing talented teachers, and making investments at scale where needed. Its broad policy agenda, aimed at ensuring outcomes over providing inputs, informs the expectations around school and teacher performance in the service of school goals, and the practices intended to achieve them.

Government schools in Victoria have three broad sets of management responsibilities:

○ *Governance and budgeting:* managing their own budgets, including the purchase of learning resources, professional development, and teachers' salaries

○ *Workforce development:* selecting and hiring teachers, developing a school professional development plan, providing mentoring and induction for staff, and sharing best practices through collaboration with other schools

○ *Curriculum and assessment:* planning a school curriculum that meets AusVELS requirements, conducting national and state assessments, and reporting to DET

Schools demonstrate the implementation of government policy in each of these areas through a five-year strategic plan, and an annual implementation plan.

School Strategic Planning

Schools must establish goals, targets, and the strategies to achieve them in each of three designated categories: student learning, student engagement and well-being, and student pathways and transitions. The process of developing the strategic plan is a reciprocal one, balancing the policy interests of DET with those of the parents and school community. This occurs through a process of school self-review, and is typically followed by engaging the community through working groups or other consultation exercises. Once endorsed by the school council, the principal submits the plan for review through the regional office of DET.

School strategic plans thus contain some common elements, including specific targets. Schools (and in particular, principals) are accountable to DET for progress towards these targets. These targets typically include quantitative measures, such as raising mean scores in literacy and numeracy on NAPLAN, and addressing the distribution of achievement within a school. Additional measures may include outcomes on the Student Attitude or Parent Opinion surveys.

Strategic plans also indicate *how* schools will achieve their goals, identifying key improvement strategies. These goals and strategies are then elaborated in schools' annual implementation plan. The specific goals, targets, and strategies will vary from school to school, depending on the student body, previous performance, and the interests of the school community.

Important in the context of teaching quality is that the approach to school strategic planning is a developmental one. There is recognition that achieving improved performance requires the ongoing development of teacher capability. Measures of staff professional development are typically embedded in school strategic plans, and teacher performance and developments processes reflect contributions to school-level goals. Thus school strategic plans connect teacher professional learning to student learning outcomes and well-being, and in turn to school and community goals, helping foster collective accountability. (See also Box 3.1.)

Box 3.1 Strategic Planning at Footscray North Primary School

Footscray North Primary School is located in the City of Maribyrnong, a suburb of Melbourne around three miles west of the city's central business district. This part of the city has experienced several waves of immigrant groups, including second- and third-generation families, as well as newer immigrants and refugees. More recently, rising house prices and outward expansion of the city has seen an influx of middle-class residents. The school is characterized by a diverse multicultural population from a range of socioeconomic backgrounds, as well as a broad range of needs for English as an additional language.

The school's strategic plan for student learning thus includes a curricular focus on raising literacy outcomes, while goals in the area of student well-being include reducing the number of absences, and improving performance on parent and student satisfaction surveys. The school uses a diverse range of key improvement strategies for achieving these goals, including enhancing the visibility of school leadership, building creating and engaging environments for student learning, and celebrating the diversity of the community. See Table 3.1.

Table 3.1 Footscray North Primary School: Strategic Intent.

	Goals	Targets	Key Improvement Strategies
Student Learning	To improve student outcomes in literacy and numeracy.	o By 2015 Year 5 Reading will indicate 50% of students are in Bands 6, 7, and 8. o By 2015 Year 5 NAPLAN data will indicate at least 15% more students are in the top two bands than Year 3 2011.	Build commitment to the school vision and values through visible leadership. Build teacher capacity and skills to implement effective teaching and learning. Create engaging learning environments. Celebrate the diversity of the school community.

	Goals	Targets	Key Improvement Strategies
Student Engagement and Well-being	To strengthen student well-being and engagement.	○ In 2015 the Parent Opinion Survey variable for social skills will score 5.6 or higher. ○ In 2015 Student Attitudes will register 4.60 or above on the variables motivation and learning confidence, with parity between boys and girls. ○ By 2015 the average number of student days absent will be 11 or less.	Build teacher capacity and skills to implement effective teaching and learning. Create engaging learning environments. Celebrate the diversity of the school community. Continue to evaluate and support current welfare programs. Continue to keep student absences low.
Student Pathways and Transitions	To consolidate transition processes for students at all points of primary education.	○ In 2014 in the Parent Opinion Survey the variable approach-ability will be at 5.8 or above. ○ In 2014 Student Attitudes will register 4.6 or above on the variable connectedness to peers.	Build teacher capacity and skills to implement effective teaching and learning. Create engaging learning environments. Celebrate the diversity of the school community. Continue to be proactive with local organizations in smoothing transition into Prep and out to Year 7. Evaluate current practice in passing information from one year to the next to maximize effectiveness and avoid lost learning time.

Salient among the key improvement strategies is the building of teacher capacity and skills. This recognition of teacher professional learning as a strategy for improving student learning is a common feature of school strategic plans in Victoria. The explicit linking of professional learning to school goals was promoted by the Performance and Development Culture policy (discussed later in this chapter).

A challenge for government schools in Victoria is that the goals in a school's strategic plan must be achieved within its allotted annual budget. This means that all schools need to carefully establish priorities and accept trade-offs in spending, and this informs the amount and type of professional learning that is undertaken. It also means that financial stewardship by principals is of great importance in the effective functioning of schools.

Resourcing Education—How Victorian Schools Are Funded

Resourcing of government schools in Victoria is based on a progressive funding formula, under which schools with a greater proportion of students from disadvantaged backgrounds receive an increased level of funding to assist those students. The issue of funding equity remains an active area of political debate in the wake of the federal government's responses to the Gonski report, which noted that Victoria had the lowest per-student recurrent income in government schools among Australian states (Gonski et al., 2012).

The anticipated increased federal funding under Gonski drew support from both major political parties at the state level, with then-State Education Secretary Richard Bolt describing it as "an essential platform to resource our school reform agenda" (DEECD, 2013a). The Australian Education Union lobbied the federal and state governments to guarantee the full Gonski funding through to 2019, particularly as the majority of the funding originally proposed was earmarked for the final two years of the program.

Although discussions around Gonski funding have stalled at the federal level, the present state government has announced it will provide additional needs-based funding to schools from 2016 (DET, 2015a).

The Student Resource Package

The funding of government schools occurs through a progressive funding instrument known as the Student Resource Package (formerly known as the School Global Budget), a process that will continue through at least the end of 2017. State government monies represent about 90% of public school funds, with around 8% contributed by the federal government, and the remainder from grants and fundraising (Bandaranayake, 2013).

Funding allocation is predicated on the idea that freeing principals to decide on the allocation of school expenditures will help achieve the best outcomes for students rather than being constrained by the "jam jars" of line item budgets (DEECD, 2013e). A government report on the Student Resource Package credits this "effective and efficient use of resources" as a major factor in strong results from national testing (NAPLAN) during 2008–2010 (DEECD, 2013e). It is a needs-based funding model, providing greater funds to schools with students from traditionally underserved backgrounds.

The amount of money that each school receives in its Student Resource Package is determined firstly by a base funding amount, which varies by grade level (see Figure 3.5). Greater per student funds are allocated for Prep, Grades 1–2, and Grades 7–11. This base is then weighted by a multiplier, primarily based on the Student Family Occupation category, a measure of socioeconomic status. Additional weighting is applied for students with disabilities, and those for whom English is an additional language. This sum comprises the bulk of each school's funding (around 92%), although additional funds can also be allocated by the state to schools for specific infrastructure work, and small targeted programs such as welfare officers for students at risk of dropping out (Bandaranayake, 2013).

Figure 3.5 Student Resource Package Funding to Government Schools.

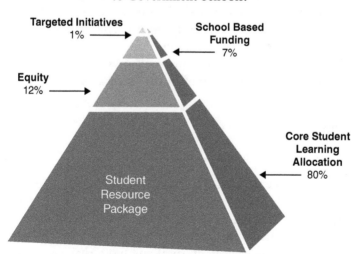

Reproduced from DEECD, 2013e, p. 39.

Victorian government schools have almost complete discretion to determine their own spending priorities. As school funds are not tagged to specific expenses, principals are expected to be adept financial managers. They must produce an annual budget for approval by the school council, undertake workforce planning to avoid either teacher shortages or excess, and allocate money effectively to balance resource purchases, professional learning, causal relief teachers, and a host of other expenses.

Principals therefore both have a great deal of flexibility in how they distribute funds to achieve school goals, but must also be judicious. The manner in which principals choose to allocate expenses can have a strong influence on opportunities for staff development and student learning. DET manages this through principal training and mentoring, and the provision of a range of planning tools and resources.

Funding Equity and Accountability

The Victorian government has signaled changes to the SRP from 2016. A state-commissioned review of funding recommended revising the present model to more closely tackle areas of disadvantage, with a view to address the plateau in the state's educational performance over the past decade (Bracks, 2015). This approach increases the proportion of equity funding, with more targeted resources for disadvantaged and struggling students, and increased accountability to see that funding matches need.

Among the report's 70 recommendations are an increase in needs-based funding. Beyond factor loadings based on student background, additional funds will be provided to target underperforming students, with the state introducing catch up funds to support students in high school who scored below minimum levels on NAPLAN in Year 5. Also recommended are new funding and initiatives to support students at risk of dropping out, or who have already dropped out of school (Bracks, 2015).

Recruitment

Meeting Supply and Demand in Victoria

In Victoria, as in much of Australia, the main human resources issue for government has been the equitable distribution, rather than the total supply, of teachers. The stability of the teaching workforce has been challenged in recent years by the use of short-term teaching contracts, and difficulties in retaining teachers in rural and more challenging schools. In the long-term, Victoria will need to attract new entrants, particularly secondary school teachers, to meet the anticipated expansion of Melbourne's outer suburbs, and at a time when both state and nation are seeking to simultaneously raise the quality of initial teacher education.

At present in Victoria, there is an increase in numbers enrolling in and graduating from initial teacher training programs. The most recent supply and demand report from the DET noted that final-year enrollments in both undergraduate- and graduate-entry programs were at a 10-year high, with 6,030 new teachers graduating in 2013. Graduate-level enrolments represent around 61% of these, a proportion that has seen an uptick in growth over the three years to 2014 (Weldon, Shah, & Rowley, 2015), even as graduate courses have moved towards two-year programs.

Overall, these numbers have grown at a rate sufficient to keep up with the growth in student numbers. In fact, public school student-teacher ratios at primary level steadily declined during 2000–2013, from 16.9 to 15.3 schools, but remained steady (at 12.2) in secondary schools. Ratios in Catholic schools are similar to those in government schools, while those in independent schools are lower still (ABS, 2010). Average class sizes in Victoria are 22.2 in primary schools, and 21.4 in secondary schools (DEECD, 2014f).

Nonetheless, Victoria will need to sustain the trend of increased enrolments if it is to keep pace with the anticipated growth in student numbers. Melbourne's population is forecast to double to 7.7 million by 2050 (MPA, 2014). More immediately, the school aged population is expected to grow by around 14% from 2010 to 2020: by 2.7% annually at primary level, and 1.1% at secondary (Weldon, Shah, & Rowley, 2015).

Sustaining a steady supply of teachers will also be needed to offset anticipated retirements from teaching. Around 36% of teachers in government schools and 38% of those in Catholic schools are over the age of 50, a proportion that has increased steadily since 2001 (DEECD, 2012a; Weldon, Shah, & Rowley, 2015). (See Figure 3.6.) With new teachers joining the workforce, around half of all teachers are under the age of 40, compared to about one third in 2003 (Weldon, Shah, & Rowley, 2015).

Overall teacher supply is, for now, meeting demand. Attractive starting salaries, the uncapping of federally subsidized places in universities, and loan support for tuition fees all contribute to making teaching an accessible career. And although teaching is not regarded as a particularly high-status occupation—TALIS 2013 found that just 38.5% of Australian teachers felt that the teaching profession was valued in society (OECD, 2014c)—this too is changing. Interview participants indicated that teachers were generally well-regarded by the community as being

Figure 3.6 Proportions of Teachers and Principals in Government Schools, by Age, Victoria 2001–2013.

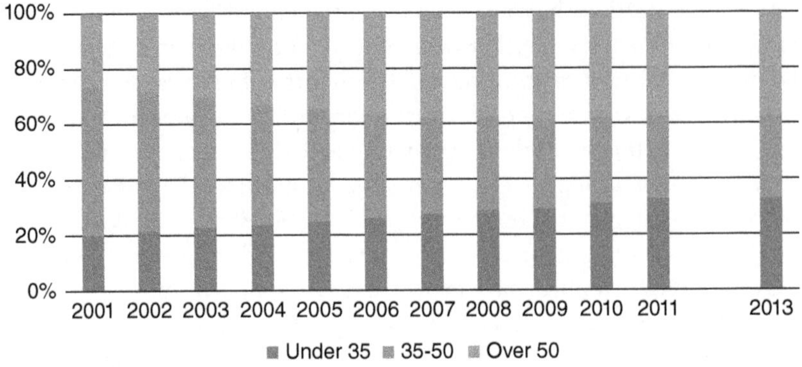

DEECD, 2012a; Weldon, Shah, & Rowley, 2015.

honest and having integrity, and that an older public view of teaching as an occupation with convenient hours for raising a family was giving way to a growing perception of teaching as a profession (Aulich, 2014).

Personal attributes and interests predominate as motivations for becoming a teacher. Among early-career teachers in Australia (those with five years teaching experience or less), a love of teaching, a desire to work with young people, and a desire to contribute to society were the most common responses. For secondary teachers, this also included "a love of subject" (McKenzie et al., 2014, p. 91). Few teachers cited salaries or the status of the teaching profession as important factors. (See Table 3.2.)

Table 3.2 Early career teachers: factors that were important in the decision to become a teacher.

Factor	Primary	Secondary
Love of teaching	80.6	63.5
Desire to work with young people	77.7	65.5
Desire to contribute to society	52.7	50.8
Holidays, hours of work	27.7	36.9
Family role model(s)	26.4	20.7
Encouragement from teacher(s) while you were at school	21.9	26
Security of employment	20.7	33.2
Love of subject	18.2	67.7
Availability of employment	13.2	23.4
Working conditions	12.1	17

Factor	Primary	Secondary
Status of the teaching profession	4.9	5.8
Attractiveness of salary	4.3	6.1
Other	2.8	3.7

Source: McKenzie et al. (2014): Staff in Australia's Schools 2013:
Main report on the survey

Distribution of Teachers, Hard-to-Fill Positions, and Recruitment Incentives

DET monitors teacher shortages and supply issues through the deployment to schools of the Teacher Recruitment Difficulty Census in February, and the Casual Relief Teacher Recruitment Census in August. Findings from these surveys show that Victoria has a high need for mathematics, science, and technology teachers at the secondary level, although these shortages have reduced in severity since 2008 (DEECD, 2012a). National data show that this issue is not restricted to Victoria, with around 20% of mathematics, general science, and physics teachers at the secondary level teaching out-of-field in 2013, although this proportion is down from around 30% in 2010 (Weldon, 2015). (See Figure 3.7.)

Figure 3.7 Out-of-Field Teaching in Selected Secondary Subjects, Australia, 2010 and 2013.

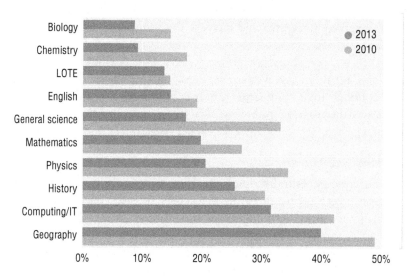

Reproduced from Weldon, 2015, p. 9.

Subject area shortages can impact upon teaching quality. A state-level audit found that the quality of mathematics and science teachers—those having adequate subject knowledge and effective teaching strategies—was identified as the most important challenge in improving education in these disciplines (VAGO, 2012). The report also found that while the number of unfilled vacancies in these subjects had fallen from 2008 to 2012—due in part to reduced teacher attrition (including fewer retirements) during the global financial crisis—further shortages were anticipated as older teachers leave the profession.

One education researcher we interviewed described a worrying cycle of underperformance in these subjects. Shortages of trained teachers in mathematics and the sciences leads to high proportions of out-of-field teaching, which are even greater in remote schools. Students taught by teachers who don't feel competent or confident in the content area are less likely to achieve at an advanced level in these fields, and less likely themselves to major in or become a teacher of that subject (Dinham, 2014).

There are also shortages in teachers of languages other than English (LOTE), particularly at the secondary level. Victoria's languages policy has set a target of all government schools offering language programs from Prep through to Grade 10 by 2025 (DEECD, 2013f), and this represents a growing priority for the state. AEU Victoria's 2009 State of Our Schools survey found that at both primary and secondary level, LOTE was the subject area most vulnerable to program cuts due to a lack of qualified teaching staff (AEU Victoria, 2010). Victoria's language implementation plan thus includes increased funding to support school language programs and increase the number of LOTE teachers (DEECD, 2013f).

Further teacher shortages are experienced in Melbourne's rapidly expanding northern and western suburbs. These areas tend to be lower socioeconomic areas, with larger numbers of immigrants and speakers of languages other than English. Schools in these areas are also more likely to experience greater difficulties in teacher recruitment and retention.

Incentives and Scholarships

Victoria does not centrally allocate teachers to schools, instead using an incentives-based approach to draw teachers towards hard-to-fill positions, supplemented by scholarships programs to attract new teachers into shortage areas (DEECD, 2013a). Policy efforts in this area during 2010–2014 also sought to further increase the flexibility of entry into teaching, including employment-based and alternative pathways, in order to attract a more diverse pool of candidates (DEECD, 2013b).

At the school-level, principals may offer one-off "special payments" of between A$750 and A$8,000 per annum to teachers (DEECD, 2014g). Principals may also opt to hire teachers at a salary level above that which the teacher has yet to attain or offer "accelerated salary progression" as an incentive to attract or retain teachers (DEECD, 2014g). In each case however, these incentives must still be funded out of the fixed annual school budget, and principals are accountable to school councils for the judicious use of limited funds.

Department-level incentives are used to attract teachers to difficult-to-fill geographic or subject areas:

o *DET's Teaching Scholarships* scheme provides stipends of between A$3,000 and A$7,000 to new graduate teachers to work in designated priority or rural schools, and/or hard-to-staff subject area. Teachers are bonded for a minimum of two years, and may receive a A$4,000 bonus after four years.

o *Science Graduate Scholarship* allocated 400 scholarships annually to graduates with a science background to help them become qualified as teachers. Grants of up to A$11,000 are available for those who teach for at least three years. Additional incentives are available for working in a rural school. (Program is on hold for 2016.)

o *Languages Teaching Scholarships*, offered through 2015, provided stipends to university graduates or present school teachers to train as language teachers, or to community members with proficiency in Victorian Aboriginal languages.

The Victoria government has in recent years allowed federally funded, alternative pathways in teaching, replacing an earlier, similar state-based model. Teach Next is a federal initiative that began in 2012 aimed as a career change program for professionals to become teachers.[5] Participants undertake an initial six-week intensive teacher training course and begin teaching while working towards a Postgraduate Diploma of Teaching through Deakin University during their first two years of teaching. The program allowed participants to transition from another career into teaching without the loss of salary that would be incurred by studying full-time. Teachers through Teach Next were placed in priority schools and subject areas.

A similar model since 2010 is Teach for Australia, which seeks to attract high-quality candidates into teaching. Six weeks of initial teacher education is followed by ongoing intensive workshops and study over two years as the candidates work towards a master's degree in teaching. Teach for Australia recipients are allocated to secondary schools in socioeconomically disadvantaged areas, and in hard-to-fill subjects; around 47% of Teach for Australia recipients are recruited to teach in the high-priority areas of mathematics and science (Teach for Australia, 2014). The program is yet relatively small, with the first four cohorts of the program (2010–2013) placing 151 teachers in schools in Victoria, 144 of these in government schools.

Perceptions of the Teach for Australia program are mixed. An evaluation report of the program found that principals in participating schools were largely supportive of the program based on the positive experiences with Teach for Australia teachers, and factors including their commitment to the school, subject knowledge, and the training and support they received (Weldon et al., 2013). However, the same report found that, although comparable effectiveness measures were difficult to ascertain, teacher training under the program was achieved at a considerably higher per-graduate total cost than that of training teachers through a standard program (Weldon et al., 2013). This latter finding has contributed to criticism of the program from the Australian Education Union, which has contended that the length of the preclassroom training period is insufficient, and such funds could be more effectively spent supporting teachers in the early stages of their careers (AEU Victoria, 2014b). Initial teacher education for Teach for Australia was initially provided by the University of Melbourne, and will be provided by Deakin University from 2015.

The Master of Teaching (Secondary) Internship is a new program in 2014 run by the University of Melbourne's Graduate School of Education (MGSE) in partnership with DET, and allows graduates to take an employment-based pathway into teaching. Based on MGSE's clinical teaching model (discussed below), the program provides supports to teacher candidates—an intern supervisor, in-school mentors, a clinical specialist, a transition coach, and demonstration classes by expert/lead teachers—to aid their transition to the classroom. Participants receive a salary during training, which takes place mainly during school holidays. Teacher candidates are employed on three-year contracts, with an 80% equivalent workload for two years, and are selected based on vacancies in hard-to-staff schools and subjects.

Although it remains to be seen whether these initiatives will be effective in addressing teacher shortages, findings from earlier programs provide some encouragement. An evaluation of DET's previous Career Change program from 2005 to 2011 found higher than average retention rates in the profession (although not necessarily in the same school), and more rapid progression to leadership roles. Key factors cited as important to the program's success were support from a mentor, frequent contact and personalized academic and induction support from university-based staff, selection by the school of candidates into the program to ensure a good fit with the school, and a reflective practice model to effectively bridge theory and practice (Moore & Pitard, 2012).

The Teaching Career and Stages

The teaching career in Victoria is increasingly framed by the national professional standards for teachers, given their role in structuring initial teacher education, professional development, and its adoption into balanced scorecards for teacher evaluation (discussed later in this report.) While the national standards set out four career stages, Victoria has yet to establish certification for the upper two levels or peg them to salary progression.

Thus although discourse around teacher experience and capability is increasingly shaped by the national standards, formal progression in Victoria remains structured by state policy, with career stages progressing from Classroom Teacher (Bands 1 and 2), to Leading Teacher (Link 3-9). Thereafter, teachers may look to advance to school leadership positions— assistant principal and principal.

There is a difference in expectation of teachers in each of the bands. Teachers in band 1 are expected to focus on developing their skills to become effective teachers, particularly in the first few years, while teachers in Band 2 are expected to take on further responsibilities, such as team- or grade-level leadership. Movement from Classroom Teacher 1 to Band 2 requires approval from a principal that the teacher is capable of assuming responsibilities within the school.

Moving from Classroom to Leading Teacher is not automatic. Teachers are hired directly into a leading teacher role, usually for a fixed period, and to help undertake a school-wide improvement agenda. In practice, the roles of Leading Teachers may vary widely across schools and include a broad array of responsibilities, ranging from: mentoring beginning teachers; taking a role in school management including hiring new teachers, or evaluating teacher performance; providing feedback on teaching; or being involved in school strategic planning. Leading Teachers we spoke with considered the adoption of these responsibilities less as part of their formal job requirements, but rather part of the expectation for leadership that accompanies any lead role in a professional working environment.

Schools will typically have a fixed number of Leading Teacher positions depending on its student population, needs, and resources. In order to meet succession planning needs, DET seeks to maintain a Leading Teacher profile of around 10% to 15% of the teaching workforce (DEECD, 2013i). Leading Teacher roles are commonly tenured for up to five years, with the teacher moving back to Classroom Teacher Band 2 if the contract is not renewed.

Teachers seeking to prepare themselves for more senior teaching positions, particularly those in Band 2, will often begin by putting themselves forward to take on additional roles within the school, such as team or grade leader, or professional learning coordinator. These roles are decided at the school level, and are considered part of the expectation of growth within the profession. The progressive adoption of responsibility with experience both signals to school management interest in, and provides preparation for, leadership roles within the school.

Salaries

Salaries for teachers in government schools are established through periodic negotiation between Victoria branch of the Australian Education Union and the Department of Education and Training, with the present *Victorian Government Schools Agreement* (Link 3-10) reached in 2013. Following a long period of negotiation centered on low wage growth (including industrial action from teachers), the agreement includes provision for annual growth of 3–7% through to the end of 2015. (A new government schools agreement is expected in 2017.)

Classroom teachers in Victoria sit on one of two salary ranges—Classroom Teacher 1, Classroom Teachers 2—with each containing five and six salary levels respectively. Beginning teachers start on A$63,400, and increment annually towards a maximum of A$95,000 at the top level of the second range (AEU Victoria & DEECD, 2013). There is an additional three-level salary range for Leading Teachers, who may earn up to A$104,000. Principals and Assistant Principals sit on separate salary scales.

 Progression through the salary levels (Link 3-11) occurs annually following a performance review process (described later in this chapter). Full-time teachers would typically move to their maximum rate after 11 years of continuous full-time employment, unless they move into a leadership role. For teachers that begin employment following their undergraduate education, this maximum salary may be reached by teachers in their mid-thirties. Thus although starting salary for graduate teachers compares favorably with that of other professions, the average teacher salary in Australia tends to be lower (about 93%) than that of other occupations for full-time, tertiary educated workers (OECD, 2014a, p. 469).

Teaching salaries in Australia also tend to have a lower ceiling than that of teachers in many other countries, with the ratio of top of scale to starting salary in Australia just 1.40, compared with an average of 1.61 across OECD countries (OECD, 2014a, p. 470). The low salary ceiling has often been cited as a limiting factor in efforts to further raise the attractiveness of teaching as a career, which must still compete with other professions for high-potential candidates. According to Dr. Lawrence Ingvarson of the Australian Council for Educational Research:

> The evidence is that Australia has been less and less willing to pay for high quality teachers. It has maintained reasonably competitive salaries at the entry stage but these rapidly become uncompetitive with other professions after five to ten years. It is this comparison that matters when high quality graduates make their career choices, not the starting salary. Where Australia falls down in comparison with high achieving countries is in the ratio of salaries at the top of the scale to that at the bottom.

> (Ingvarson, 2012)

Teachers in Victoria do not receive merit pay, but the Victorian government has explored this policy on several occasions, including trials programs at several schools from 2010 to 2012. However, a DET submission to the Australian Government's Productivity Commission indicated that although merit pay trials were found to have motivated school leaders to carefully apply performance management processes, they had had only limited direct impact upon teaching effort (DEECD, 2012d).

In a 2011 discussion paper, the then-DEECD recommended expanding salary and nonsalary incentive schemes to reward effective teachers, together with facilitating the dismissal of teachers deemed to be underperforming (DEECD, 2012b). However, merit pay for teachers was vigorously opposed by the Australian Education Union, and was ultimately dropped. Teachers interviewed for this project acknowledged weaknesses in the system for the evaluation of teacher performance, but described merit pay as antithetical to school culture in Victoria and to teaching as a collective endeavor. This evidences a tension between the incorporation of market principles and teacher professionalization in state policy formation.

Teachers we spoke with also remained confused over terminology between career levels in the national standards, and state salary scales (especially Lead versus Leading Teacher). Teachers and policymakers we interviewed indicated that aligning salaries with the national standards could help strengthen the standards as the accepted professional grades, and might also provide options for retaining high-achieving teachers in the classroom. As AEU Victoria Deputy President Justin Mullaly described:

> What we argue is that there's actually a real logic in incentivizing people to stay in the classroom. We want our high-performing people ... to stay in teaching and to stay in the classroom. That's where they can be most effective. We think that there's a real need to recognize that in salary.

Working Conditions

In addition to salaries, working conditions for teachers are important, with research showing they are a major factor in teacher retention (Darling-Hammond, 2010; Ingersoll & Strong, 2011). The Victorian Government Schools Agreement also establishes expectations around the responsibilities of teachers, including face-to-face teaching, preparation and grading, school trips and extracurricular activities, and mentoring of other teachers. The average working hours are expected to be 38 hours a week, and the agreement also sets a ceiling on the number of weekly instructional hours—22.5 hours for primary teachers, 20 hours for secondary teachers, and 18.7 hours for secondary teachers that have responsibility for coaching school sports teams. It is also expected that teaching workloads be shared across teachers in a school:

> Class size, preparation and high quality content, correction and assessment are major factors impacting on improving instructional practice. Teachers should have the opportunity to perform all of their duties within a reasonable timeframe and have fair and reasonable conditions and students should have ready access to their teachers. In this context, the work allocated to a teacher should, as far as practicable, provide for an equitable distribution of work across all teachers in the school.
>
> (AEU Victoria & DEECD, 2013)

Guidelines on maximum class sizes are also included in the agreement. For primary schools with students from Prep through to Grade 6, average class size should be no greater than 26 students, and Prep-Grade 2 having an average of just 21 students. For secondary schools, in teaching grades 7 to 12, classes should be no greater than 25 students.

The agreement also provides conditions for maternity and other parental leave, a not inconsequential issue for teachers given that around 80% of primary and 59% of secondary teachers in Victoria are female (McKenzie et al., 2014). Teachers on parental leave receive 14 weeks of leave at full pay, or 28 weeks leave at half-pay. Teachers can also establish job protection for parental leave for up to seven years, providing them with opportunities to return to teaching.

Short-term Contracts

One of the most pressing concerns for teachers in Victoria over recent years has been the proliferation of the use of short-term contracts. The growth in the use of contracts was associated with teacher job uncertainty and high staff turnover. DET and AEU have moved to constrain the incentives that facilitate the excess use of such contracts and monitor their use in the Victorian Government Schools Agreement 2013.

Short-term contracts provide important flexibility for schools, such as for parental leave, or unanticipated fluctuations in school rolls. However, a surplus of teachers, particularly at the primary level, increased competition for teaching positions in Victoria over the past decade. This allowed schools to increase their use of short-term contracts both as a tool to trial teachers, and to subsequently decide to either renew or terminate the short-term contract. As schools were previously not obliged to pay short-term contract teachers during the holiday periods (between contracts), this provided a financial incentive to schools to keep even experienced teachers on successive short-term contracts.

As a result, the use of such contracts in Victoria grew disproportionately. Teachers reported that it was also not uncommon for teachers to be on contract for several years, and to have additional part-time jobs to supplement their income while seeking to secure a permanent teaching position. Together, this led to considerable discontent among teachers, and strained efforts to attract high-potential individuals to selected teaching over another career. Thus short-term contract use was a major factor in industrial action by teachers in 2012 and 2013.

Teaching contracts are more prevalent among early career teachers. AEU's annual beginning teacher survey showed that around 56% of teachers in the state with less than five years' experience were on fixed-term contracts in 2013. Around 28% of these were for less than 12 months, and 46% were for 12 months (AEU Victoria, 2014a). Three-quarters of beginning teachers surveyed indicated that the requirement to reapply for positions has had a negative effect on their teaching (AEU Victoria, 2014a).

The use of short-term contracts can also complicate efforts to raise teaching quality in Victoria. Teachers on contract, which can be as short as six weeks or a school term, may be less likely to receive the same length and quality of induction and mentoring, or have opportunities to take on further responsibilities within school teams. This has potential negative consequences for staff cohesion and stability, and the retention, professional development, and effectiveness in instruction of classroom teachers.

In 2013, AEU Victoria and DET moved to close this loophole. Schools are now required to offer ongoing employment where there exists an eligible teacher, and cannot roll over contracts indefinitely. In addition, fixed-term contracts have been amended to include a pro rata payment for holiday periods, removing one of the financial incentives for excessive short-term contract use (DEECD, 2013i).

Hiring: Getting a Job as a Teacher in Victoria

Teachers in Victorian government schools are employees of the state. Although their salaries are drawn from the school's budget, teachers are paid directly by DET, are subject to the relevant human resources guidelines, and have department email addresses.

As the state does not centrally allocate teachers, DET operates a job vacancies website, Recruitment Online, which allows qualified teachers to locate vacancies and apply for positions. Under its Teacher Graduate Recruitment Program, certain program vacancies may be tagged as specific to graduate teachers aiding them to find their first teaching roles.

There are also limited supports for teachers who are seeking work as a result of becoming excess teachers—those teachers whose positions at their school are no longer needed due to changes in student enrollment, school organization, or educational programs. As described by senior teacher, Seona Aulich, previously excess teachers had priority in reassignment to vacancies, but this also carried some risk to their reputation:

> [P]reviously, there was a bit of a stigma I suppose attached to excess teachers, because if a principal had to put someone in excess at their school, they're probably not gonna put their best teacher. That's changing. The fact that excess teachers are now getting jobs on merit is changing the stigma.

Under new rules, excess teachers are required to be interviewed for any vacancy for which they are suitably qualified (DEECD, 2014h), although they are not automatically guaranteed employment. Teachers retain their status as permanently employed while in excess, are assigned regular duties such as team or substitute teaching, and are assigned a redeployment coach to help them find another teaching position and/or undertake additional training.

Selection

Selection decisions for employment are made at the school level, but following state policy guidelines (Link 3-12). Prospective teachers apply directly to schools, with applications reviewed by a school-based, teacher selection panel. Each panel is comprised of three or more people—typically an assistant principal, senior teacher, and classroom teacher—which short-lists candidates, conducts interviews, and provides a recommendation to the principal, who makes a final decision on employment based on the merits of individual candidates.

However, during interviews with teachers we also found that the professional practice (practicum) element of initial teacher education programs had a significant impact on employment prospects, and provided an effective, informal method of matching teachers with schools. The practicum element was commonly viewed by final-year teacher candidates as a job trial, where their successful performance could aid employment for the coming year, as described by senior teacher Seona Aulich:

> [T]hey become part of your planning sessions. They attend meetings after school. They are effectively a teacher in this school for the three or four weeks that they're there. We [Victorian schools] have a merit-based system for employing staff. If you have had a really successful fourth-year round, and there are jobs coming up for graduates at the school the following month, as they often are—September-October, jobs will be advertised; university finishes [in] October-November— it's all about the same time. It's very much … a student teacher's best interest to put their best foot forward at a school that they may like to gain employment at.

Another teacher we spoke with indicated that the positive impression she had made during the professional placement at an outer-suburb school subsequently helped her land a teaching job. With no immediate vacancies upon completion of her qualification, she volunteered at the school and then went traveling abroad during the summer vacation. The school later contacted her when a maternity leave position became available. She received a phone call while traveling inviting her to submit an application, did her interview by video, and returned early from her travels to begin work.

This highlights a tension between a labor market for teacher, and the potential benefits of allocative methods. School-based decisions allow schools to select teachers they know are a good fit for its culture, students, and community. This can be especially important in the case of rural schools, where the teacher may be working in a small town, is more embedded in community life, and is more likely to have close interaction with students and parents outside of school hours. Employing a teacher who undertook professional practice in a rural school may reduce the likelihood of teacher turnover, and also suggests benefits from closer university-school partnerships.

However, the absence of a central mechanism for teacher allocation means that schools in rural areas, those located far from a university, may have a harder time finding teachers. This can place pressure both on schools to locate teachers that are a good match, and on university placement coordinators.

Preparation

Overview: Teacher Training and Registration in Victoria

Teachers in Victoria receive their initial teacher education (ITE) at research universities, or at one of the small number of private colleges or TAFEs (technical and further education colleges) that offer ITE. More significantly, since 2001, Victoria has also required that all teachers be registered with the Victorian Institute of Teaching (VIT) in order to be permitted to teach in schools. Teachers must provide evidence they have the required competencies for teaching as measured against state, and since 2013, national teacher professional standards. ITE programs must also be accredited to prepare teachers against the same standards. Each of these has bearing on the content of ITE programs.

More recently, the move to national standards and new reforms in ITE are beginning to move the balance of ITE programs towards the graduate level, and especially two-year programs. Other national initiatives seek to increase the entry standards for new teacher candidates, and assure the quality of graduates. Each may be viewed as part of an historical passage of increasing teacher professionalization that has taken place progressively over almost a century, but has accelerated in the past decade.

Yet the state-based nature of education policy implementation, coupled with federal-level funding of universities, complicates the supply and distribution of teachers, and limits the feedback mechanisms and policy levers that the state government has available to raise teaching quality. Nonetheless, scaling up effective school-university partnerships has been a centerpiece of education reform initiatives in Victoria, albeit often through federal funding. Innovative university-level initiatives are also contributing to raising the quality of initial teacher preparation in Victoria, each of which is discussed below.

Accreditation of Teacher Education Programs

Initial teacher training in Victoria, as in other Australian states and territories, typically takes place in traditional university settings. At present, there are 99 accredited teacher education programs across 12 institutions in the state, which includes nine universities, two technical institutes, and one Christian-based education provider (VIT, 2014a).

The purpose of accreditation is to ensure that all ITE programs train new teachers in accordance with the criteria set out in the Australian Professional Standards for Teachers, and is expected to help increase the portability of qualifications received by teachers in Victoria to other states in Australia (although Victorian-trained teachers would still need to meet individual state registration guidelines).

Accreditation is a reciprocal process between VIT and ITE providers, is based on nationally agreed on standards and processes adopted in 2011 (Link 3-13) (AITSL, 2011a), and updated in 2016 (see Chapter One). Universities supply evidence of program design and rationale, assessment requirements, admissions data, graduate outcomes, professional experience outcomes, evidence of partnerships, feedback data, and policy documents to demonstrate their programs meet each of the 37 focus areas of the standards (AITSL, 2013). VIT convenes a four-person panel—three from its accreditation committee, and one from out of state—to review program data, and to conduct site visits as needed to verify and address specific issues. The panel then makes a recommendation to VIT's full accreditation committee.

Accreditation is, in essence, a peer review process that seeks to reinforce and enhance teacher professionalization through engagement with sector representatives. VIT's 23-person accreditation committee is comprised of 3 members of the VIT council and 20 noncouncil members from universities, primary schools, secondary colleges, the independent and Catholic school sectors, the Victorian Curriculum and Assessment Authority, and DET. The intention is to get input from stakeholders that represent the jurisdictions where the ITE program is delivered, and to support the Graduate Teacher Standards of the APST (AITSL, 2011a).

In the area of professional practice, for example, guidelines require that school-university partnerships allow candidates to experience working with a variety of learners, and to gain an appreciation of the diversity of schools and communities. Partnerships must have arrangements for qualified supervisors, and for candidates' practice to be assessed against the standards. There must also be mechanisms for identifying, counseling, and supporting teacher candidates who may be at risk of not successfully completing the practicum element of the program (AITSL, 2013).

Participants interviewed for this study generally regarded the accreditation process as successful. Both VIT and universities commented that their institutional relationship was largely positive, with universities having opportunities for representation on, and input into, VIT's committees (Paproth & Cosgrove, 2014). This provides some indication that the process is becoming educator- or sector-led. Nonetheless, VIT's role in accreditation has placed some constraints on the academic autonomy traditionally enjoyed by university schools of education.[6] As noted by one higher education representative:

> We have a great relationship with the VIT that is tested at times. That's one of the key changes: that we are beholden to an external review and accreditation where most of the areas in the university are not. We write our courses and frame them around the professional standards provided to us by the Institute for Teaching. Therefore our practices [are] shaped by government policy, even by proxy. If we were to separate ourselves from that, then we risk our programs not being accredited.... [O]ur graduates would still graduate from the university with a legitimate degree, but they would not be able to gain registration to be teachers in schools in this state.

A corollary is that multicampus universities have had to make changes to their teacher training curricula to ensure consistency of content between their campuses. While this has meant some decreased latitude for campuses to tailor ITE courses to local communities, it has also provided a number of advantages. As the teaching of diverse learners is part of the national teaching standards and embedded in program accreditation, it provides greater assurance that all students, including those in rural areas, will have access to teachers who have passed the same quality standard no matter where they received their initial teacher education. It also gives greater flexibility for teacher candidates to begin their study at one campus, and complete it at another.

VIT representatives noted that the accreditation process was not a qualitative assessment *per se*. It certifies that institutions either met or did not meet the standards, but does not describe *how well* they were met. Nonetheless, VIT staff regarded the process as rigorous. All accreditation committee members are trained in using the teaching standards for program review, and as VIT Director of Special Projects Fran Cosgrove notes, accreditation panels go through several cycles of checking and review:

> I've sat on four or five of these panels. As yet, no one has gone through the gate completely unquestioned. There are always little bits that need to be fixed up or further explained or changed. [The accreditation committee manager] will then communicate with the institution who will make the changes ...

> It will then, after a period of usually several months, come back to the entire committee. [A]n approval will be given on the recommendation that comes from [the accreditation committee manager] on the basis of work that has been done by the institution. We'll give it the tick of approval or we'll ask for more.

VIT Chairperson Don Paproth noted that particularly the professional practice element of programs required a significant amount of detail and time to document, and was the most difficult to accredit.

Other participants we spoke with were more circumspect about the prospects for the accreditation process to produce real change in raising teaching quality. University of Melbourne Professor of Education Stephen Dinham noted that the accreditation process itself was a rigorous exercise for universities, but that the potential positive impacts of accreditation on teaching quality would be more fully understood when courses are reaccredited:

> The big thing will come when these newly accredited courses are reaccredited. What's supposed to happen is rigorous attention to the impact—the quality of the graduates and the impact they're having in teaching.

Professor Dinham also cautioned that as policy compliance can become a ritual over time, reaccreditation should seek to avoid becoming a rushed process that might not provide the kind of data that evidences the effect of practice.

Content of ITE Programs

Curricula for initial teacher education programs have historically been the domain of the universities, informed by educational research, and further shaped by the specific institutional context. Accreditation is leading towards greater consistency of ITE curricula, although universities may differentiate themselves through specializations and concentrations. The largest extent of variation among universities has tended to be in the implementation of the professional practice (practicum) element, which has also been the focus of several state-level inquiries (Parliament of Victoria, 2005).

Teaching to students from diverse backgrounds is a common component of ITE programs. For example, among the national professional teaching standards, ITE programs must prepare graduate teachers to understand:

- *Students and how they learn:* including student and child development (physical, social, and intellectual); differentiated teaching for students from different backgrounds; strategies for teaching Aboriginal and Torres Strait Islander students; and strategies for students with different learning needs, including disabilities
- *The content of the school curriculum and how to teach it:* including assessment and reporting, and emphasis areas—literacy, numeracy, ICT, and knowledge of Aboriginal and Torres Strait Islander histories, cultures and languages
- *How to create safe, supportive, and inclusive learning environments:* how to deal with challenging behaviors, and how to support safe use of ICT (AITSL, 2011b).

Primary school teachers are trained as generalists, typically teaching all but specialist subjects such as LOTE, music, and physical education. New national reforms require that ITE programs offer a specialization, such as mathematics, a science, or an additional language (TEMAG, 2015b). The intent is that teachers will be able to share this knowledge with colleagues to build school capacity. Some universities in Victoria already offer a specialization. An example is the master of teaching (primary) at the University of Melbourne, in which candidates may specialize in mathematics or science teaching, which comprises a quarter of the total program content.

Undergraduate Programs

Undergraduate programs remain a common pathway into especially primary teaching. Monash University's Bachelor of Education (Hons) program (Link 3-14), illustrates how program elements are commonly structured into four-year undergraduate ITE in Victoria. Candidates program receive a grounding in the pedagogy of each of literacy and numeracy, and with additional but fewer units in arts, sciences, humanities, and other subject areas. They may also elect additional courses to strengthen their abilities in one of the target areas of literacy, numeracy, or languages.

The Monash degree program is comprised of four major themes: education studies, curriculum studies, discipline studies, and professional studies.[7] Education studies focuses on the core work of teaching, including pedagogy, development, learning inquiry, differentiated teaching, and assessment. It also addresses legislative and policy elements, as well as provide a familiarity with issues relating to society, culture, and indigeneity.

Curriculum studies looks at the content that teachers teach, and in particular the sequencing of the AusVELS curriculum and its related pedagogical concepts. As with many other ITE programs in Victoria, there are many more study units (here twice as many) for literacy, numeracy, and science, than with health, arts, humanities/social science, and other subjects, reflecting national and state emphasis areas.

Discipline studies is designed to strengthen teacher candidates' own capabilities in one of three selected streams—Leadership in English and Literacy, Leadership in Mathematics, or Languages Other Than English (LOTE). The requirement that all schools offer a language other than English is reflective of the diversity of the student population in Victoria, and the increased need for teachers with second language skills. Thus students in this stream study their language of choice within the relevant university department. By contrast, those that elect English and mathematics take a sequence in the fundamentals of that discipline, but with a focus on communication of concepts. This approach both supports the emphasis on curriculum and pedagogy in the curriculum stream, and helps meet accreditation guidelines that teachers' own abilities be among the top 30% of the population.

Professional studies denotes the practicum element, typically phased in across the course of the program. (See Table 3.3.) Teaching responsibility is progressively incremented, building from classroom observation, to joint teaching, and to full class control by the final year. The extent and timing of control is negotiated between the teacher candidate and supervising teacher during the placement.

The period of professional experience may vary across institutions, although a minimum of 80 days for undergraduate programs and 60 days for graduate programs is embedded in teacher registration and course accreditation processes.[8]

Table 3.3 Example of Minimum Practicum
Requirements: B.Ed. (Hons), Monash University.

Year of program	Number of days in practicum
Year One	10
Year Two	10
Year Three	20
Year Four	40

Graduate Programs

An increasing number of teacher candidates are entering teaching through graduate-level programs. These are required for secondary school teachers, but are also increasingly common among those entering into primary teaching. Master's programs typically consist of two years full-time equivalent study, as universities move to phase out one-year graduate diplomas. The master's degree is commonly taken in four semesters across two years, although some programs also offer 1.5 year completion by including a summer trimester study option.

Teacher candidates complete sequences in curricular content and pedagogy. For primary teacher candidates, these are typically two semester courses each on literacy and numeracy, and one semester course each on science, humanities, and the arts. For secondary candidates, this typically involves at least two semesters of secondary content and focused on the pedagogy of the candidates' major.

As secondary teaching candidates commonly enter ITE with undergraduate degrees in their major subject, these courses focus on the way content is structured in the curriculum, how this content builds across the secondary career towards senior school qualifications, theories of assessment, planning for teaching, and pedagogical approaches.

Most master's level teacher education programs also require a substantial research component. Teacher research skills are of increasing importance as a professional learning tool, and to develop research and inquiry competencies in students, extending them beyond the curriculum.

There is some variation among universities as to how research is integrated into the curriculum. For example, master's candidates at Monash University undertake either a professional learning project intended to contribute to improving teaching and learning within an educational setting; or a practice-based education research project intended to "develop students' capacities to generate and analyze evidence as a basis of professional practice" (Monash University, 2015).

Candidates at Victoria University may elect either an 8,000 word capstone research project coupled with an oral presentation, or a 15,000 word master's thesis, while those at Deakin University typically complete a research methodology sequence, culminating with a 12,000 word research thesis. The goal is for candidates to use "the skills of inquiry required by a teacher-researcher to gather evidence, analyze and reflect on practice" (Deakin University, 2014).

Innovations in Initial Teacher Training in Victoria

Much of the innovation in ITE takes place at the level of the university, including emphasis on enhancing the professional experience element of programs. For example, the University of Melbourne's Master of Teaching program involves teacher candidates being placed in schools two days a week during their studies. It seeks to tightly integrate theory and practice through an interventionist clinical practitioner model, discussed in greater detail in Box 3.2.

Similarly La Trobe University completed a pilot program of school-based teacher preparation, in conjunction with DET and Charles LaTrobe P–12 College, a multicampus school. Under its Teaching School program, teacher candidates spend two days a week in teaching practice. A broadband link connects the school and university, bringing classes both into and out of the school, facilitating demonstration and observation, and giving candidates the opportunity to experience an evidence-based inquiry approach to teacher training (Darling-Hammond, 2013). Candidates also have an allocated space at the school, allowing them to keep up with their university studies during the day, and facilitating formal mentoring opportunities and informal interactions with experienced teachers.

An additional innovative pilot program in Victoria is the Global Practicum, developed by five universities in Victoria in conjunction with the Victoria Council of Deans of Education (VCDE). Run twice annually, the program sees 8–10 students from each university undertake a month-long period of professional practice in a school in Malaysia. Teacher candidates receive mentoring from two university faculty who travel to Malaysia to observe and provide feedback to students.

The program has benefits for both teacher candidates and university faculty. Candidates are able to situate their teaching practice in a broader context, and contrast their in-school experiences of curricula, school organization, and teacher professional collaboration in Australia with those in Malaysia. As one teacher educator explained, the sharing of supervision and mentorship responsibilities also increases communication among university faculty, who must generate shared understandings around observation and feedback to teacher candidates on their practice:

> That's a fantastic collegial experience for the people who go. Also, it gives a bit of interaction with colleagues conducting teacher education in other areas. It creates some consistency in the practice of teacher education across Victoria, because [the participants] are working together, and mediating, moderating behaviors between [them]. That might be about how students are reported on, what the expectations are in the classroom, [and] how they're prepared.

A further project seeks innovative ways to improve teacher education in the science, technology, engineering, and mathematics fields to address a cycle of falling enrolments and teacher shortages in these subjects. Beginning in 2014, the Reconceptualizing Maths and Science Teacher Education Programs (ReMSTEP), is a three-year collaborative venture by four Victorian universities—Deakin, La Trobe, and Monash universities, and the University of Melbourne—funded by the Australian government. Initiatives under the scheme include giving teachers professional practice experience in research environments, engaging undergraduate science students in schools to attract new teacher candidates, and including science specialization options into ITE programs at the primary level.

Box 3.2 Clinical Practice: MTeach Program at Melbourne Graduate School of Education (MGSE)

The M.Teach program at the University of Melbourne is characterized by extended professional experience, and high levels of support to bridge university and school. The program also incorporates several of the elements of recently introduced ITE reforms. It was inspired by ideas from the Teachers for a New Era project—specifically, that teaching is "an academically taught clinical profession" (Carnegie Corporation, 2001), and drew upon lessons from the clinical experiences of MGSE Dean Field Rickards in the field of audiology (Rickards, 2014). A central principle of the program is that it is based in clinical practice, that is, teaching and working in schools alongside experienced teachers. Candidates spend two days a week in schools across the four semester program, and an additional 2–4 weeks near the end of each semester.

The program begins with a careful selection process. Candidates are evaluated based not solely on academic transcripts and working experiences, but also on their disposition and suitability for teaching, as explained by MGSE Deputy Director of Teaching and Learning, Larissa McLean Davies:

> [W]e spent many hours actually looking at the profiles of the candidates coming in and looking at where their strengths were ... It's not an overall score at the end. It's a much more nuanced way of looking at different bands [on the Teacher Selector] and looking at that in combination with GPA.

A second principle is that candidates are trained as clinical interventionist practitioners in a model that emphasizes evidence of students' learning and learning needs, research and selection of an intervention strategy, and assessment of the effectiveness of that intervention. The development of differentiated teaching strategies is thus a key element: Candidates are trained to identify different levels of development within a class, and direct teaching to 4–5 instructional groups (Griffin, 2014).

The program takes a developmental approach to student learning— understanding the student's present stage of learning, locating their zone of proximal development, and determining what is needed to help that student advance. This practice-based research process draws upon the work of MGSE Professors Patrick Griffin in measurement and assessment, and John Hattie in interventions and effect sizes. As Professor Griffin notes, the emphasis on guiding students along a path of increasing competency increases teachers' focus on process as well as outcomes:

> [T]he idea of evidence is pretty clear. Almost all of our graduates would talk about skills not scores, and all of them would talk about evidence not inference as a way of monitoring growth. And they would all talk about readiness to learn, rather than achievement levels.

It also encourages teachers to research, select, and trial teaching interventions to advance learning, some of which may be not be familiar. This also mirrors the Timperley cycle of teacher inquiry at the heart of the VIT's teacher registration and evidence-based professional learning approaches, in which teachers reflect upon student learning in order to guide their own learning. (See Table 3.4.)

Table 3.4 Interventionist Practitioner Cycle of Inquiry (Rickards, 2012).

Aspire	What is the student ready to learn in _____ and what is the evidence for this?
Analyze	What are the possible evidence-based interventions and what is the associated scaffolding process for each?
Apply	What is the preferred process and why is it preferred?
Anticipate	What is the expected impact and how will you check?
Appraise	What happened and what resultant decision was made?

The MTeach approach is thus both grounded in education research, and is coherent with the policy environment in which graduate teachers will eventually work. Teacher candidates and graduate teachers interviewed for the project indicated that they felt confident in their ability to gather evidence of student and teacher learning, which facilitated their registration process with VIT.

A significant feature of the program is the support that candidates receive to integrate theory and practice. It employs clinical specialists, university-employed teachers with deep familiarity of program content, working in tandem with teaching fellows, school-based teachers with significant experience in teacher coaching. The two are in constant communication, reviewing and giving feedback on candidates' lesson plans, observing lessons, and provide coaching.

The two positions work closely with mentor teachers in schools to support them in applying the clinical teaching methods in their mentorship roles, and in turn helping to shape the culture of the school. They support the teacher candidate's transition from academic studies to teaching, ensuring that candidates are effectively drawing on their practice experiences, and tightly integrating them with their studies.

The clinical teaching framework of diagnosis, intervention, and assessment also forms the basis for the evaluation of teacher candidates in the program. Each candidate's semester is capped with a Clinical Praxis Exam, in which they are assessed on their ability to draw on the clinical inquiry method, drawing together theory and practice. This contrasts with traditional university settings in which each course is typically assessed with a separate exam. The Clinical Praxis Exam requires teacher candidates to reflect on each aspect of this cycle, and detail their research supporting a particular intervention. Their findings are then presented before a university panel of faculty and practitioners. Thus candidates' readiness is assessed in an integrated way, based not solely on what they have learned, but on how they are able to apply this knowledge in their teaching practice.

Improving Clinical Practice in Victoria

In addition to recent federal efforts, emphasis on improving professional practice has also been a focus of state-level policy efforts, and the subject of several government inquiries. This includes a 2005 report by the Victorian Parliament, which found a number of concerns, particularly the quality and consistency of supervision of preservice teachers. The report found that many supervising teachers in schools were reluctant to take on the role of assessing, or to provide "bad grades" to a teacher candidate during the practicum (Parliament of Victoria, 2005).

The parliamentary report found there was greatest buy-in from the school and supervising teacher where there existed strong school-university partnerships that provided a win-win situation for both school and university, providing a focus for recommendations. Among the successful elements were longer periods of professional practice that allowed collegial relationships to form between supervisor and teachers and candidates, and in which the teacher candidate participated in school and community activities that extended beyond the classroom. The report noted these partnerships were highly valued by principals "because they place preservice teachers in schools for sufficient time to allow them to make a real contribution to curriculum development and teaching in the school" (Parliament of Victoria, 2005).

The report identified Victoria University's Project Partnerships as one such model. Regarded as practice-theory oriented (rather than theory-practice), teacher candidates work with teachers on addressing local learning priorities. Under this model, schools identify specific learning needs, and candidates are assigned related tasks. The relationship between candidate and supervising teacher is shifted from that of the one-way transmission of knowledge, to one in which the candidate is integrated into a school team. Candidates typically receive longer than minimally mandated time in school, and work on authentic tasks valuable to the school's curricular or teaching needs. In return, the candidate's involvement alleviates time pressures on school teachers and helps control the costs of supervision (Parliament of Victoria, 2005).

School Centres for Teaching Excellence

With higher education a largely federal responsibility, school partnerships are an area in which the state, as administrator of government schools, can have a more direct influence in the area of initial teacher education. Building on successful partnership models like those above, DET developed the School Centres for Teaching Excellence[9] initiative in 2010 to foster innovative clinical practice in ITE in Victoria. Stronger university-school partnerships is also coherent with new federal reforms in ITE.

The SCTE model created seven clusters to build schools' capacity to provide professional placement experiences for teacher candidates, establish research partnerships between universities and schools, and more closely link theory and practice in ITE. Each cluster comprised one or more universities, several schools, and a DET regional office. Several teacher candidates were assigned to a school and a mentor, returning to the same school for their professional placement throughout the year, serving to build closer relationships between school students and teacher candidates. In all, 6 universities, 65 schools, and around 1000 teacher candidates have taken part in the program (DEECD, 2014j).

Each cluster is able to take a different focus in its approach. For example, one focused on giving candidates extended experience teaching in rural communities. The cluster extended the mentor model to a whole-of-school approach in order to give candidates greater exposure to a range of classes and levels, and giving them greater voice in the classes and projects they chose to observe as part of their practicum. The approach also increased candidates' contact with parents and the community, an important element in reducing teacher attrition in rural settings (DEECD, 2014j).

DET documents suggest that the partnerships model offered several positive outcomes for professional practice. Firstly, it fostered closer communication between university- and school-based educators, feeding back into university curricula. ITE programs can be designed with closer connection to practice, and tailored to local circumstances. In another cluster, the university tailored a curricular unit on early literacy to address needs in oral language development identified by one of the schools (DEECD, 2014j).

Secondly, the model emphasizes longer internships and a greater involvement by the teacher candidate in the life of the school. This may be two days a week in the school, followed by a traditional block placement. Teacher candidates on longer placements are more likely to be invited to school faculty or team meetings. In clusters where teams of teacher candidates are placed together in a school, this provides increased opportunities for mutual support.

Thirdly, partnerships models can help foster professional collaboration among teachers at cluster schools, supporting the development of mentor cultures. This shifts the role of supervision away from a one supervisor, one teacher candidate model, to one of shared supervision. This in turn feeds back on assessment for candidates, becoming more of a team exercise, increasing the number of sources, and quality of information on which candidates' feedback and assessment may be based.

Fourthly, clusters have helped draw together primary and secondary schools. For example, teacher candidates in training for secondary education in one cluster undertook observational visits to primary schools as part of their practicum, and conduct reflections on practice with teacher candidates in primary education programs. Other clusters focused on implementation of ICT in student learning, and on combined professional practice for candidates across different years of their ITE program.

The success of the School Centres for Teaching Excellence pilot program in raising the quality of teaching preparation is reflected in its continuance as Teaching Academies of Professional Practice from 2014 (DEECD, 2014j), as part of the New Directions policy framework. This new program expands the model to create 12 clusters, and includes schools from rural and regional areas, and from both government and nongovernment sectors (DEECD, 2014i).

Box 3.3 School-University Partnership: A Developmental and Evidence-Based Approach to Literacy

A visit to Footscray North Primary School in Melbourne's western suburbs, a partner school with the University of Melbourne, reveals both a commitment to the developmental approach to literacy—long a feature of schooling in Victoria (Griffin, 2014)—and the continual use of evidence to support decision making in curricular choices and lesson planning.

The school caters for a broad range of students and learning needs. The area is diverse and multicultural, originally inhabited by indigenous Kulin peoples, later settled by Greek and Italian immigrants, and with subsequent waves of immigration from Vietnam and East Africa.

The school largely serves students from lower socioeconomic backgrounds, but recent expansion of the city center has also drawn in students from the middle classes, as Principal Sharon Walker describes:

> About 80 percent of our students come from an English as Additional Language background. We also have high-needs students, children from impoverished backgrounds. We have children here who range from refugees who've really just landed, up to families whose parents are here on AusAID scholarships, and they're doing their professorial degrees at the local universities. We have a range of children and a range of backgrounds, and [this] makes it such a rich place to work.

Adorning the walls of the school are posters that echo its values and goals, and which draw upon the strength of its diversity: "integrity, inclusion, and respect," "international mindedness," and "higher order thinking."

Raising literacy outcomes for its diverse student body is a school strategic goal. However, its developmental approach to learning encompasses broader student well-being. This is reflected in the curriculum with the "Kids Matter" and "Bounce Back" programs to support students' social and emotional well-being, and other curricular units are adapted to celebrate the school's cultural diversity and reflect a global perspective. The school also employs multicultural education aides and welfare offices to help teachers better understand their students' home cultures, to support communication between students and teachers, and to help integrate newly arrived families into the community.

Entering into a classroom at Footscray North, the strong focus on literacy with a developmental and personalized approach is immediately visible. The teacher points to the top of the white board and two magnetized red arrows reading "Learning Intentions" and "Success Criteria." Today's lesson is on using alliteration, with the goal to write a poetic structure employing this technique. This is part of making teaching and learning visible, in which the teacher and students are clear on what they are learning, and how they will know if they have done so. Down at students' eye-level, three colorful charts with descriptors and smiley faces help students distinguish the characteristics of books and resources that are "Just Right," and suited to their current level of reading development.

Most salient are the bright red, rectangular book boxes centrally placed on every desk, each labeled with a student's name. Principal Walker explains that this is one of the school's literacy nonnegotiables (a term we found in common practice in schools we visited), that every child in the school have continual access to their own book box. Each student receives a box on the first day of school, and carries it with them to their new class at the end of each school year. Each is different, stocked with around 6 to 10 books, including a minimum of 3 "just right" texts, 1 difficult/challenging text, 1 magazine, and 1 nonfiction item, used during daily independent reading times, and changed regularly to meet the particular child's present reading level and interests. Each also contains a reading log and reading journal, in which students, parents, and teachers record and monitor progress—notes from student-teacher conferences, outcomes from formative assessments, book selections, and progress in home reading—enabling multiple layers of support for student literacy.

Returning to the school's multipurpose room, we are joined by Mary Dowling, a senior teacher, literacy coach, and University of Melbourne Teaching Fellow, who explains how a developmental approach is built into the school's use of assessments to inform teaching. Multiple formative and summative assessment strategies are used to gather evidence of learning, including Guttman Charts, colorful arrays that indicates the zone of proximal development—the competencies each student is ready to learn next—providing a guide for instruction. As Ms. Dowling explains, the formative assessments are designed to cover a range of constructs and competency levels:

> Testing's differentiated, so they don't all get the same test. There's teacher knowledge there, and there's some estimation. Some kids may have to be tested more than once ... They're looking at around a 45 to 75 percent accuracy rate. Because if they get all of them right, it tells us nothing. If they get too many of the questions wrong, it also tells us nothing about their ZAD [Zone of Actual Development] and then subsequently their ZPD [Zone of Proximal Development].

Each student response is recorded in a spreadsheet, coded 1 or 0, and color-coded—green if correct, or red if incorrect. Reordering the spreadsheet—horizontally by increasing difficulty of learning construct, and vertically in terms of student competency—produces the Gutt-man chart (Link 3-15). The colored boundaries indicate each student's current level of skill acquisition and where they need further development. This provides a quick visual representation of where the teacher can focus her/his teaching efforts, and how s/he can differentiate teaching for students and cohorts, important in school with a diverse range of learners. As Assistant Principal Davide Lombardi recently reported:

> We have a grades 3–4 class where some kids are working at a year 1 level in maths and we have three or four students working on year 9 maths … It's incredibly challenging to balance, but there is no guesswork; all our decisions are based on evidence.
>
> (Trioli, 2015)

The developmental and evidence-based approach have proved successful in raising school outcomes for Footscray North. The school's Year 3 to Year 5 growth on NAPLAN in reading and numeracy have eclipsed both the mean growth for Australia schools, and those with similar student profiles.

Ongoing Challenges in Initial Teacher Education

Despite these positive innovations, there remain ongoing challenges to ITE in Victoria. These emerge in part from the difficulty in alignment of university funding, with both teacher registration and teacher supply determined at the state level.

Australian universities are primarily federally funded. In order to keep courses and programs financially viable university-wide, shortfalls in enrollment (and thus funding) in one part of the university may be addressed through increased enrollment in others. Thus the number of seats in ITE programs does not directly correspond to the teacher demand at the state level, and can place the business interests of the university in tension with their education school's role in educating teachers for jobs primarily within the state. The uncapping of federally funded also allowed some universities to increase teaching enrollments, contributing to oversupply and shortages in some areas highlighted earlier.

While not all universities responded in this way, an interview with one teacher educator illustrated how these tensions can manifest in ways that challenge sustaining improvement in teaching quality through ITE programs. Firstly, a supply imbalance of teacher candidates can complicate placements for professional practice, a requirement for candidates to graduate and become registered. Particularly final-year candidates in shortage areas are attractive for schools, which may use professional placements as opportunities to trial and vet potential teachers:

> [S]chools are often utilizing particularly [one-year] graduate diploma programs. They know that those students will be ready for the labor market at the end of this year. Come November, there can be interviews and job offers made to those people within the year. It can very often be a way for schools to market test what's going on from which university. Are graduates [from this particular university] getting more of what we need in our school? 'Is this physics teacher going to be the right fit for us? We know that we've got two physics teachers who've put their hand up to retire this year,' or whatever it might be that shapes demand.
>
> (interview with teacher educator, 2014)

Feedback to universities on the demand for new teacher graduates is often felt at the professional placement phase. Although universities generally have good relationships with schools, an oversupply of teachers in some subject areas can mean trying to quickly establish new relationships and school placements, which may view candidates as an additional burden.

> We know that informally, the humanities generally are [already] well-catered for... Doesn't really matter who the provider is ... there's certainly an abundance of those teachers being prepared in the market place. It's hard to get them positions in schools because they're full up. They [schools] say, 'You know what? We've got four places that we can offer. If it's about humanities and the social sciences, no. We want to use those places to get some science people in, [or] maths.

Secondly, increased enrollmentss can have impacts on class sizes in some ITE programs. This can mean hiring sessional tutors, and less face-to-face time for candidates with professors. It can mean fewer opportunities for professors to visit and observe candidates during their professional placement, putting greater responsibility on reporting from supervising teachers. Larger class sizes can also impact the space for teacher education within the university and potentially impact on quality.

> You structure your teaching in a particular way. Over the years, I've been working with groups of students between let's say 30 and 35 students. That's been optimum because the maximum class size

in a government school you're working into is 27... It's a "like" environment. They get an understanding of when they're doing micro-teaching within that room, within that group, this is how I'm positioned. Those groups are now between 45 and 50, which means we have to ... in some cases, change the physical environment they're located in. The rooms aren't big enough to do the work we do. Because we're teaching [the practice of] teaching as highly intellectualized craftwork, there needs to be space for doing. That's something that is often disregarded in the university thinking. They have a conventional lecture theater, bus row seat approach to what's going on in the learning environment.

They're the types of changes where the necessary changes to organizational behavior around improving the business model of the university and being more efficient alongside being more effective often disrupts the way we've historically conducted teacher education.

Thirdly, some universities have moved to increase the flexibility of ITE programs, moving a number of their curricular modules online, and in conjunction with weekend intensive classes. This flexibility in delivery makes ITE available to a more diverse population (particularly career-changers and those in rural areas), and can attract into teaching those who may not otherwise have had the opportunity.

However, in a policy environment oriented to strengthening ITE, the same teacher educator questioned whether online learning can offer the same quality of pedagogical experience, whether it leads to a less cohesive ITE program and whether candidates may miss out on the mutual support and learning environment offered through a traditional cohort model:

[I]f I talk personally, I feel an anxiety about the things that get converted into online environments, that they can't be intellectually deconstructed in the moment. We rely enormously on the student being able to cope with what's being presented to them. I concern myself that we will lose wonderful prospective teachers to not necessarily disengaging, but poorly aligned pedagogies.

For me as a teacher educator ... we would have some of that, but we would maintain our face-to-face base, because we're in a people business. We are looking to develop and build, and reveal engaging teachers who are gonna work with young adolescents. It's about communication and people skills, content knowledge, experience. All things that are better manifest in a person-to-person exchange.

Induction, Mentoring, and Teacher Registration

Induction and mentoring have seen considerable growth in coverage and quality in Victoria. As a result of policies implemented over the past decade, mentorship for beginning teachers has expanded to encompass nearly all schools in the state. This expansion was initially led by policy requirements from DET, but driven soon thereafter by the teacher registration process that connected mentorship to state and now national teaching standards. At the national level through AITSL, state education ministers endorsed updated guidelines in 2016 intended to further improve the quality and consistency of induction practices across states and school systems. Induction and mentorship have been further underpinned in government schools through formal recognition in the collective bargaining agreement between state and union, allowing beginning teachers reduced teaching workloads in the first year. Together, these have resulted in near universal mentorship for beginning teachers that uses the national teaching standards to help bridge ITE and teaching practice for early career teachers.

Induction is predominantly school-based. DET provides guidelines and online resources to support schools in the induction and mentoring of beginning teachers. Schools are expected to provide administrative materials and school policies, hold an orientation day, and allocate a "buddy" and a mentor to support each teacher in their transition to the school. DET documents characterize the purposes of induction as providing a sound understanding of school and profession, assistance to improve teaching practice, empathetic moral support, and support for VIT registration (DEECD, 2013g).

DET guidelines outline three induction phases. The first—Getting Started—provides information on how to connect to the school community, and how to establish a relationship with a "buddy," who can provide an informal introduction and orientation to the school. The second—Getting Settled—deals with administrative matters (such as salary payment and taxation), report writing, parent-teacher conferences, and establishing a relationship with a teacher-mentor. Beginning teachers are expected to plan for observation times, when their mentor can observe their teaching, and engage in a reflective conservation to provide feedback aimed at improving their teaching practice. The third phase—Getting Inspired—deals with classroom management, the use of ICT, classroom observations, goal-setting and planning for professional development, and collecting evidence of learning against the professional teaching standards as part of the VIT teacher registration process.

DET's Performance and Development Culture policy includes induction and mentoring, and requires that schools do the following: provide comprehensive induction materials to teachers; have in place effective mentoring for teachers; provide initial training for mentor teachers; and regularly monitor and evaluate induction supports (DEECD, 2009). All government schools participated in accreditation under the policy between 2005 and 2009, with around 97% achieving accreditation to at least Level 1 (of three), embedding a culture of mentorship in the state. Accreditation was also voluntarily undertaken by many Catholic and independent schools. Although accreditation is no longer compulsory, government schools are expected to continue to self-assess and monitor progress against this policy framework (DET, 2013).

Teacher Registration in Victoria

The implementation of the Performance and Development Culture policy by the DET also coincided with the introduction of mentorship as part of the VIT registration process. This helped inform the framing of induction in DET policy, "ensuring that induction support and mentoring are aligned with VIT and Department guidelines" (DEECD, 2009). As VIT Director of Special Projects Fran Cosgrove explained, linking mentoring to teaching standards helped expand the view of mentorship from one of collegial friendship and emotional support to one based on professional conversations around teaching competencies, and centered on student learning:

> We said, "If we're gonna do this, it has to be a professional relationship, and we have to set up that professional relationship. We have to define it through the standards and this full registration process."

> We would argue we've driven that … We've used that regulatory stick to drive the carrot of support through induction.

The VIT process thus more formally structures the induction environment for beginning teachers, and includes those in both government and nongovernment schools. New teacher training graduates enter the workforce with Graduate Teacher status, and enroll as provisionally registered with VIT. Teachers then have up to two years to progress from provisional to full registration, although this is typically achieved in the first year.

Registration serves four critical functions related to induction. Firstly, it requires the collection of evidence of teaching competencies that are embedded in the work that they do in the classroom. Teachers are asked to focus on a particular aspect of practice, and implement an action plan based on an inquiry question and related to a particular aspect of the standards. This was by design, to establish a pathway for continual improvement of one's teaching practice, rather than a one-off compliance approach where teachers merely check boxes (Paproth & Cosgrove, 2014).

Figure 3.8 Timperley Cycle of Teacher Inquiry and Knowledge Building.

Source: VIT (2013), Evidence of Professional Practice for Full Registration

Secondly, teachers are encouraged to use the Timperley cycle of teacher inquiry and knowledge building, as framed in the national standards, to reflect on their practice. (See Figure 3.8.) Teachers identify students' needs and an area of teaching practice to meet those needs, develop and implement their action plan over a period of 4–6 weeks, and assess the effectiveness on student learning. This approach helps scaffold teacher induction into a cycle of professional learning that experienced teachers use in maintaining their own registration, and provides a common language for discussing one's practice. VIT Director of Special Projects Fran Cosgrove described the process:

> [T]hey [beginning teachers] come up with an inquiry question. Then they're building up their capacity and knowledge around how you approach that through observation and discussion with others. That can be school-based, but they might also do professional reading, [or] undertake professional development activities that are outside their school or within their school.
>
> [W]e then ask them to use that knowledge to develop an action plan of how they're going to approach their teaching practice to focus on

that particular area of learning they're going to improve in their students. We ask them to do that through interaction with their mentor, [and] to implement that in their classrooms over a period of time. This is where we ask the mentors to be as involved as they can. The whole idea is that you've got a colleague at your shoulder who can see things you might not, who you can talk about the implementation with.

[I]t's then a case of looking at the artifacts of learning. What did the students produce? How do you know? What are the questions you asked? Did they learn things you didn't expect? Did some learn some things and others not? Why?

Then, it's their reflection on that. What does that mean for my practice? What does that mean for this inquiry? Does that move into another kind of an inquiry? [T]he last thing is really what have I learned from this as a practitioner? Then you start the whole cycle again.

Thirdly, the registration process is predicated on the provision of a school-based mentor observing classes and helping teachers reflect on their progress. Provisionally registered teachers provide evidence of professional conversations with an experienced teacher that are focused on student learning. Induction support for beginning teachers is characterized by VIT as "induction for professional learning" and a first step to ongoing teacher professional learning (VIT, 2014b). Evidence collection and the embedding of mentorship and professional dialog in the registration process are thus by design, and are intended both to help define, and drive support for, teaching practice (Paproth & Cosgrove, 2014).

However, this process also requires mentors having the necessary competencies to support the development of teaching practice, and provide feedback that is not received as evaluative or judgmental. This has been helped by the Teacher Mentor Support Program jointly delivered by VIT and DET since 2004, and supported by Independent Schools Victoria and the Catholic Education Offices.

The two-day Teacher Mentor Support Program, which operates in the first semester of each year at various locations across the state, is designed to give experienced teachers the knowledge and skills they will need to mentor beginning teachers (DEECD, 2014e). Participation by mentors is not compulsory, but the program has had good coverage with around 12,000 mentors trained over the past decade (Paproth & Cosgrove, 2014). The course focuses on identifying beginning teachers' learning needs, promoting collegial support, using a collaborative inquiry approach to develop teaching practice, and having evidence-informed professional conversations (VIT, 2014b). The course also emphasizes mentors' own knowledge of the professional standards, required for their own maintenance of registration. Thus mentor training and mentorship increases buy-in to the standards from experienced teachers, helps support professional dialog, and provides a common language for doing so.

Fourthly, registration connects teacher induction to school leadership and school-wide goals. Each school is required by VIT to convene a panel comprised of the principal, mentor, and another experienced teacher who reviews the teacher's evidence and recommends approval (or postponement) of full registration to VIT. This helps build induction and mentoring into the culture of the school, and provides a foundation for ongoing professional learning and connection to the teaching profession in a decentralized schooling environment.

The process is a departure from traditional models, in which teachers work in isolation, and teaching practice is the sole domain of that teacher. Combined with the national teaching standards, it provides a pathway for continual improvement by linking student learning with reflective teaching practice and ongoing professional learning. As former AITSL Chair Anthony Mackay explains:

> [T]hink about the nature of the early years, induction, orientation, coaching, mentoring, observation, feedback. Any profession that really wishes to say that it's going to make a difference through the quality of its practice just absorbs, accommodates, embraces all of that, and understands there's going to be a commitment over your professional life.

Supports for Induction

A key support for induction is the provision of planning time for beginning teachers. Since 2004, and through collective bargaining between AEU and DET, teachers in their first year have their workload reduced by at least 5%. This equates to around 1–2 hours a week of additional allocated planning time to support teacher learning and increasing their effectiveness (AEU Victoria & DEECD, 2013). Beginning teachers typically use this time to observe an experienced teacher's class, gather evidence of their practice for registration, have professional conversations with their mentor, or evaluate student data and plan classes. While mentors do not receive additional release time under the agreement, principals are required to ensure that mentors are able to undertake the role within a 38-hour working week.

Both VIT and AEU provide training support programs for new teachers. VIT runs a series of free seminars for provisionally registered teachers throughout the state during the second and third terms of each calendar year. These sessions brief teachers on the full registration process, provide resources for collecting evidence of practice, and connect teachers with VIT staff for further registration assistance. AEU provides a free day-long workshop to its members in their first five years of teaching, addressing some of the key challenges for graduate teachers such as managing teaching workloads, familiarization with performance and development processes, and dealing with extreme student behaviors.

Induction and Mentorship in Practice

The exact form of induction and mentoring processes in Victoria depends to some extent on school leadership, and the availability and experience of mentors, which may vary with a school's size and geographic location. Nonetheless, in schools visited for this study, we found several commonalities.

Mentors were usually selected from the same grade level and/or professional team within the school. This meant that mentors and beginning typically had the same class timetables, and the same periods of allocated planning time (designated nonteaching hours). This arrangement provided greater opportunities for collaborative planning, and professional conversations around the content and pedagogy of the classes.

In primary schools, teachers were often assigned classrooms adjacent to that of their mentor. This provided additional opportunities for informal conversations and interactions, and a quick source of support.

However, the alignment of mentor and teacher by grade level, subject, or location in the school was less frequently possible in the case of secondary school teachers. As senior teacher Seona Aulich explains:

> It's more challenging in secondary schools, because there might be a secondary school teacher who's in the PE [physical education] faculty who's been partnered with someone from maybe a health background, but they're actually in two different offices in different corners of the school. They don't have that incidental conversation that generally those primary teachers get to have all

the time, because we [primary teachers] work a lot more closely together.

This finding was supported by VIT data showing that provisionally registered teachers in primary schools were more likely to report a high quality mentoring experience than those in secondary schools.

Effectiveness of Teacher Induction

Together, VIT and DET policies have seen a significant increase in the coverage and quality of induction and mentoring in the state. VIT data show that rates of mentorship among beginning teachers increased rapidly from below 50% prior to the enactment of the registration process, to remain between 93% and 99% over the past decade (Paproth & Cosgrove, 2014; VIT, 2014). (See Figure 3.9.)

An early report into the effectiveness of VIT's support for provisionally registered teachers found strong evidence that it had led to significant increases in teachers' collaborative engagement with colleagues, and in their professional learning. However, it also found the extent to which

Figure 3.9 Percentage of Beginning Teachers with Mentors.

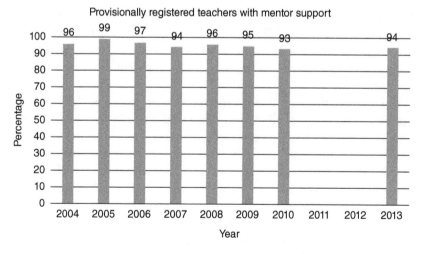

Reproduced from VIT, 2014, p. 11.

this occurred was influenced by the level of support and encouragement from school leadership. According to the report by the Australian Council for Educational Research (Ingvarson et al., 2007):

> School leaders in high impact schools ensured that: induction programs for new teachers were in place; care was taken in selecting appropriate mentors; VIT training for mentors and PRTs (provisionally-registered teachers) was supported; time was set aside for mentors and PRTs; and that VIT procedures for assembling evidence and making recommendations were implemented faithfully.
>
> As reported by PRTs, school leaders in low impact schools were more likely to take a rather cavalier approach to the registration process. School leaders in these schools did not see themselves as partners with the VIT in supporting beginning teachers and assuring the quality of new entrants to the profession. PRTs in these schools were more likely to comment that ... their school had let them down. (2007, p. 49)

Nonetheless, the report found that negative experiences were rare. Mentor teachers and principals indicated they regarded the VIT process as fair and valid, and valued the opportunity for the profession to have a significant role in seeing that new teachers met the standards (Ingvarson et al., 2007).

There is also evidence to suggest that the mentoring process has positively influenced the classroom practices of beginning teachers and helped develop their teaching knowledge. Data from AEU's New Teachers Survey in 2005 and 2007 showed that teachers generally rated the workload required for registration as being high, but were also more likely than not to regard the work as being impactful on their teaching performance (AEU Victoria, 2005, 2007).

VIT surveys also showed that around 90% of provisionally registered teachers indicated that they made beneficial changes to their teaching through feedback from mentors and/or experienced teachers. Ninety-four percent agreed that working collegially in the classroom with an experienced teacher had allowed them to see what good professional practice looks like and had focused their professional reflection on engaging students and student learning. In addition to mentee benefits, over 95% of mentors agreed that had experienced professional learning benefits from their involvement with mentoring a provisionally registered teacher (VIT, 2014).

A more established culture of support for mentorship also developed as registration and national standards become more firmly embedded.

A 2013 evaluation report found that 89% of teachers and mentors reported satisfaction with support and encouragement from school leaders, and with timely and adequate support from the school. A similar percentage indicated that their school understood the challenges of beginning teachers and that this was reflected in the responsibility allocated to the provisionally registered teacher (VIT, 2014). As the report notes:

> [T]he full registration process uses the support of the entire profession in Victoria to develop the practice of provisionally registered teachers to the Proficient Teacher level.
>
> (VIT, 2014)

While acknowledging the complexity of factors involved, VIT also cites the support for provisionally registered teachers as contributing to the retention of new teachers in the profession (Paproth & Cosgrove, 2014). VIT data found that approximately 78% of provisionally registered teachers surveyed in 2013 indicated that the full registration process had increased the likelihood they would stay in teaching, a figure that has steadily increased from previous years (VIT, 2014). (See Figure 3.10.)

Figure 3.10 Provisionally Registered Teachers' Agreement That the Evidence-Based Process Has Increased the Likelihood They Will Stay in Teaching.

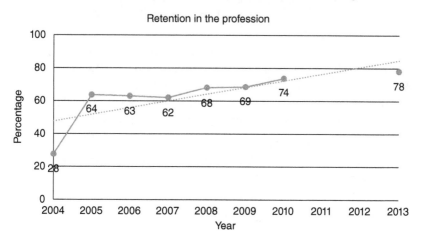

Reproduced from VIT, 2014, p. 14.

Box 3.4 Mentoring graduate teachers

Seona Aulich, a senior teacher at Rosanna Golf Links Primary School in Melbourne's Eastern Suburbs, described to us the range of activities that graduate teachers may experience in their first year in the classroom. With 12 years of teaching experience, she is one of several teachers in the school assigned to mentor graduate teachers. Formal mentoring is required for their registration, but also comprises a range of informal contact opportunities that support learning for beginning teachers.

Mentorship is one of the expected roles of senior teachers like Seona. As DET Human Resources documents note, Range 2 teachers are expected to "model exemplary classroom practice and mentor/coach other teachers in the school to engage in critical reflection of their practice and to support staff to expand their practice" (DEECD, 2013h).

In 2013, Seona served as a mentor for a new graduate, describing the process as having become more structured in recent years:

> [A]t various times [the graduate teacher] will come in and sit in in my grade, for example. She'll watch me teach. Then I'll go and observe her, just to make sure communication lines are well and truly open to ask questions. It's quite a formalized process.

Periodic meetings between the graduate teacher and the assistant principal were also established. Although part of formal induction, these sessions were generally casual in nature, intended to provide a check-in opportunity on the graduate's progress in adapting to the school and to teaching.

Unlike her mentee, who had her teaching workload reduced by 1–2 hours a week, Seona did not receive additional noninstructional time for mentoring activities. Instead, she was apt to characterize her mentoring role not just part in terms of her formal allocation, but also as part of her professional obligation to support colleagues:

> That [mentoring] would be something that I would be expected to do [as a senior teacher]. [The graduate teacher] is someone you're working with anyway. You don't want to see someone struggling in their job, so you do whatever [you can].

Efforts were also made to provide frequent opportunities for informal contact and support:

The mentor becomes that person that they get to go and ask those questions—there's none too ridiculous ... [I] had a great relationship with my graduate. Phone calls all the time, and questions, and I'd send her through my planning in case she was getting a little bit snowed under. Or staying back and just going through data and making sure that she knows exactly what she's doing, because it can be a pretty overwhelming start. There's no easing in—it's you jumping in the deep end.

Seona's mentee also has access to induction activities beyond the school. After the first school term (late March) she attended a meeting held by the local school network. This provided an opportunity for graduate teachers from various schools to share their experiences and to build peer networks. She was also invited back to visit her alma mater to share her experiences with teacher candidates, and received an additional two days off during the year to attend external training workshops.

The Organization of Schooling in Victoria

Organization within Schools

The way schools and their curricula are organized, and the time available to teachers, structures teachers work and can influence teaching quality. Victorian schools have control over how they are organized, but within national and state guidelines. Curricular decisions are framed by the AusVELS curriculum (Victorian curriculum from 2017), which applies to all government schools; and decisions about staffing and hours of work must be meet the guidelines of the collective bargaining agreement with AEU. Such decisions are commonly made by the principal and school leadership team in communication with the school council. For example, at Footscray North Primary School, organization of staffing, curriculum, and timetable are made by a consultation committee comprised of school leadership and staff representatives.

Organization thus varies across government schools, with the arrangement of grade levels providing an example. It is estimated that around half of all students in government primary schools in Victoria are taught in composite (multilevel) grades. One common model is Prep, then combined Grades 1/2, Grades 3/4, and Grades 5/6.

Schools also have flexibility in establishing curricular programs, so long as they are able to demonstrate that they are meeting the learning objectives as set out in AusVELS. Primary students will typically have their classroom teacher for literacy and numeracy, and spend a smaller number of hours each week in specialist subjects such as physical education, library skills, and art. Science may be taught by students' classroom teacher, or as a specialist subject, depending on the school and its learning goals. The specialized teaching of literacy and numeracy at the primary level as occurs in some countries is rare in Victoria, although not precluded by policy, as schools have autonomy in deciding how they meet the curricular learning objectives.

Box 3.5 Structuring the curriculum at Rosanna Golf Links Primary School

Rosanna Golf Links Primary School is located in Melbourne's more affluent eastern suburbs, around 10 miles northeast from the city's central business district, and has around 425 students from Foundation (Prep) through to Grade 6. The school uses a composite system, combining seven grades into four levels:

- Foundation
- Junior School: Grades 1 and 2
- Middle School: Grades 3 and 4
- Senior School: Grades 5 and 6

Students have their regular classroom teacher for the main learning areas such as literacy and numeracy. Each week they have several specialist subject periods. These include ICT, Auslan (Australian Sign Language), physical education, science, the arts, and library. The school also has a specialist Deaf facility—one of only around 20 in government schools in the state—to help provide inclusive learning for Deaf students. An example timetable of specialist subjects is show in Figure 3.11.

The school's curricular offerings are emblematic of the flexibility available to schools in Victoria. For example, students in Foundation year undertake two two-hour sessions weekly of activity-based learning (known as the ABL program). During these sessions, four classrooms are set up with play-based activities covering themes based on: literacy, numeracy, science, and inquiry studies. Students

Figure 3.11 Timetable of Specialist Subjects at RGLPS.

ROSANNA GOLF LINKS PRIMARY SCHOOL - TIMETABLE TERM 2 2014

MONDAY

SPECIALIST	9.00 – 10.00	10.00 – 11.00	11.30 – 12.30	12.30 – 1.30	2.30 – 3.30
PLANNING	ASSEMBLY		LEVEL 5/6 PLANNING		
Science	APT	1/25	5/6W	5/6W	3/4D
PE	APT	1/28	Prep T	Prep M	2/5E
Art	APT	1/41	5/6V	5/6A	3/4H
LOTE	APT	Present Program	5/6A	5/6W	3/4E
Music	APT	Instrumental	Instrumental	Instrumental	Instrumental
ICT/Library	Instrumental	1/40	5/6B Jule B	5/6B Jule B	Prep P
RE			Prep M / Prep S	Prep P / Prep T	5/6A & 5/6W / 5/6V & 5/6B

TUESDAY

SPECIALIST	9.00 – 10.00	10.00 – 11.00	11.30 – 12.30	12.30 – 1.30	2.30 – 3.30
PLANNING	FOUNDATION PLANNING		LEVEL 1/4 PLANNING		
Science	Prep T	Prep M	3/4M	3/4M	5/6AI
PE	Prep P	Prep S	3/4L	3/4P	1/2P
PE	5/6W	5/6B	1/4W	3/4M	
Art	Prep M / Prep S	Prep P / Prep T	3/4P	3/4D	1/2L
LOTE	5/6W	5/6B	3/4D	3/4L	5/6B
Music	Prep S / Prep M	Prep P			
ICT/Library	5/6A	5/6W			

WEDNESDAY

SPECIALIST	9.00 – 10.00	10.00 – 11.00	11.30 – 12.30	12.30 – 1.30	2.30 – 3.30
PLANNING	LEVEL 1/2B PLANNING		LEVEL 1/2A PLANNING		Prep M
Science	1/2L	1/2D	5/6V	1/2B	5/6B
PE	3/4D	APT	3/4M	3/4L	1/2D
Art	APT	1/2L	1/2S	1/2L	1/4W
LOTE	1/2L	APT	1/2B	1/2P	5/6V
Music	1/2D	1/2D	APT / 1/2P	APT / 1/2B	Instrumental
ICT/Library	1/2L	1/2L	1/2P	1/2S	1/2P

Level 4

THURSDAY

SPECIALIST	9.00 – 10.00	10.00 – 11.00	11.30 – 12.30	12.30 – 1.30	2.30 – 3.30
PLANNING	1/2LA	1/2PA	Prep P	Prep Sa	OF AS FACILITY PLANNING
Science	APT	5/6A	5/6V	5/6W	1/2B
PE	APT	Prep M	Prep S	Prep P	5/6B
Art	3/4P	3/4H	APT	APT	Prep T
LOTE	Instrumental	Instrumental	Instrumental	Instrumental	
Music	3/4H	3/4W	1/2E	1/2E	
ICT/Library			1/2B & 1/2S	1/2D & 1/2P	Prep S
RE			APT / 1/2P	1/2E & 1/2L	

FRIDAY

SPECIALIST	9.00 – 10.00	10.00 – 11.00	11.30 – 12.30	12.30 – 1.30	2.30 – 3.30
Art	1/2S	1/2D	Instrumental	1/2S	Prep S
Music	Instrumental	Instrumental	1/2D	Instrumental	
ICT/Library	3/4L	3/4P	3/4L & 1/4P	1/2D	
RE			3/4H & 1/4W	1/4D	
Sport				1/2L	Prep T

Level 4

Time bands: MORNING RECESS (between 11.00 and 11.30); LUNCH RECESS (between 1.30 and 2.30).

are free to move between the classes exploring the different themes, engaging in activities, and then are encouraged to write about their experience. The activity provides opportunities for developing socio-emotional learning, independent inquiry, as well as practicing writing skills.

Like all government schools, RGLPS is required to have a languages program. The school selected Auslan for its language other than English (LOTE) offering, taking advantage of the Deaf facility for hearing-impaired students. All students receive weekly Auslan instruction in half-hour classes for Grades Prep–2, and hour-long classes for Grades 3–6. Additional classes are made available for teachers and parents.

The school also incorporates several school-wide learning themes into its curriculum. It is part of the Sustainability Victoria Resource Smart program (receiving state accreditation), in which schools take action to save energy and water, reduce waste, promote biodiversity, and in the process embed learning opportunities for students centered on sustainability into the curriculum. Examples include a frog pond—constructed by a team of Grade 3/4 students—and vegetable gardens within the school. These facilities are then integrated into the school's science program to give students hands-on learning opportunities and to teach responsibility for the environment.

Organization of staff and timetabling is also a school responsibility. The assignment of responsibilities (and salaries), and the number of allocated planning and meeting hours for teams must all be factored into school budgets. Teachers are often organized into grade-level teams and professional learning teams (and in some schools these are the same). Timetabling by grade-level teams can facilitate collaborative planning during times where students are receiving specialist instruction.

Depending on its size, a school may employ between one and three assistant principals, or assign reduced teaching roles for senior staff to undertake leadership responsibilities. For example, Willmott Park Primary School has two assistant principals—one for school administration, policy, and management; the other for teaching and learning. Among senior teachers, it has two professional learning coordinators tasked with identifying individual and team learning needs, conducting whole-school professional learning, and providing teacher observation and feedback. The school also has grade-level team leaders who coordinate planning and help ensure consistent delivery of the curriculum across classes in each grade; and a preservice teacher coordinator to facilitate supervision for teacher candidates on professional placement.

The way schools organize themselves may also be reflective of the school strategic plan. At Footscray North, the Principal, Assistant Principals, Leading Teacher, and Intervention Teacher meet to evaluate school-wide data and identify potential areas of concern or that may need intervention. As part of an action plan to create more effective and engaging learning environments, the school has also adopted the Kids Matter mental health and well-being framework.[10] It has thus formed a Kids Matter Community Group that includes teaching staff that helps organize events to create stronger connections between parents, the community, and the school.

Box 3.6 Organizing time at Willmott Park Primary School

Willmott Park Primary School is located in Craigieburn in the northernmost suburb of Melbourne, a rapidly expanding area with new housing developments into what was once the city's rural fringe. Willmott Park's student population has likewise grown dramatically, by nearly a hundred—to 715—in less than two years. Many of the students are from immigrant backgrounds, and there is a significant proportion of students from language backgrounds other than English.

The variation in students' English literacy abilities has been a contributing factor—together with recent professional learning in instructional leadership—in a push towards the effective use of student data to guide learning. This has given the school a strong emphasis on the efficient use of time focused on student learning, and the use of collaborative planning to ensure consistency across classes and grades.

The school uses straight age grades to organize classes, intentionally timetabling all core classes within each grade at the same time. The purpose is two-fold. Firstly, grade-level classroom teachers have the same teaching times and noninstructional periods. This maximizes the available time for collaborative planning. Secondly, it helps keep all grade-level classes in step with curricular units. Assistant Principal Deborah Crane said that at any given time, a principal or professional learning coordinator should be able to walk into a given class and know what the learning objectives are, aiding coordination between teachers and school leaders (Hughes & Crane, 2014).

Weekly class schedules at Willmott Park are mapped onto major learning objectives for each class during each of the four school terms. This additional planning helps keep teachers in step not just with curricular expectations, but is designed to facilitate consistency in pace across classes within a grade. Schedules can be adapted depending on the progression of each class and any difficulties encountered.

Teachers have at least two hours a week of allocated planning time, depending on their role. Each grade-level team has a weekly collaborative planning session. As with other meetings at the school, the number of participants is intentionally restricted to encourage active teacher participation, a move that Principal Hughes felt impacted positively on teaching quality:

> Professional conversations within their teams are incredibly powerful, and setting those up with a critical mass of three or four people in a team is important. We used to have structures here where we'd have six or seven or eight, and that was far too big to have valid professional conversations, because there'd be a couple of "passengers" that just sit there. With three or four everyone's involved and the conversations are highly professional. That's been a significant factor.

Time within meetings is valued, and follows the same structure and format: celebrating successes; weekly planning for learning; data for improvement; ideas and hints for improving the teaching and learning of units; administrative matters; occupational health and safety, parent concerns, and student welfare/behavior. Meeting notes (Link 3-16) are posted on the school's internal website making them accessible to all staff members, a process intended to encourage transparency and consistency across the school.

The set format and formalized notes serve specific purposes. Weekly planning for student learning and evidence of improvement are given priority in the agenda, and the majority of the meeting time is dedicated to their discussion. Principal Hughes noted that this helped maintain professional conversations, avoiding loss of time on issues that are peripheral to student learning:

> [Administrative matters] should only be ten percent of the conversations. The rest of it should be official pedagogy.

Teachers use these collaborative meeting times to discuss upcoming curricular expectations. They review the books and materials that will be presented to students during that week. Teachers also share additional lesson resources, and draw attention to elements for emphasis in the materials. They identify and discuss success criteria for learning elements asking "how will we know that the students have grasped the material?" Teachers also compare their recent learning objectives, resources, and assessment data against the AusVELS curricular progression points.

As with other schools we visited in Victoria, Willmott Park teachers regarded the effective use of noninstructional time as a valuable part of their professional work. As such, it was thus commonly used for collaborative planning or professional learning, and focused on student learning progress.

School Networks

A key support for teaching quality in Victoria has been the use of school networks and clusters for the sharing of knowledge and good practice among schools—an acknowledgment that the teaching profession itself is a core resource for school improvement. During the second wave of reforms, DET funded 72 senior education officers. Each was assigned to a school network to develop regional network leadership teams and to help them work through a process of collaborative improvement. These teams became hubs for the deployment of coaches and professional development activities such as classroom walks and instructional rounds to observe practice and to connect policy with improving school practice. As one policymaker described it:

> What that period did was enable and require principals and other school leaders to critically observe classroom practice and reach an understanding of what good classroom practice looked like, and an acceptance that in their own schools much of the practice wasn't very

good. It provided both a capacity to do something and a stimulus to do something at the same time ...

We reached a view that it was network-based activity that was going to improve outcomes, to build capacity and give us the opportunity to get inside the classroom door.

Under the Towards Victoria as a Learning Community policy, the state stepped back from its direct support of capacity-building through the networks, opting to give schools the autonomy to form collaborative networks on the basis of common interest rather than geographic proximity, a move intended to foster the development of a "self-improving system." However, many teachers we interviewed were skeptical of the motivation, and inclined to view the move as a cost-cutting exercise. Describing the reaction of principals to the move, an official noted:

They find it really hard. They don't like it very much. In a sense they feel a bit abandoned by the system. Some principals do, but some principals are really happy that they don't have to go to meetings and be part of a collective capacity building activity, so it's a question of balance. I'd have to say there are more that feel unhappy about it than who feel happy, but that will take some time to work through.

Despite the reduced direct role of government, we found that school networks continued to play an important role in the school professional development activities. Consultation in 2015 by the state government found support from principals to again increase resources to networks in order to support well-being and capacity building for principals and teachers (DET, 2015b).

School Review and Improvement

School accountability is an area of active policy interest in Victoria, with several policy developments and changes in recent years. Common to each of these developments, however, is a cycle of reflective inquiry, professional engagement, and feedback, and the use of networks to promote continual improvement focused on student learning.

In 2013, a new school review process was introduced, based in a peer review approach and guided by a School Performance Framework (Link 3-17). The principles underpinning the review process included: student learning at the core; equity and inclusion as paramount; fostering a culture of accountability; and matching accountability with support (DEECD, 2013c). The review process begins with a school self-evaluation that is formally the responsibility of the principal and school council, although schools were encouraged to engage the whole school in the process, including teachers, students, and parents.

Schools could opt for a peer review, typically by two school principals and an externally accredited reviewer, which was intended to capture elements of best practice for dissemination across the system. Schools that failed to meet key thresholds were flagged for a priority review from DET to identify areas of improvement for a program of intervention: "Interventions will focus on strengthening the capacity of teachers and leaders to build the school's ability to self-improve, and to sustain improvement" (DEECD, 2013c, p. 11). Intervention programs were to target support for capacity building and school improvement, including structured peer support programs or coaching for principals in areas such as: leadership, teaching and learning, school governance, strategic partnerships, and literacy and numeracy.

From 2016, DET is transitioning to a new School Improvement Framework, based around four statewide priority areas: excellence in teaching and learning; professional leadership; positive climate for learning; and community engagement in learning. Schools are asked to focus on the following initiatives to improve student well-being and learning:

- Building practice excellence
- Curriculum planning and assessment
- Building leadership teams
- Empowering students and building school pride
- Setting expectations and promoting inclusion
- Building communities

Schools will use a cycle of self-evaluation and diagnosis, prioritization and goal-setting, development and school planning, and implementation and monitoring. The process for school accountability thus parallels the developmental approach to teacher professional learning noted earlier, drawing upon expertise within the system, and focused on feedback, development, and continual improvement.

Professional Learning

School-based, Evidence-supported Professional Learning

Professional learning in Victoria is embedded in the day-to-day work of teachers and connected to student outcomes. Under national- and state-level policy frameworks, teachers are encouraged to both individually and collaboratively assess a variety of student data, locate student learning needs, and thus target their professional learning on student learning. This evidence-based, professional learning cycle provides a shared rationale for professional learning between policymakers and practitioners.

The professional learning practices in government schools were shaped by the second wave, with investments in teacher capacity building, including literacy and numeracy coaches, and the formation of school networks together with policy that valued teacher learning, as articulated in the Performance and Development Culture and Professional Learning in Effective Schools frameworks. They have been further shaped by the teacher registration processes underpinned by professional teaching standards. School-based, teacher-led, and evidence-supported professional learning is thus a feature of the policy environment shaping teaching quality in Victoria.

Box 3.7 A coherent professional learning plan—Footscray North Primary School

With a diverse multicultural student population, many of which are from English as an Additional Language (EAL) backgrounds, Footscray North Primary School has a strong focus on improving student literacy. It has built its professional learning plan around increasing growth in student outcomes, such as between Years 3 and 5 as measured by NAPLAN scores. These growth targets are compared both with state averages, and with those of matched schools with similar characteristics.

A school-wide professional learning plan is one of the school's key improvement strategies. It is a sustained, long-term approach, which sets common themes for teacher professional learning each year. In her first two years at Footscray North, Principal Sharon Walker began by focusing on teachers' knowledge of the school curriculum:

> There are many things that I have transferred from high-performing schools to here. [Firstly,] to have a very clear curriculum. To

be very mindful of what we are trying to teach here. We spent the first couple of years ensuring that every teacher knew what the curriculum was. It sounds pretty basic, but we call it a guaranteed and viable curriculum. So that if you come to our school, you'll know what you need to teach.

More recently, the school has focused on improving capability in assessing student abilities and growth, the selection of teaching strategies for improvement, and evaluating their effects.

Professional reading forms one core strand of professional learning at the school, and is planned at least a full year in advance. For 2014, *Visible Learning for Teachers* (Hattie, 2012) was a common text read progressively throughout the year, and in 2015, Marzano's *Nine Instructional Strategies* (Marzano, Pickering, & Pollock, 2001). As described by Principal Sharon Walker, these materials are discussed in meetings at multiple levels, giving coherence to the school's professional learning:

> All of our staff are expected to engage in professional reading. [We] would have a couple of whole-staff meetings where we look at that as a staff. Then, we have a professional learning team level, where that team unpacks it. Then, we have our coaches supporting. It's never a one-off. Our teachers are very well supported in implementing new strategies.

Teachers at Footscray North emphasized the importance of a professional learning strategy that was sustained and connected to school-wide goals to lift teacher capability. Mary Dowling, Leading Teacher, a teacher coach, and Teaching Fellow with the University of Melbourne, emphasized the value of a structured, coherent, and ongoing professional development program to improve teaching quality:

> It's not isolated sessions ... We don't have necessarily an hour on open-ended questioning on a random staff meeting night. [In such a case,] you might take bits and pieces, and you might not do anything with it. All our professional learning now is well planned in advance. It will live through the whole year. It will filter down through the coaches, and their agenda in the classroom, through the learning logs, through the learning walks, and back up again through leadership. We'll keep using that cycle all the way through.

They used to drive me up the wall. You'd go to these one-off sessions. You might get one little idea and think, "Oh, I could do that, but that's it." How do you know it's embedded in practice? How do you know teachers have shifted in their practice? You just wouldn't know. Whereas with this model, I think it's relentless, 'cause it just keeps going on, and on, and on. There's lots of support through the coaches. Then there's that sort of evaluating, monitoring process where I go in with the coaches. We look at learning logs. We look and see if it's actually happening in the classroom.

At Footscray North, coaches are a key part of the professional learning strategy to see that new teaching strategies are being implemented in the classroom. According to Principal Walker:

What we knew was that these coaches are absolutely crucial in skilling our teachers ... [T]he coaches' role is to ensure that the practices that our teachers are using in the classrooms are the high-performing practices. So there's no, "I'm gonna give this a go, and it doesn't work, and I'm gonna forget about it."

Teachers at Footscray North also undertake additional study. The leadership team meets once a week, participates in action research in the use of data to inform literacy and numeracy, and is involved in the Assessment and Learning Project through the University of Melbourne. Classroom teachers study online teaching modules in numeracy through the Australian Mathematical Sciences Institute.

Release time for teachers is an important part of professional learning. Allocated planning time is used for professional readings, and additional release time is used to analyze student outcomes data. With a diverse school population and broad range of learning needs, Footscray North's teachers use data to gauge each students' progress and employ differentiated teaching strategies in their class.

The emphasis on research to inform continual improvement and development for even experienced teachers is a core part of professional learning at the school, as Principal Walker describes:

This is, "Good on you for teaching for 20 years, but we are a highly professional group." [T]here's not one profession that is not always looking forward. We're part of that, a professional group, a highly professional group, that is informed by fantastic research. That's who we are.

Characterizing Professional Learning in Victoria

There are several practices that characterize professional learning in Victoria. The first is school-wide professional learning plans, usually articulated in annual implementation plans. Professional learning activities are informed by the goals and targets of school strategic plans, and the student population and their learning needs. This reflects a broadly held view that structured and ongoing teacher professional learning is a key facet of school improvement, and underlines the importance of principals as instructional leaders (Kent, 2014).

The second is that the delivery of professional learning activities is often school-based. This is often related to particular student learning needs, but may also be a function of cost. The state does not directly provide professional development but instead takes a "panel" approach to assure there are sufficient professional development providers meeting minimum quality requirements in key learning areas. As DET Executive Director or Priority Policy Ian Burrage explains:

> We don't put money into stimulating the market. We have panels …
> We run a tender and get a group of people who [meet] our standards …
> [W]e quality assure them, [but the] schools pay for them themselves.

Thus funding for professional learning, including paid release time to attend, comes out of the school's global budget, and decisions on professional learning activities outside the school are made judiciously.

For example, at Rosanna Golf Links Primary School (RGLPS) in a central eastern suburb of Melbourne, teachers interested in external professional learning fill out an application indicating the desired activity and how it relates to individual and team development goals, and school leadership teams decides. As senior teacher Seona Aulich explains, limited budgets restrict the number of external professional development activities staff can attend:

> Our [professional learning] budget is A$20,000. We've got 19 grades [teachers], plus seven teachers of the Deaf, plus education support staff … plus five specialist teachers. Probably looking at that money to be shared around 35 people.

> Normally, the average price for a course would be about A$300 for a day. Then I need to then have myself replaced back at school—a day at school, there's a flat rate for CRTs [causal relief teachers]. That's

about A\$320 or so that schools are out of pocket. Out of a A\$20,000 budget, it gets eaten away quickly.

The third is the use of student data to inform teacher professional learning. In each of the schools we visited, there was a firm focus on gathering and interpreting multiple forms of data at each of school, class, and student levels. NAPLAN was commonly used at the school level. At grade- and class-level, evidence was frequently focused on progression in literacy and numeracy. Analysis of these data was then used to inform professional learning. As described by professional learning leader and classroom teacher Tania Ellul:

> It depends on their individual needs and it's also about their data. Looking at how their grade is scoring on different types of tests, and the areas of improvement for the grade. It could come from the teacher, or it could be just something that I can notice in their data that the students aren't, perhaps, performing and trying to collaborate with that teacher to work out how they can improve their data, and obviously increase their students' learning.

Fourthly, there was increasing use of peer observation, feedback on teaching, and/or the use of coaches to improve practice. Follow-up observations may also be used to see that professional learning is informing classroom teaching. For example, among the school-wide professional learning goals at Rosanna Golf Links Primary School was the incorporation of higher-order questioning strategies into Theories of Action Rubrics.[11] Planned professional learning activities included peer observation and collegial discussion in teaching teams to assist teachers in implementing these approaches.

Other schools make use of coaches in order to help teachers incorporate new strategies into their teaching. For example, Footscray North Primary School employs literacy and numeracy coaches who conduct classroom walks and peer observation. Gantt charts are also used to see that all teachers in the school have access to coaching during the year. Importantly, coaches did not to evaluate performance, but were there to facilitate professional learning into classroom practice and ensure consistency of delivery across classrooms.

Finally, professional learning is the responsibility of teachers. The process of reflective inquiry, in which teachers identify their students', and thereby their own, learning needs is connected both to teacher registration and to annual individual performance and development plans (see Appraisal below).

Box 3.8 The use of data at Willmott Park Primary School

During a visit to Willmott Park Primary School, on the Melbourne's northern metropolitan fringe, we discussed the collection and use of data in school planning with Principal Gavin Hughes and Assistant Principal (Student Learning) Deborah Crane. Willmott Park placed perhaps the greatest emphasis on data collection and analysis among the schools we visited, but was emblematic of a broader shift towards the increased use of evidence-informed decision making and planning for both student and teacher learning.

The only external testing conducted was NAPLAN, required by all schools in Australia each May. Assistant Principal Crane said that NAPLAN was useful at the school level, as it allowed both comparison with similar schools, as well as tracking growth of students from Year 3 to Year 5, providing confidence that the school was providing learning growth for their students (Hughes & Crane, 2014).

The remainder of data at Willmott Park are collected locally, largely in the core areas of literacy—reading, writing, speaking, and listening—and numeracy. Assessment schedules were issued for each school term, comprising a series of formative assessments, and using an array of methods. In Grade 4 literacy, for example, data sources included the following:

- PROBE2: a reading comprehension tool
- Running records: to check reading fluency, accuracy, and self-correction
- English Online Interview: an interview-based diagnostic assessment for students in Grades P-2
- On Demand Testing: an online, adaptive series of tests in literacy and numeracy developed by the Victorian Curriculum and Assessment Authority, and linked to the state curriculum and learning standards (VCAA, 2013a)
- Teacher anecdotal notes based on student observations, and conversations with students and other teachers
- Student writing samples, with a moderation process to ensure consistency among classes
- Additional teacher-developed assessments if/as needed

Several aspects stood out from the way Principal Hughes and Assistant Principal Crane described the use of data in the school. Firstly, data were used primarily for school internal purposes, such as diagnostic assessments to ensure consistency in learning and delivery, and early identification of potential problems in specific constructs or skill areas. An exception was required biannual reporting to the state on progression against AusVELS standards.

Secondly, multiple forms of assessment data were triangulated to build a stronger picture of learning progress. Data were also analyzed in multiple ways at each of the student, class, and cohort levels. In interviews with teaching staff, discussion frequently returned to data analysis as a tool to inform curriculum and planning. Staff at the school nonetheless appeared to be critical and thoughtful users of data and assessment, as illustrated by Hughes and Crane in discussing how the school selects its assessment methods:

Crane:	Evan and I did a PL [Professional Learning program), Principals as Literacy Leaders. It makes us now look at what testing are we doing? How old is that test? Who created the test? What cohort of children did the study, to [understand] that it's a relevant age for that testing? We have to look at the validity of the test.
Hughes:	We have to examine the validity of the test for the purpose that we're doing ... Because there's a lot of invalid testing out there that perhaps people are using. We've spent a lot of time really investigating that.
Crane:	Yes, and trying to keep current because if we're doing the same running records or same testing of reading that I did when I first started here 14 years ago, children are different now. The content levels are a little bit different. The expectations might be the same as in the level, but the way that we do it has changed. We've gotta keep moving ahead ... getting feedback from teachers. Are you happy with the results that you're getting from Probe? Is it giving you enough information to guide your teaching and learning? If not, then I have to re-source and go find other data sources.

Thirdly, data collection and analysis at the school informed planning. Assistant Principal Crane worked with team leaders to analyze learning and attendance data each term. These were used at grade-level meetings, for example, to help focus discussion on areas of the curriculum that may need greater emphasis, and planning mini-lessons to help address particular areas of weakness. Principal Hughes further explained that to ensure students at all achievement levels in a cohort were improving, data from one year could be used to inform and monitor progress the next:

> We have all the data that Deb's collected over the year. We compile that to get a profile at that level—Grade 2 for example. Then that data is given to all the Grade 3 teachers for the coming year. We add on a full-year's natural progression plus five percent and that's their goals for the year. That gets broken down into weekly increments where they're having conversations with the data that Deb's feeding back. It all leads to achieving that goal. Halfway through the year we see if they're on track or behind. If they're behind on achieving a particular goal, say numeracy, then an intervention is made there to do something else in their planning.

Transparency in the availability of data and common practices in their analysis also informed professional conversations focused on teaching and learning, and building a sense of collective responsibility.

Principal Hughes and Assistant Principal Crane described an improvement in the quality and use of data by Victorian schools as one of the major changes over the course of their careers. They noted that teachers would previously develop tests solely for their own classes as a check on student retention of the material. The greater availability of data tools and increased awareness of how to interpret assessments had allowed the school to compare progress with state and national curricular standards, and feed information back to create a culture of evidence-informed planning and decision making.

Professional Learning Polices in Victoria

Policies Shaping Professional Learning Practice

Professional learning in Victoria has been shaped by both national and state policies. The *Australian Charter for the Professional Learning of Teachers and School Leaders* establishes the principles that should underpin professional learning, specifically that it "will be most effective when it is relevant, collaborative and future focused, and when it supports teachers to reflect on, question and consciously improve their practice" (AITSL, 2012b).

This national charter served to further embed the state's expectations for the teacher professional learning. DET guidelines in the form of the *Professional Learning in Effective Schools* (Link 3-18) document articulated the expectation that professional learning be focused on student outcomes, make use of data, and be collaborative. It also suggested the practices that should be used, such as professional learning teams, action research, peer observation, and lesson study—underpinned by the "seven principles of highly effective professional learning" (DET, 2005). (See Box 3.9.)

Box 3.9 The Seven Principles of Highly Effective Professional Learning

Principle 1:   Professional learning is focused on student outcomes (not just individual teacher needs).

Principle 2:   Professional learning is focused on and embedded in teacher practice (not disconnected from the school).

Principle 3:   Professional learning is informed by the best available research on effective learning and teaching (not just limited to what they currently know).

Principle 4:   Professional learning is collaborative, involving reflection and feedback (not just individual inquiry).

Principle 5:   Professional learning is evidence based and data driven (not anecdotal) to guide improvement and to measure impact.

Principle 6:   Professional learning is ongoing, supported, and fully integrated into the culture and operations of the system—schools, networks, regions, and the center (not episodic and fragmented).

Principle 7:   Professional learning is an individual and collective responsibility at all levels of the system (not just the school level), and it is not optional. (DET, 2005)

The state Performance and Development Culture framework, which based around the above principles sought to craft a school culture built around collaborative behaviors and professional dialog (DEECD, 2009). From 2005 to 2015, schools were accredited across five elements, one of which was having "a professional learning strategy (that) reflects individual, team, and collective development needs" (DEECD, 2009). Its emphasis on improving student learning outcomes as the focus of teacher professional learning, together with investments in the formation of strategic networks and the use of coaches, helped move teaching in Victoria from a "my classroom, my rules" culture towards a deprivatized one in which teachers are more comfortable with observations, peer collaboration, and coaching conversations (interview with M. Victory, 2014).

Connecting Professional Learning Policy with Teacher Registration

The process for renewing teacher registration in Victoria further supports the principles of professional learning outlined above. Maintenance of registration is required to teach. All Victorian teachers must document a minimum of 20 hours of professional learning each year,[12] and show how this learning addresses at least one standard in each of the seven domains. Victoria is presently the only state in which registration maintenance is done annually, but this allows it to connect professional learning both to teaching standards, and to annual teacher performance and development plans (Paproth & Cosgrove, 2014).

Unlike in neighboring New South Wales, VIT doesn't accredit professional learning providers or activities. In both states though, the process is designed to be teacher-led, and teachers have flexibility in the choice of professional learning, so long as they are able to reflect upon and record how the activities have influenced their professional growth against the standards. VIT encourages teachers to use the Timperley cycle of reflective practice outlined earlier, as a model for professional development.

Both state and federal governments are investing in a range of resources to support teachers' familiarity with the standards and the registration process. For example, AITSL has developed a range of "illustrations of practice." Each of these video resources provides an exemplar of teaching practice tagged to a specific teaching standard and career stage. It has also created a mobile application to help teachers collect evidence of their own standards-referenced professional learning.

At the state level, DET has created the Evidence-Based Professional Learning Cycle (Link 3-19) website. Paralleling the Timperley cycle, teachers can access videos and written resources showing how other teachers in the state have identified both students' and their own learning needs, sought out professional development activities, applied their learning in the classroom, and assessed its impact. Similarly VIT has created an online *MyVIT* tool, allowing teachers to record and upload evidence of their professional learning.

Regional Offices and School Networks in Professional Learning

School networks are an important element of support for professional learning to schools, coordinated through DET regional offices. Networks can serve to engage schools with departmental policies, offer professional learning activities to support those policies, and feed information back from schools to shape policy implementation. For example, school networks, organized through department regional offices, used instructional rounds to investigate problems of practice.[13] Evidence drawn from these rounds and from education research was used to develop regional professional learning strategies that could then be disseminated back out to schools. This ensured that policy was grounded in practice and more closely tailored to the needs of network schools. The Curiosity and Powerful Learning strategy of the Northern Metropolitan Region provides one such example (DEECD, 2011). (See Figure 3.12.)

Figure 3.12 Curiosity and Powerful Learning Framework Schematic.

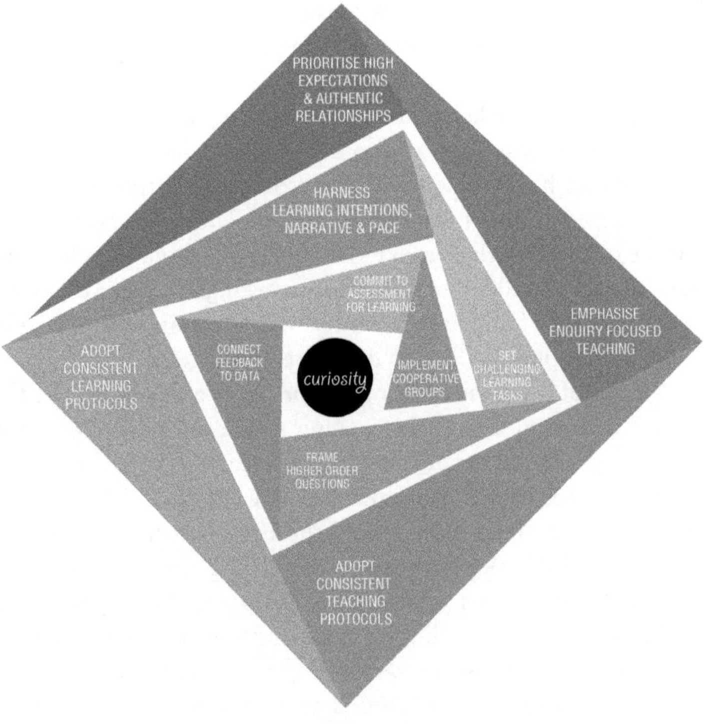

Reproduced from DEECD, 2011.

As senior teacher Seona Aulich describes:

> It wasn't just a book that was published—it was actually something that was working within the schools. There were a number of PD [professional development] days as a whole staff that we attended with other schools in our local area. We were given a whole lot of support material to go with that. If I was going into a classroom with a focus on higher order questioning, then there was rubrics [to help us understand:] "What does it actually look like?" As a school, we were doing this probably two or three times a term, we were doing follow-up PD and unpacking the whole concept and what that looked like [in practice]. It was a really nice thing. It was something that everyone was able to get on board with too. We want to develop curious learners.

The effects of these policies were to provide a common language for teaching and effective professional learning, and to provide coaches to directly support school improvement and individual teaching practice. Networks provided a mechanism for reciprocal information transfer between DET and schools connecting policy with school needs, and allowed for the sharing of practices across schools at low cost. Teacher Seona Aulich explains how the school networks function to provide professional learning:

> Across our networks, once a term we have network meetings. I'm a grade five/six teacher. All the grade five/six teachers will get together from the schools within our cluster. The idea is to share best practice. Last week we had a network professional development where there were 12 sessions running. These sessions were run by classroom teachers who are doing something particularly well in their classrooms. [For example,] I went to a literacy session for middle years' literacy at a different school. You're seeing something new that you haven't seen before, but there's no cost at all to the school. We're trying to continually do that sharing of best practice, not just within the school, but within network schools.

Following a change of government, the state scaled back its direct involvement in centrally led networks under the Towards Victoria as a Learning Community policy, instead supporting schools to form self-determined networks (DEECD, 2012c, 2013). Teachers and principals we interviewed underscored the ongoing importance of networks in individual and school professional learning. As explained by Willmott

Primary School Principal Evan Hughes and Footscray North Primary
Principal Sharon Walker:

> Within the old region we had subgroups called local networks. They
> are in most cases still in existence. We had a very strong one here
> which is all the schools in the outer north called the Hume network
> of schools. In fact we've got a conference this weekend where we'll
> probably get about a hundred leaders of schools attending. We've
> driven that agenda ourselves. There's no department involvement.
> It's just the network setting, the professional learning, organizing the
> speakers, doing the whole lot ourselves.
>
> (interview with e. Hughes & D. Crane, 2014)

> We're saying, We know the work. We know what needs to be
> done. We actually go out and look for people who can support
> us in that work, because it's not coming from above. We don't
> want to lose the momentum. With funding having gone, and the
> structures that we were used to have gone. Yeah, so we're looking.
> We're not stopping.
>
> (interview with S. Walker, 2014)

In June 2015, new Education Minister James Merlino began consultation with the education sector on the use of regional offices, and emerging policy aims to increase the state's involvement in networks.

Additional Professional Learning Supports and Resources for Teachers

Although there is a strong emphasis on teacher-led, school-based professional learning in Victoria, DET provides a range of additional resources
and supports for teachers' learning. These are often coordinated in partnership with other organizations that can offer specific expertise. They
include:

- o International study tours: jointly run with the Asia Education
  Foundation, DET helps fund 1–2 week study programs primarily to Asia, to deepen teachers' knowledge of language, culture,
  and history of the region, and link teachers' experiences with the
  AusVELS curriculum
- o Languages professional learning: DET provides annual funding to
  a range of languages organizations to support their professional
  learning offerings for LOTE teachers

o Managing challenging behaviors workshops: delivered jointly with The University of Melbourne, provided training for 480 teachers and staff in 2013

DET offers a range of online resources on which teachers can draw for additional supports, such as the Abilities-Based Learning and Education Support program that provides resources for curriculum, pedagogy, and assessment to adapt teaching practice for students with disabilities and additional learning needs. Other organizations such as AEU and the Independent Education Union play a role in professional learning. Their co-owned Teacher Learning Network provides standards-referenced professional learning workshops, courses, and resources free or at reduced cost to their members.

There have also been federal funds to support professional development in Victoria. The Australian Government Quality Teaching Program (AGQTP), which ran from 2000 to 2010, funded a range of professional development projects for government, Catholic and Independent school sectors. The goals of the AGQTP were to "equip teachers with the skills and knowledge needed for teaching in the 21st century, provide national leadership in high priority areas of teacher professional learning need, improve the professional standing of school teachers and leaders" (ACARA, 2013b). AGQTP funds have since been incorporated into the National Education Agreement, however program documents remain accessible as professional learning resources.

Appraisal

Victoria began implementation of a new teacher evaluation system in 2014. Connected to teachers' annual salary review cycle (described below), it incorporates the principles of the nationally agreed on Australian Teacher Performance and Development Framework, with its focus on student outcomes, a clear understanding of effective teaching, and frequent, meaningful feedback that informs professional practice (AITSL, 2012a). It also builds upon the elements of Victoria's Performance and Development Culture framework emphasizing teacher and school improvement, and including goal-setting that is tied both to the national professional standards for teachers and to student achievement. Teacher evaluation is also an aspect of teaching policy that has undergone considerable review and scrutiny in recent years.

The Evaluation Process

Teacher appraisal (known as performance and development, or P&D) in Victoria is determined by state policy, but takes place entirely at the school level. Principals are ultimately responsible for teacher performance, but assistant principals, senior teachers, or other members of the school management team may also provide input. The process is cyclical and takes place on the same annual timetable for all teachers in all government schools, from May 1 to the following April 30, with the following steps:

- *planning* in April/May to prepare and agree on performance plans with the principal
- mid-cycle *review* in September/October to discuss the teacher's progress
- *assessment* in March/April of the teacher's performance against the national professional standards for teachers

The next planning cycle is informed by outcomes of the previous year.

Performance and development, as the name suggests, is intended to connect teachers' performance against specified standards and goals with their development through professional learning opportunities and feedback on their work. It is underpinned by principles of collective efficacy, peer collaboration, and professional accountability (DEECD, 2014d). DET has sought to ground its appraisal policy in research, and harness the process to build collective capacity by fostering a visible culture of instructional practice, and of schools as professional learning communities.

Teacher performance is linked to school improvement and student learning in several ways. Firstly, teachers' individual P&D plans are closely aligned to school goals, and the three broad categories: student learning, student engagement and well-being, and student pathways and transitions. Among these, student learning goals are the most tangible, and outcomes on a variety of assessments feed into teachers' plans. Senior teacher Seona Aulich explains:

> As a staff, we look at whole-school data a lot, and we look at trends. Collectively, we're accountable as a school. We set new goals for our strategic plan and our annual implementation plan from looking at the previous year's data. What realistically can we improve for the following year? That's where our PDP (performance and development plan) goals are coming from.

Figure 3.13 Example of a Balanced Scorecard Approach.

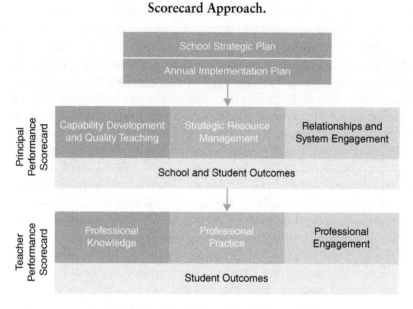

Reproduced from DEECD, 2013b, p. 15.

Secondly, appraisal is tied to professional teaching standards. In May 2014, the state introduced a balanced scorecard approach, in which teachers are assessed in four domains (see Figure 3.13). The first three are the domains of the national professional standards—professional knowledge, professional practice, and professional engagement—while the fourth is student outcomes. Teachers and principals together discuss and set goals in each domains using appropriate standards, levels, and descriptors. Schools have considerable flexibility in the type of professional learning, portfolios of evidence of performance, and have discretion in the relative weighting of each domain in assessing individual teacher performance (DEECD, 2014d).

Teachers that have adequately met the goals in their plans receive an annual salary increment. In practice, this happens for almost all teachers, and is an area in which the government has sought to use financial incentives as a mechanism to lift teacher performance (see below). In 2016, the government has indicated it will adapt the balance scorecard model further. Referred to as a "whole-of-practice" approach, it will retain the cycle of planning, goal-setting, and feedback in the professional knowledge, practice, and engagement domains of the standards, and in student achievement, engagement, and well-being.

Teacher Appraisal and Improving Teaching

Embedded in the process are two mechanisms which direct the focus of appraisal towards professional learning and student outcomes. Under the Performance and Development Culture framework, teachers' individual P&D plans should include team goals and also be aligned to school goals. This is intended to promote collective accountability: teachers are accountable to each other by furthering team goals and to the community through strategic plans. Moreover, by situating individual plans in the context of team goals, the process is intended to help foster collaborative practices.

By tying the process to national teaching standards, teacher appraisal also becomes connected to the annual maintenance of registration to teacher professional learning. Evidence of professional learning in practice becomes evidence both for registration and appraisal. It connects a school-based process to state policy, to national professional standards, and to a common discourse for teaching quality.

Teachers and principals are thus expected to undertake professional conversations based around teaching standards and continual improvement—student learning needs, teachers learning to engage students, and evaluation of impact on student learning. In this way, the P&D process provides another mechanism for teachers to be reflective about their own teaching practice. This helps further embed the national standards as a common language for discussing teaching quality, given that principals and senior teachers may themselves be less familiar with the standards than more recently trained teachers.

Performance against individual plans is based on multiple forms of feedback. This typically includes feedback on classes observed by peers, information from student and parent surveys, or structured observations (DEECD, 2014d). Recent international survey data showed that nationwide, Australian teachers were more likely to receive feedback on their work from members of the school management team (57%) or other teachers (51%) than they were from their school principal (27%) (OECD, 2014c).

Box 3.10 Teacher evaluation and feedback at Willmott Park Primary School

Visiting Willmott Park Primary School, the P&D process had recently been restructured to reflect new state policy guidelines. Performance plans are agreed through discussion with the school principal, incorporating individual and team goals for grade-level from Prep through Grade 6.

The school had developed a matrix of suggested improvement goals for individual plans (Link 3-20), organized under the three domains of the teaching standards—professional knowledge, professional practice, and professional engagement—to assist teachers to connect their performance plans to teaching standards and school goals. Teachers could select six improvement goals—two from each domain—then use these together with evidence from student achievement data to create S.M.A.R.T. goals that included specific targets.

Structured feedback was based on periodic lesson observation throughout the year from one of the Professional Learning Leaders, and supplemented by occasional informal walk-throughs by the Assistant Principals and Principal, which together contributed information towards appraisal conversations. The observations were structured to follow a common format based on the e^5 instructional model promulgated by DET under the Performance and Development Culture framework. Observations are recorded using a Professional Learning Reflections (Link 3-21) template, under the following rubric and prompts:

- **Engage:** *Establishes learning goals.* Are students engaged? How can you tell?
- **Explain:** *Develops language and literacy in curricular areas.* What is the teacher saying?
- **Elaborate:** *Facilitates substantive conversation.* What are students saying?
- **Explore:** *Prompts inquiry.* What are the students doing?
- **Evaluate:** *Feedback.* Where is the teacher evaluation? Where is the student evaluation?

Feedback to teachers is further structured around Powerful Learning protocols adopted by the Northwestern Metropolitan office of DET, focused on developing curiosity in learners. The strategy suggests the ingredients of a lesson for analysis, such as lesson pace, questioning style, the assignment of purposeful tasks, feedback (to and from students), and assessment of learning (DEECD, 2011).

Continual Review and the Politics of Teacher Evaluation

Although teacher appraisal serves primarily a developmental focus, it also has perhaps been more contested than other aspects of policy related to teaching quality in recent years. The Performance and Development

Culture framework described earlier situated teacher appraisal as part teacher professional learning, and in the context of school improvement. As school leaders hold the primary responsibility for teacher appraisal, principals' training in conducting the process was a key part of the initial policy development.

However, a state audit report in 2010 found significant variability in its implementation. While the majority of teachers and principals felt that the appraisal process was increasing the quality of teaching, it also found that around 5% of schools had not implemented a teacher P&D cycle, around 25% of principals felt unprepared to address teacher underperformance, and around 25% of teachers failed to identify professional learning activities—despite it being a core part of the performance and development culture framework (VAGO, 2010). Findings from this and similar reports provided much of the rationale for nationally agreed on framework, and the new state teacher P&D process.

Senior teachers we interviewed for this study agreed that teacher appraisal had become more rigorous over recent years, and that there had been significant differences in their practice across schools. As senior teacher Seona Aulich explains:

> To be honest, the process [then] was fairly passé. Previously, I think from school to school, you would find that they were doing very different things. You would have some principals that would have an informal chat like this for 15 minutes. "You're doing a great job." Then that would just sign you off.

According to senior teacher Mary Dowling, the increased use of evidence in teacher performance has reduced the variability in teacher evaluation that existed previously:

> It varied so much about who you had for an interview. Because in some cases, you'd get really grilled. If it was with someone else, you might talk about the footy [Australian Rules Football] for half the time. It was well-known that it really depended on who you got for the interview. All things involving teacher evaluation and teacher performance are much tighter now than they were in those times, but what I experienced was trying to come to grips with new regulations and various standards, rather than just saying, "Oh, yeah, we know he's a good teacher because the parents are all crazy about him, and the kids love him." Schools have to be much more accountable now. It's very much evidence-based.

Different methods of increasing the effectiveness of teacher appraisal have been trialed in Victoria, evidencing a tension between market-like and professionalizing approaches to policy (Darling-Hammond, 2012). On the one hand, the introduction of the Performance and Development Culture framework and e[5] instructional model sought to more closely link annual teacher appraisal with professional learning, classroom practice, and school improvement. On the other hand, trials with salary bonuses in some schools were run during 2010 and 2011. In 2013, DET intended to use financial incentives to shape appraisal, by constraining automatic annual salary increments, dismissing low-performing teachers, and including bonus payments to high-performing teachers. As one DET senior policymaker explained:

> [I]n the most recent industrial agreement with the teaching profession through the unions, poor performance that can't be improved will lead to dismissal. That's been agreed … We would have liked to have introduced a performance-related bonus scheme as well, because we have a significant number of teachers who are at the top of their pay scale. There is no financial incentive or reward for their continued high performance. We'd like to have a situation where both in terms of professional experience and practice, but also in terms of financial reward, really good performance is recognized.

As DET Executive Director of Priority Policy, Ian Burrage noted this came from the government's view that financial incentives could be effective in increasing school and teacher engagement with the appraisal process as a mechanism for improving teacher performance:

> All the stuff we're doing on the performance arrangements now and where the controversies come and we are trying to choke [automatic annual] progression … It's not because of the finances … [i]t's because we see that where we put some stakes on the appraisal process, it gets treated infinitely more seriously. That's our theory.

Teachers interviewed for this study were skeptical of this perspective, and showed concern about a potential narrowing conception of teacher effectiveness, and an increased focus on student test scores as the primary measure of student outcomes. Senior teacher Seona Aulich described the above proposed policy responses as antithetical to the culture of teaching in Victoria:

> People are not interested in the whole performance pay concept at all. Teachers are fairly irate about it. [T]eachers are groups of people that

work very closely together and care about one another and there are no secrets in a school. If [one] fails, then everyone knows about it … Then you start to break down the culture of the school …

[P]articularly in a primary school, you've got all these roles that may not necessarily contribute to the academic success of the student or a school, but are really important in the running of the school … You've got a staff that are really connected. Part of it is because of this [school] culture that this particular teacher has a very large part in. What if that teacher isn't necessarily producing academic outcomes here? Should that teacher then fail?

It's this holistic view of what a teacher is. Maybe you've got children in your grade who perhaps have been incredibly shy. I'm the teacher this year who managed to get the student to open up. It may be that next year the student is going to flourish academically. Now his or her school attendance has greatly improved, and s/he is actually smiling. All that sort of stuff. How do you measure that?

While the new system specified that annual salary increments would not be automatic, performance pay trials were ultimately not extended into policy. This was due, in part, to resistance from teachers expressed via industrial action.

The agreement on salary increments and performance policies between DET and AEU also highlights the role of the educators' union in Victoria as contributing to teacher professionalization. Although at times strongly tested, there is frequent and ongoing dialog between DET and union officials, both formally and informally in the context of policy development (Mullaly, 2014). The union has sought to position itself as an advocate for raising teaching quality. According to AEU Victoria Deputy Vice President Justin Mullaly:

We see ourselves as both an industrial advocate for our members but also as a professional body in that sense. What we're very much interested in doing in that professional space is making sure that our members are getting access to the kind of support that they need to develop their work and that it's done in a way that actually is supporting their work.

In discussion of teacher appraisal, Mullaly described that AEU was generally supportive of appraisal as a mechanism for raising teaching quality, but stressed that such processes must take account both of the resourcing context for schooling, and of the effects of any process on teacher collective efficacy:

> One of the key issues that our members were confronting was the desire of government to introduce performance pay. To that extent, there's probably not a better example of the nexus between a union's role industrially and a union's role professionally.

> It was something that was very much the antithesis of what we wanted to see in our schools, largely around the impact it would have on collegiality [and] on the benefit that comes from teachers being able to freely and fairly work with each other, on the basis that it's through that kind of collaboration that ideas get shared and that students are in the best place to be—having teachers that have well resolved and developed teaching and learning plans that're going on into the classroom.

In sum, the teacher appraisal process represents a balance between competing perspectives on how teacher performance relates to school improvement. It maintains some of the levers common to appraisal in other sectors, such as salary progression conditional on meeting certain minimum performance standards. Yet it also incorporates the features of a professionalizing approach to policy, by linking appraisal to collective performance and professional learning. In aligning its appraisal process with the national standards, it aids coherence both across levels of governance, and with policies in initial teacher education, induction, and professional learning.

Leadership

> *In Victoria's highly devolved system, principals must be the driving force behind improvements in teaching quality and performance.*

> (DEECD, 2013b)

With Victoria's system of self-managing schools, principals and school leaders are tasked with a tremendous number of responsibilities. These include the following: resource allocation; accountability to the community and DET for continual improvement in student learning; and personnel management, including teacher appraisal and planning for professional learning. Principals must both be adept organizational and financial managers, and have strong instructional leadership skills. Thus the success of the self-managing schools model in Victoria depends in good measure on the ability of the state to maintain a steady flow of, and effectively train, aspiring school leaders.

This represents an ongoing challenge, particularly with increasing enrollments. Principal attrition rates in the state are fairly high—around 9% per annum—and there is concern that both the volume and increasing complexity of principals' work may complicate efforts to attract a greater number of teachers into leadership roles (Darling-Hammond, 2013). The present system relies largely on self-identification by interested individuals, or by informal nomination from members of school networks. DET has therefore begun developing a new talent identification system that will work with school networks to identify potential talent and draw new candidates into leadership training programs.

There is no mandated formal qualification or licensure requirement for becoming a principal in Victoria. Although most principals of schools have higher-level university qualifications, such as Master's degrees, applicants are only formally required to be a trained and registered teacher. However, in consideration for principalship, it is expected that applicants show evidence of demonstrated capabilities in each of the five key selection criteria set out in DET's 2007 *Developmental Learning Framework for School Leaders* (DEECD, 2012e; Matthews, Moorman, & Nusche, 2007).

There have however been moves towards voluntary certification for principals. The Principals Australia Institute, a nonprofit organization founded by several principals' associations, has created and is trialing an Australian Principal Certification program based on the Australian Professional Standard for Principals (Link 3-22).

Leadership Framework and Skills

DET has long viewed leadership capability as representing a set of knowledge and skills that can be learned and developed over time, rather than a fixed set of attributes (Matthews, Moorman, & Nusche, 2007). This was reflected in the department's 2007 Developmental Learning Framework for School Leaders (leadership framework), which identified five domains of the knowledge, skills, and dispositions of effective school leaders to create the conditions for quality teaching and learning (DEECD, 2012e; DET, 2007), including technical leadership, human leadership, educational leadership, symbolic leadership, and cultural leadership. Each was further elaborated into a set of leadership profiles with descriptors of increasing proficiency across each domain.

Given the importance of the development of leadership capabilities to school improvement in Victoria, the state has maintained a level of investment in the direct provision of leadership training. This stands somewhat in contrast to the government's policy approach in other areas. The bulk of this investment comes via the Bastow Institute of Educational Leadership—a specialized leadership training institute.

A recent review of the Developmental Learning Framework commissioned by the Bastow Institute found that while the domains and capabilities of the framework contained the same elements as other highly regarded leadership frameworks internationally, it could be further improved with an increased emphasis of the "practices that promote an accountable community with shared educational values, a focus on student learning, collaboration, reflective dialog and deprivatization of practice," and recommending the state move towards adopting a new standards framework based on the Australian Professional Standard for Principals (Ingvarson, 2013). Like the Developmental Learning Framework, the Standard addresses the characteristics of effective leadership, and sets out what principals are "expected to know, understand and do to succeed in their work." (AITSL, 2011) It embeds a cyclical model of planning and acting, reviewing, and responding that is centered on student learning emphasizes the collective and analysis of data in decision making.

Figure 3.14 Australian Professional Standard for Principals Leadership Lenses.

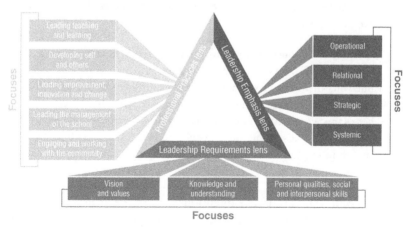

Source: AITSL, 2014a.

The leadership framework has now been superseded by the Australian Professional Standard for Principals, with leadership profiles and descriptors that serve to guide the development of principals, grouped according to three lenses—leadership requirements, professional practices, and leadership emphasis—and focused on the role of the principal in enabling and leading high-quality teaching and learning (see Figure 3.14). This will be used in conjunction with a new state framework for improving student outcomes, and emphasizing strategic resource management, leadership of quality teaching, and strengthening community engagement. The standard and profiles thus now inform the program offerings on school leadership at the Bastow Institute.

Leadership Training and the Bastow Institute

The Bastow facility itself is striking. The building façade is the red brick clad, original school building of State School no. 307 founded in 1882, one of the first school sites in Melbourne. In sharp contrast, the recently renovated interior is a spectacular piece of modern architecture with ceiling-high glass window panels connecting at oblique angles. There are courtyards and standing tables in purpose-designed open-plan conversational spaces. The basement houses an electronically networked lecture theater, capable of seating around 100 people, while simultaneously webcasting to many more. The building itself is perhaps emblematic of where the government sees it has a strong direct lever in school improvement, and of the way a tradition of school education can be married with a forward-looking vision for education. As Bastow Director Bruce Armstrong explains:

> It's symbolic of your employer investing in the development of your knowledge, skill, and disposition to lead and teach ... to say ... "we value you." It was to be symbolic both in its infrastructure, and with how we conceptualize change at a school level or system level ... There's this wonderful, contemporary, modern, forward-looking fit-out, and I think it's saying that if you're to be a leader, you have to have a futures perspective.

The institute sits wholly within the DET. Its leadership offerings are thus a reflection both of policy intentions, and of the professional learning needs for principals in Victoria. Since its opening in 2009, Bastow has had 7,000 teachers and principals undertake training at the facility, making it the largest provider of educational leadership training in the state.

The Bastow curriculum was developed in 2009 following a research exercise that drew on school leadership research internationally. It combined the developmental learning leadership model with elements of the Teaching for Understanding framework of Harvard's Project Zero, emphasizing a performances of understanding approach in which learning can be represented and expressed multiple ways. Course curricula are also being updated to incorporate the Australian Professional Standard for Principals.

Leadership trainees are encouraged to attend in pairs or teams to reinforce learning beyond the institute, and courses are structured so as to help principals translate the skills they learn in course workshops back into the school setting. As described by Director Armstrong:

> One of the big shifts in our courses from pre-Bastow to Bastow was that people would need to come and go through performance assessments. And it was within action learning, so you'd learn a little bit, [then] you'd go back to your site. You'd have a challenge project or a school-based change project or a peer-led project that you would identify, looking at your school context, and needs, and stage of development. Then you'd come back [to Bastow] and talk about your learning and there'd be a formal and information assessment and feedback.

Candidates' learning needs are identified using the iLead 360° survey tool. The tool asks candidates and their colleagues to reflect upon the candidate's leadership practice, job performance, and professional learning. Survey information is used to identify the specific domains and capabilities in which candidates may need more training. Candidates then undertake a series of modules to meet those learning needs.

Under the TVLC and New Directions policy initiatives, Bastow's course structure has been redesigned to move from a modules approach to a career-stages approach. Its major program offerings are for:

o Emerging leaders: *Impact* for teachers in their first 3–5 years of teaching

o Middle leaders: *Create* for teachers leading teams in schools

o Aspiring Principals: *Unlocking Potential* for assistant principals or leading teachers

○ New principals: *Evolve* for those new to principalship

○ High performing principals and retired principals: courses from principal coaching to Master's degrees in Instructional Leadership, designed for those have the potential to be system leaders

Each of these programs is contiguous with the next. By identifying potential leaders earlier, DET intends they can be staircased into ongoing leadership training at Bastow throughout their career.

DET is developing a new system for the identification of leadership talent within the state. The 2014–2015 plan sought to train up to an additional 400 teachers as emerging leaders; 200 middle leaders, those already working in leadership roles; 100 aspiring principals to complete a Principal Preparation Program; 200 existing principals, providing them with specialized coaching; and 80 high-performing principals as network leaders (DEECD, 2013b).

More recently, Bastow has undertaken four new initiatives to streamline its operation and increase its effectiveness. Firstly, it has sought to form closer partnerships with universities in leadership development, enabling leadership trainees to receive university credit for some of their Bastow coursework. This move serves to support content rigor and access to university knowledge for Bastow, as well as providing a mechanism for leadership trainees to reengage with universities and perhaps complete additional qualifications. For example, some units in instructional leadership are taught by Melbourne Graduate School of Education faculty, with participants receiving university credit towards a Master of Instructional Leadership. Bastow also entered into a credit transfer arrangement with Monash University for its Master of Leadership program for principals and middle leaders.

Box 3.11 Bastow and MGSE: Master of Instructional Leadership

The Bastow Institute provides a limited number of scholarships for a Master of Instructional Leadership program offered through the University of Melbourne. The 1–2 year program, taught largely over weekends and school holidays, focuses on principals' use of evidence to understand the impact of teaching in their school on student learning, and fostering teacher collaboration and deprivatization of practice to drive school improvement. It begins by teaching principals how to use school data to calculate effect sizes at the level of classrooms and grades, and down to individual students. Principals study how to interpret the impact they have as instructional leaders on student learning, and how to work with staff in the school to raise their effectiveness.

Professor John Hattie, one of the course instructors, explained that a key leadership challenge for principals is how to make these data available and visible to staff in a way that is nonthreatening, and can establish a common conception or standard for progress in student learning:

> The one [method] that I use the most is the bookmark method. We have a levels-based curriculum, not a years-based curriculum, which makes this a lot easier. We ask the teachers, to bring out artifacts of kids' work ... We get them to place two pieces of work, a pre- and a post-, usually over eight to ten weeks. We ask the teachers to first individually put it across a [curricular] line, then have a debate [on student progress]. And then they go back and do it again as a group.

> The role of the principal is to moderate that debate. If you get it wrong, teachers will never do this exercise again, because you're questioning their judgment. It's a massive skill. I take them through simulations on how to do this, point out the traps that you fall into, and get them to understand what happens.

The program also helps principals learn to create learning communities within the school and improve instructional practice. As Professor Hattie further notes, the emphasis is on school leaders harnessing teacher knowledge and expertise already be present in the school:

> I think we have to stop the days where we expect everybody in the school to be expert at everything. One of our tasks is to say to them, "If you [as principal] don't have that, you've got 20 or 30 other people in your school ... Your job is to create the right narrative, not necessarily do everything ... " I think the mistake is that we think that a teacher's an expert with [everything]—we haven't got enough money for that.

Secondly, the institute is moving towards the generation of some of its own revenue. Part of this action involves moving from fully subsidized courses to a copayment from participants. Presently, this is in the area of 5% to 10% of total cost. Participants would then pay around A\$350–700 for its programs.

Thirdly, the institute is extending its work to both increase access to, and more closely meet the needs of, schools and leaders in rural and regional Victoria. One strategy involves increasing the online offerings and webcast materials to reduce the need for candidates to travel to the Bastow facility in Melbourne, but will also involve training delivered in the regions. As noted by Director Armstrong:

> We've got a lot of our colleagues that are in small, rural schools, regional contexts, and so we want to be able to do service delivery that's responsive to the needs of networks of principals, so that we can help inform that quite underdeveloped space of what teaching professional learning looks like in the context in which they work. That is really going to be the powerful lever to get improvement. It's done in a way that's challenging but respectful. It opens up their practice to the scrutiny of others but in a way that maintains relational trust.

Bastow has also begun to offer courses in coaching for school leadership teams. Each team studies together at the Institute, looks at their own school's data, seeks to develop their team work, and designs an improvement project for their school. Director Armstrong explains that by working with the whole leadership team at once, it has the potential to change school cultures:

> It's very powerful because that's when you start to get not [just] little pockets of reform in one or two teachers' classrooms. Often the prevailing organizational structures or cultures can mitigate against innovation and reform in a school and can be exhausting for teachers, and they give up. By bringing everybody together with a sense that we're going to lead this together, you get this whole school endeavor, which I think is absolutely critical.

Beyond Bastow, DET provides an induction toolkit for new principals, online learning modules, and partners with professional associations to provide a range of professional learning opportunities. For example, the Principals as Literacy Leaders program, developed by the

Australian Primary Principals' Association, was offered through the Victorian Principals' Association. The five-day program focused on the use of data/evidence to evaluate school literacy needs, and building principals' capacity to build and lead professional learning communities for improving literacy in their school. DET provided funding to subsidize the program, and funded 10 hours of ongoing coaching to support principals in implementing the program in their schools.

Box 3.12 Development of Aspiring Leaders

We met with Kelly Morrow, recently appointed as a first-time principal of Rosanna Golf Links Primary School, east of Melbourne's central business district. Morrow's trajectory is an example of the progressive leadership opportunities, mentorship, and resources applied to leadership development.

Principal Morrow began her career with several years of contract teaching. This gave her experience in a variety of different school contexts that helped prepared her for leadership. Four years at a primary school in a low socioeconomic area with many students from LOTE backgrounds provided opportunities to take on additional responsibilities, and she received strong mentorship from senior teachers. This was followed by nine years of teaching in a fast-growing, high-immigrant community, where students needs opened up a range of team leadership roles.

Formal school leadership training began when her potential was identified by school network leaders, and was asked to join the Principals Internship Program. Although discontinued in 2012, this 6-month program matched 12 aspiring leaders with other principals from the same school network. Aspiring leaders shadowed principals, receiving close mentorship and support. Morrow was matched with a principal based on skill sets and personality. Although initially reluctant, given that her mentor principal was located in a suburb over an hour away, Principal Morrow described the good match with her mentor as a key part of the program:

> The best part of mentoring is that I have a fantastic relationship with my mentor still, and [when] you get stuck and you're on the phone [with them]: "How do you deal with this? What do you do?"

Mentorship was paired with formal training in school leadership at the Bastow Institute, including in-person and online modules, and research grounded in school practices. On completion of this training, Morrow was placed into an acting assistant principal role, before becoming principal in late 2014.

Summary

A focus on strengthening the quality of the teaching workforce has been a characteristic of educational improvement strategies in Victoria. The policy approach to achieving this has changed over time, with changes in government, and as the state has sought to address a plateau in performance. The early 2000s were characterized by investments in teacher professional learning and coaching, from 2010 to 2014 on harnessing teacher knowledge to create a self-improving system, and more recently signs of renewed government investment, and continuing alignment with national standards and guidelines. Yet successive governments have tended to leave earlier reforms intact, providing a degree of long-term stability in educational governance.

Education policies in the state are oriented towards students and their learning needs, with a focus on improving equity of opportunity. School strategic plans place significant emphasis on student learning, with particular attention to literacy and numeracy, but also support student learning transitions, and student overall well-being. School funds are needs-based, providing greater resources for historically disadvantaged students, and recent funding recommendations are aimed at intervention in student disengagement and underperformance.

The state's system of autonomously managed schools has lent itself to the use of market-like mechanisms in policy areas such as the distribution of teachers and the availability of professional learning providers, and in trials for teacher appraisal and remuneration. The system provides flexibility for school leaders to shape school curricula and target resources to meet the needs of their particular students, but also risks wide variability among schools. Effective school leadership is thus a key concern for the state, and these mechanisms have been balanced by state investments in educator and leadership development, and in the use of national standards to improve consistency. Recent policies have sought to identify and develop leadership potential earlier in the teaching career.

Policy efforts in Victoria have also contributed to a transformation of teaching practice over the past 15 years from an individual, to an increasingly collaborative profession. Policy elements have included support for mentoring and induction, feedback on teaching from multiple sources, and professional learning plans that are aligned to team and school goals. Significant value is placed on the role of school networks to connect schools and school leaders, and to collaborate and share knowledge, resources, and practices for mutual support and improvement.

Teaching in Victoria is increasingly evidence-informed. Teachers collect multiple forms of evidence of student learning, which feed into lesson planning and professional learning. This is bolstered by a teacher registration and induction process that encourages reflective inquiry and the gathering of evidence of professional learning that is centered on student learning needs. The process also requires professional conversations with school leaders and mentors, reinforcing teacher collaboration.

Professional teaching standards underpin these policy areas, creating a common discourse for teaching quality. This connects the knowledge and skills of graduate teachers, with those of experienced teachers, and provides a pathway for professional learning. Teaching is thus increasingly understood as a continuum of learning that continues beyond initial teacher education and throughout one's career. This is reflective of a developmental approach not solely towards student learning, but also towards teacher professional learning and school improvement.

Furthermore, state policy is increasingly aligned with nationally agreed policies in areas ranging from curriculum and assessment, to teacher education, registration, and professional learning. Teacher performance and development plans are aligned to meet both school goals, and national professional teaching standards. The result is the construction of a coherent policy system to support teacher and student learning.

Notes

1. See: http://ausvels.vcaa.vic.edu.au/Overview/Strands-Domains-and-Dimensions
2. Examples of progression points descriptors are available at: http://www. vcaa.vic.edu.au/documents/auscurric/progressionpoints/ausvels-englishprogressionpoints.pdf
3. School councils—comprised of the principal, a teacher, and elected parents and community representatives—provide input into school strategic plans, hiring recommendations for principal, and approval of school budgets.
4. From 2007 to 2015, the Department of Education and Training (DET) was known as the Department of Education and Early Childhood Development (DEECD).
5. The program suspended its new intake in 2015, but it continues for existing scholarship recipients.

6. Schools of education are not unique in this regard. Other professional studies in Australian universities—such as engineering, architecture, and medicine—are also subject to forms of professional accreditation.

7. Detailed information on courses and study objectives may be found here: http://www.monash.edu.au/pubs/handbooks/courses/D3001.html

8. The standard for length of professional placement has been in place since 1998 as articulated in the Guidelines for the Evaluation of Teacher Education Courses from the former Standards Council of the Teaching Profession (Parliament of Victoria, 2005), and is now incorporated into the national standards.

9. Video resources on School Centres for Teaching Excellence are available on the Department of Education and Training's website at the following URL: http://goo.gl/QLFTLU

10. See http://www.kidsmatter.edu.au/primary

11. Theories of Action Rubrics, developed by a regional school network, are teaching protocols such as using collaborative group work, harnessing learning intentions, setting challenging learning tasks, connecting feedback to data, and framing higher order questions. See also http://www.aiz.vic.edu.au/.

12. All teachers are required to be maintain registration annually by 2016. Teachers first registered before 2011 on a five-year registration cycle must document 100 hours across a five-year period. (See http://www.vit.vic.edu.au/.)

13. See "Instructional Rounds in Education: A Network Approach to Improving Teaching and Learning" (City, Elmore, Fiarman, & Teitel, 2009).

CONCLUSION

Dion Burns and Ann McIntyre

AUSTRALIA HAS TRADITIONALLY been a strong performer on international education assessments; however these results have, in the majority of states, declined over the past 10 years. Policy initiatives at both the state and national levels have aimed at addressing both this decline and unequal performance across the system along several axes. Among educational initiatives, much of the focus has been on policies that support increasing professionalization of teachers and raising teaching quality. The chapters in this book have provided examples of how these reforms have played out in different state contexts—with Victoria highly decentralized and NSW utilizing more state control but moving towards increased local control. Viewed together, we identify the following five themes that characterize education policy formation in these states.

Theme One

Part of the transformation of teaching and of policy that informs teaching quality in Australia over the past decade has been the renewed attention to the occasionally conflictual, but generally complementary, goals of excellence and equity in education. A desire to raise the overall quality of the system is driven in part by the country's international competitiveness ambitions as a sizeable and largely export-driven economy. However, it is the Melbourne Declaration (and its antecedents), and the commitment to a quality education for all children, that provides a vision for education in Australia and that has been dominant in framing education and the development of national policies supporting teaching quality. Explicitly referencing the need for investment and support for indigenous youth and disadvantaged learners, the Declaration has helped draw focus to the equitable resourcing of education. As the text of the Declaration notes:

> As a nation Australia values the central role of education in building a democratic, equitable and just society—a society that is prosperous,

cohesive and culturally diverse, and that values Australia's Indigenous cultures as a key part of the nation's history, present and future.

(MCEETYA, 2008)

This increased focus on equity can be seen in teaching policy, such as the
accreditation of ITE programs against the national teaching standards—
specifically those that speak to knowledge of Aboriginal and Torres Strait
Islander cultures, identities, and languages; and strategies for teaching
learners from diverse backgrounds—and which require programs to prepare teachers with competencies that meet these standards.

Theme Two

A threefold focus is evident in education policy formation and implementation in Australia.

- The establishment of a suite of national policy frameworks for
  teacher quality, and a national framework for curriculum and
  student assessment.
- State governance of educational policy enables state adaptation
  of the national frameworks to address student demographics and
  state policy contexts.
- An increased emphasis on local school authority for action to
  enable the implementation of policy in order to support classroom
  teachers to achieve the best outcomes for students.

This structure enables Australia to balance the need for central action
to address significant educational inequalities across the nation, while
preserving the state-based provision of education. As noted in the Victoria chapter, state compliance with national standards alone may be insufficient as a driver of quality. The increased emphasis on local authority
in policy implementation thus enables flexibility for schools to adapt
curricula and instruction to meet the needs of school communities and
students, and to allocate resources at a local level to meet teacher professional learning needs. Nonetheless there is significant variation in effective policy implementation among states and schools, and addressing this
variation will be an ongoing challenge for administrating authorities.

Theme Three

The development of a cohesive national framework for the development
of teacher quality. The framework includes the Australian Professional
Standards for Teachers, the Australian Professional Standard for

Principals, the Australian Performance and Development Framework, and the Australian Charter for the Professional Learning of Teachers and School Leaders. These built upon and strengthened many of the policies and practices already in place in NSW and Victoria, giving these states an advantage in bringing state policies and standards into line with national frameworks.

These frameworks are intended to be mutually complementary, to connect several aspects of the teaching career—initial teacher education, induction and mentoring, professional learning, performance and development, and career progression—under common standards, to guide the development of teacher quality, and to provide a clear platform for describing and assuring best practice. These frameworks also serve as a basis for raising the status of the profession through enabling standards-based assessment of teaching practice from graduate to lead teacher career stages. This is expected to be further enabled by ongoing reforms aimed at establishing exit standards and quality benchmarks for professional practice in initial teacher education.

Theme Four

There is a strong focus on evidence-informed decisions to support teaching and learning. This includes evidence of teaching practice and standards assessed through observation, outcomes, and professional portfolios of evidence aligned to standards. Evidence-based professional learning is articulated against professional standards.

Student outcomes data are collected and analyzed to guide student and teacher learning and school improvement. Teacher discussions we observed often addressed evidence of understanding whether children were progressing, and differentiated teaching strategies to support ongoing student learning. This use of evidence is also supported by the registration process, suggesting benefits of system coherence between regulatory agencies, teacher educators, and the government.

Theme Five

Reforms at both national and state levels have built upon expertise from within the profession. Many of the policy and practices that shape the work of teachers have been developed in conjunction with the profession. For example, the national standards were crafted through consultation with teachers and school leaders. This helped attract tremendous buy-in to the standards and avoid the resistance to implementation, or a "check box" compliance response, that can occur when policy is simply imposed. In our interviews, we found significant support for the national professional teaching standards from a broad range of stakeholders and that these were helping to create a common discourse around the elements that constitute quality teaching.

Similarly, professional associations and educator unions have had a role in shaping the conditions in which teachers work. Teacher unions have sought to balance their roles as industrial organizations with that of teacher professionalization bodies, such as through investment in teacher professional development and negotiating release time for beginning teachers to learn from colleagues, receive mentorship from senior teachers, and gather evidence towards their teacher registration to facilitate their induction into teaching. Professional collaboration is also increasingly understood as a core part of teachers' work, codified in national professional teaching standards, and further supported by intentional policy moves at the state level.

Australia's strong cultural egalitarianism and ethos of fairness and equity exists in balance with the desire for educational excellence. The innovative drive for continual improvement has enabled the states of Australia to collaboratively develop a comprehensive suite of reforms that are designed to influence the quality teaching and the learning of students. These reforms center on the importance of the teaching profession and the critical role of education in shaping the future.

Appendix

METHODOLOGY

THE INTERNATIONAL TEACHER POLICY STUDY employed a multimethod, multiple case study design in order to investigate the policies and practices that support teaching quality within education systems. Seven jurisdictions across five countries were selected for the study based upon their highly developed teaching policy systems, as well as indicators of student performance on international assessments such as the Programme for International Student Assessment (PISA). In larger countries, both national and selected state or provincial policies were examined to develop an understanding of the policy system. In these cases, the state or province was treated as a case nested within the larger country case.

The same research design was followed in each jurisdiction, with adaptation to local circumstances. The research was conducted in several phases:

- o First, we conducted extensive document analysis, including education policy documents and descriptions of curriculum, instruction, and professional development practices and programs in primary, secondary, and higher education institutions. Reviews of the academic literature within and about each jurisdiction were also completed.

- o These were supplemented with analyses of international, national, and, where applicable, state data sources. Quantitative data were used to support document analysis prior to the interview phases, and later, to triangulate findings from interviews. Quantitative data sources consulted included OECD Teaching and Learning International Survey, PISA, Australian Bureau of Statistics, Australian Curriculum, Assessment and Reporting Authority, NSW Department of Education and Communities data, and data from the Victoria Department of Education and Training.

○ Two interview phases were conducted in 2014, beginning with interviews with policymakers and education experts in each jurisdiction. This was followed by interviews with agency administrators, principals, teachers, teacher educators, and other education practitioners. In each case interviews were audio- or video-recorded and transcribed for analysis.

○ The interviews were supplemented with detailed observations of activities in schools and classrooms, along with other key meetings and professional learning events.

Each jurisdictional team consisted of one or more locally based researchers, and one or more U.S.-based colleagues. This approach provided both an insider perspective and an external lens on the data in each. Key lessons and themes from each jurisdictional case study have also been drawn together in a cross-case publication that serves as a companion to the individual studies.

In the case studies of the states of New South Wales and Victoria, we interviewed 63 respondents as follows: 17 teachers, 9 principals and assistant principals, 15 policymakers, 10 university faculty and staff, 5 teacher candidates on placement, 5 union representatives, and 2 professional learning providers.

Observations and interviews were conducted in the NSW Department of Education of Communities, Universities of Melbourne, Sydney, Wollongong, and La Trobe University, Canley Vale Public School, Engadine High School, Footscray North Primary School, Homebush West Primary School, Rosanna Golf Links Primary School, and Willmott Park Primary School. These schools were selected to provide a diversity of schooling sizes, locations, and socioeconomic contexts. At each school we interviewed the principal, assistant principal, and at least three teachers. Teachers from a range of experience levels and responsibilities were selected to provide contrasting perspectives. Other interview participants included teacher coaches, professional learning providers, association and union leaders, and directors of regulatory authorities.

Interview data were supplemented with qualitative data drawn primarily from observations of key meeting and learning events. These included classroom instruction in mathematics and reading, grade-level planning meetings, and school instructional rounds. Additional data sources included the following: school strategic plans, annual school implementation plans, school budgets, grade and class instruction and assessment schedules, minutes of planning meetings, teacher schedules, classroom observation and evaluation forms, and teacher appraisal forms.

REFERENCES

Aboriginal Affairs NSW. (2015). Connected communities. Retrieved May 24, 2016, from http://www.aboriginalaffairs.nsw.gov.au/connected-communities/.

ABS. (2010). *Schools statistics* (No. 4221.0). Canberra: Australian Bureau of Statistics. Retrieved from http://www.ausstats.abs.gov.au/ausstats/subscriber .nsf/0/69FF2D323E81F5F7CA25785500127A08/$File/42210_2010.pdf.

ABS. (2012a). *Characteristics of Aboriginal and Torres Strait Islander Australians, 2011. Population distribution and structure, (No. 2076.0).* Canberra: Australian Bureau of Statistics. Retrieved from http://www.abs .gov.au/ausstats/abs@.nsf/Latestproducts/2076.0Main%20Features11020 11?opendocument&tabname=Summary&prodno=2076.0&issue=2011& num=&view=.

ABS. (2012b). Main features—2011 Census counts—Aboriginal and Torres Strait Islander peoples. Retrieved February 24, 2015, from http://www .abs.gov.au/ausstats/abs@.nsf/Lookup/2075.0main+features32011.

ABS. (2013). *Schools* (No. 4221.0). Canberra: Australian Bureau of Statistics. Retrieved from http://www.ausstats.abs.gov.au/ausstats/subscriber.nsf/0/ BB371F975498C9D7CA257CA00011DB22/$File/att3250h.pdf.

ABS. (2014a). *Australian demographic statistics* (No. 3101.0). Australian Bureau of Statistics.

ABS. (2014b). *Regional population growth, Australia, 2012–13* (No. 3218.0). Canberra: Australian Bureau of Statistics. Retrieved from http://www.abs .gov.au/ausstats/abs@.nsf/Products/3218.0~2012–13~Main+Features~ Main+Features?OpenDocument#PARALINK2.

ABS. (2014c, August 27). Education significant barrier to jobs for Aboriginal and Torres Strait Islander people (Media Release). Retrieved February 24, 2015, from http://www.abs.gov.au/ausstats/abs@.nsf/ Latestproducts/4102.0Media%20Release102014?opendocument&tabna me=Summary&prodno=4102.0&issue=2014&num=&view=.

ABS. (2014d, August 27). Exploring the gap in labour market outcomes of Aboriginal and Torres Strait Islander peoples. Retrieved February 24,

2015, from http://www.abs.gov.au/ausstats/abs@.nsf/Lookup/4102.0main
+features72014.

ABS. (2015, May 2). 4221.0—School, Australia, 2014. Retrieved May 27,
2015, from http://www.abs.gov.au/AUSSTATS/abs@.nsf/DetailsPage/422
1.02014?OpenDocument.

ABS. (2016). *Estimates of personal income for small areas, 2012–13* (No.
6524.0.55.002). Canberra: Australian Bureau of Statistics. Retrieved from
http://www.abs.gov.au/AUSSTATS%5Cabs@.nsf/0/974D8F81A12F336B
CA257521000D8620?Opendocument.

ACARA. (2012). *The shape of the Australian Curriculum: Version 4.0.* Sydney:
Australian Curriculum, Assessment and Reporting Authority (ACARA).
Retrieved from http://www.acara.edu.au/verve/_resources/the_shape_of_
the_australian_curriculum_v4.pdf.

ACARA. (2013a). *National Assessment Program—Literacy and numeracy.
Achievement in reading, persuasive writing, language conventions and
numeracy: National report for 2013.* Sydney: Australian Curriculum,
Assessment and Reporting Authority (ACARA).

ACARA. (2013b). *National report on schooling in Australia 2011.* Sydney:
Australian Curriculum, Assessment and Reporting Authority (ACARA).
Retrieved from http://www.acara.edu.au/verve/_resources/National_
Report_on_Schooling_in_Australia_2011.pdf.

ACARA. (2014). *National report on schooling in Australia 2012.* Sydney:
Australian Curriculum, Assessment and Reporting Authority (ACARA).

ACE. (2012, August 30). Response to "New directions for school leadership
and the teaching profession." Australian College of Educators.

AEU. (2016, May 17). Report shows Gonski makes a difference. Retrieved
May 19, 2016, from http://www.aeufederal.org.au/news-media/news/
report-shows-gonski-makes-difference.

AEU Victoria. (2005). *New teachers survey 2005.* Melbourne: Australian Education
Union. Retrieved from http://www.aeuvic.asn.au/newteacherssurvey2005.pdf.

AEU Victoria. (2007). *New teachers survey 2007.* Melbourne: Australian
Education Union. Retrieved from http://www.aeuvic.asn.au/newteachers-
survey2007.pdf.

AEU Victoria. (2010, March). Victorian languages strategy discussion paper:
An AEU response. Australian Education Union—Victoria Branch.
Retrieved from http://www.aeuvic.asn.au/aeu_languages_strategy_
submission.pdf.

AEU Victoria. (2014a). *New teachers survey 2013.* Australian Education
Union—Victoria Branch.

AEU Victoria. (2014b, June 23). Disadvantaged schools deserve properly
trained teachers. Retrieved February 23, 2015, from http://www.aeuvic
.asn.au/526565.html.

AEU Victoria, & DEECD. (2013). Victorian government schools agreement 2013.

AIHW. (2012). *Australia's health 2012*: Canberra: Australian Institute of Health and Welfare.

AIHW. (2014). *Australia's health 2014: The 14th biennial welfare report of the Australian Institute of Health and Welfare.* Canberra: Australian Institute of Health and Welfare.

AITSL. (2011a). *Accreditation of initial teacher education programs in Australia: Standards and procedures.* [Carlton South, Vic.]: Australian Institute for Teaching and School Leadership. Retrieved from http://www.aitsl.edu.au/verve/_resources/Accreditation_of_initial_teacher_education_file.pdf.

AITSL. (2011b, February). *National professional standards for teachers.* Australian Institute for Teaching and School Leadership.

AITSL. (2011c, July). *Australian professional standard for principals.* Australian Institute for Teaching and School Leadership.

AITSL. (2012a). *Australian teacher performance and development framework.* Australian Institute for Teaching and School Leadership. Retrieved from http://www.aitsl.edu.au/verve/_resources/Australian_Teacher_Performance_and_Development_Framework_August_2012.pdf.

AITSL. (2012b, August). Australian Charter for the Professional Learning of Teachers and School Leaders. Australian Institute for Teaching and School Leadership. Retrieved from http://www.aitsl.edu.au/docs/default-source/default-document-library/australian_charter_for_the_professional_learning_of_teachers_and_school_leaders

AITSL. (2013, May). Accreditation of initial teacher education programs in Australia: Guide to the accreditation process. Australian Institute for Teaching and School Leadership. Retrieved from http://www.aitsl.edu.au/docs/default-source/default-document-library/guide_to_the_accreditation_process.

AITSL. (2014a). Australian professional standard for principals and leadership profiles. Australian Institute for Teaching and School Leadership. Retrieved from http://www.aitsl.edu.au/docs/default-source/school-leadership/australian-professional-standard-for-principals-and-the-leadership-profiles.pdf?sfvrsn=2.

AITSL. (2014b). *Initial teacher education: Data report 2014.* Melbourne: Australian Institute for Teaching and School Leadership.

AITSL. (2015). *Initial teacher education: Data report 2015.* Melbourne: Australian Institute for Teaching and School Leadership.

ARACY. (2013). *Report card: The well-being of young Australians.* Canberra: Australian Research Alliance for Children and Youth. Retrieved from http://www.aracy.org.au/documents/item/126.

Atweh, B., & Singh, P. (2011). The Australian curriculum: Continuing the national conversation. *Australian Journal of Education*, 55 (3), 189–196.

Aubusson, P. (2011). An Australian science curriculum: Competition, advances and retreats. *Australian Journal of Education, 55*(3), 229–244.

Australian Bureau of Statistics. (2013, June 2). Schools, Australia, 2012. Retrieved November 12, 2013, from http://www.abs.gov.au/AUSSTATS/abs@.nsf/DetailsPage/4221.02012.

Australian Department of Education. (2013). *Guide to the Australian Education Act 2013.* Canberra, Australia. Retrieved from aeaguide.education.gov.au.

Australian Government. (2008). Australian curriculum, assessment and reporting authority Act 2008, Pub. L. No. 136 (2008). Retrieved from http://www.comlaw.gov.au/Details/C2014C00453.

Australian Government. (2014a). *Review of the Australian curriculum: Final report.* Canberra. Retrieved from https://docs.education.gov.au/system/files/doc/other/review_of_the_national_curriculum_final_report.pdf.

Australian Government. (2014b). *Roles and responsibilities in education part a: Early childhood and schools* (White Paper No. Issues Paper 4). Canberra, Australia: Department of the Prime Minister and Cabinet. Retrieved from https://federation.dpmc.gov.au/sites/default/files/issues-paper/issues_paper_4_part_a_early_childhood_schools.pdf.

Bandaranayake, B. (2013). Formula-based public school funding system in Victoria: An empirical analysis of equity. *International Journal of Educational Leadership Preparation, 8*(2), 191–207.

Biddle, N. (2011). *Defining the COAG targets within NSW: Background paper.* Sydney: Centre for Aboriginal Economic Policy Research.

Blackmore, J. (2004). Restructuring educational leadership in changing contexts: A local/global account of restructuring in Australia. *Journal of Educational Change, 5*(3), 267–288. http://doi.org/10.1023/B:JEDU.0000041044.62626.99.

Blackmore, J., Bigum, C., Hodgens, J., & Laskey, L. (1996). Managed change and self-management in schools of the future. *Leading and Managing, 2*(3), 195–220.

BOSTES. (2014). *BOSTES submission to the Australian government review of the Australian curriculum.* Sydney: Board of Studies, Teaching and Educational Standards NSW. Retrieved from http://www.boardofstudies.nsw.edu.au/australian-curriculum/pdf_doc/review-aust-curriculum-bostes-submission.pdf.

BOSTES. (2015). *Parents' guide to the NSW primary syllabuses (incorporating the Australian curriculum): Helping parents to understand their child's progress through primary school.* Sydney, Australia: Board of Studies, Teaching and Educational Standards NSW. Retrieved from

https://k6.boardofstudies.nsw.edu.au/wps/wcm/connect/f316419e-11c4–
4d9a-840f-0d686d1e3668/parents-guide-2015.pdf?MOD=AJPERES.

Bracks, S. (2015). *Greater returns on investment in education: Government schools funding review.* Melbourne, Australia: Victoria State Government. Retrieved from http://www.education.vic.gov.au/Documents/about/department/government-schools-funding-review-march.pdf.

Bradley, D., Noonan, P., Nugent, H., & Scales, B. (2008). *Review of Australian higher education: Final report [Bradley review].* Canberra: DEEWR.

Brennan, M. (2011). National curriculum: A political-educational tangle. *Australian Journal of Education, 55*(3), 259–280.

Carnegie Corporation. (2001). *Teachers for a new era.* Retrieved from http://carnegie.org/fileadmin/Media/Publications/PDF/Carnegie.pdf.

City, E. A., Elmore, R. F., Fiarman, S. E., & Teitel, L. (2009). *Instructional rounds in education: A network approach to improving teaching and learning.* ERIC.

COAG. (2012, June). *National partnership agreement on rewards for great teachers.* Council of Australian Governments. Retrieved from http://www.federalfinancialrelations.gov.au/content/npa/education/rewards_for_great_teachers/national_partnership.pdf.

COAG. (2013). *National partnership agreement on improving teacher quality: Performance report for 2012.* Canberra: Council of Australian Governments.

Commonwealth of Australia. Australian Education Act 2013: An act in relation to school education and reforms relating to school education, and for related purposes, Pub. L. No. 67 (2013). Retrieved from http://www.comlaw.gov.au/Details/C2013A00067.

Commonwealth of Australia Constitution Act, Financial assistance to states (1901). Retrieved from http://www.austlii.edu.au/au/legis/cth/consol_act/coaca430/s96.html.

Darling-Hammond, L. (2010). *The flat world and education: How America's commitment to equity will determine our future.* New York: Teacher College, Columbia University.

Darling-Hammond, L. (2012). Teaching and the change wars: The professionalism hypothesis. *Leading Professional Practice in Education, 124.*

Darling-Hammond, L. (2013). *Developing and sustaining a high-quality teaching force (Global Cities Education Network).* Stanford, CA: Stanford Center for Opportunity Policy in Education. Retrieved from https://edpolicy.stanford.edu/sites/default/files/publications/developing-and-sustaining-high-quality-teacher-force.pdf.

Deakin University. (2014). School of Education at Deakin University. Retrieved December 8, 2014, from http://www.deakin.edu.au/arts-ed/education/.

DEC. (2011). *National assessment program—Literacy and numeracy (NAPLAN) 2011: Regional results.* Sydney: NSW Department of Education and Communities. Retrieved from https://www.det.nsw.edu.au/media/downloads/about-us/statistics-and-research/key-statistics-and-reports/naplan-regional-results.pdf.

DEC. (2012). *Five-year strategic plan: 2012–2017.* Sydney, Australia: NSW Department of Education and Communities. Retrieved from https://www.det.nsw.edu.au/media/downloads/about-us/how-we-operate/strategies-and-plans/corporate-plans/fiveyrs-strategic-plan.pdf.

DEC. (2013a). *Great teaching, inspired learning: A blueprint for action.* Sydney, Australia: NSW Department of Education and Communities. Retrieved from http://www.schools.nsw.edu.au/media/downloads/news/greatteaching/gtil_blueprint.pdf.

DEC. (2013b). *Rural and remote education: A blueprint for action.* Sydney: NSW Department of Education and Communities. Retrieved from https://www.det.nsw.edu.au/media/downloads/about-us/our-reforms/rural-and-remote-education/randr-blueprint.pdf.

DEC. (2013c). *Terms of settlement. Referencing salaries and conditions award: Section 5.2 performance and development processes for principals, executives and teachers 2014–2016.* Sydney, Australia: NSW Department of Education and Communities.

DEC. (2015a). *2015 teaching workforce supply and demand.* Sydney, Australia: NSW Department of Education and Communities. Retrieved from https://www.det.nsw.edu.au/media/downloads/about-us/statistics-and-research/key-statistics-and-reports/workforce-plan-4-school-teachers.pdf.

DEC. (2015b). Every student, every school: Personalised learning and support. Presented at the Public Schools NSW conference, Sydney, Australia.

DEC. (2015c). National data collection for students with disability. Presented at the Public Schools NSW conference, Sydney, Australia.

DEC. (2015d). *Performance and development framework for principals, executives and teachers in NSW schools.* Sydney, Australia: NSW Department of Education and Communities.

DEC. (2015e, February 13). Media release: NSW welcomes focus on teacher standards. Retrieved from http://www.dec.nsw.gov.au/about-us/news-at-det/media-releases1/nsw-welcomes-focus-on-teacher-standards.

DEECD. (2009). Performance and development culture: Revised self-assessment framework. Retrieved from http://www.education.vic.gov.au/Documents/school/principals/management/perfdevculture.pdf.

DEECD. (2011). Curiosity and powerful learning. Department of Education and Early Childhood Development. Retrieved from http://www.aiz.vic.

edu.au/Embed/Media/00000025/Curiosity-booklet-single-pages-for-web-21-Oct-11.pdf.

DEECD. (2012a). *2010–2011 teacher supply and demand report*. Melbourne: Human Resources Division, Department of Education and Early Childhood Development. Retrieved from http://www.education.vic.gov.au/ Documents/about/careers/teaching/TeacherSupplyDemandRpt.pdf.

DEECD. (2012b). New directions for school leadership and the teaching profession: Discussion paper. Retrieved from http://www.eduweb.vic.gov.au/ edulibrary/public/commrel/about/teachingprofession.pdf.

DEECD. (2012c). *Towards Victoria as a learning community*. Melbourne: Communications Division for Flagship Strategies Division, Department of Education and Early Childhood Development.

DEECD. (2012d). *Victorian government submission: Productivity commission draft research report: Schools workforce*. Melbourne: Department of Education and Early Childhood Development. Retrieved from http://www .pc.gov.au/__data/assets/pdf_file/0003/116832/subdr95.pdf.

DEECD. (2012e, December 1). Principal selection policy. Department of Education and Early Childhood Development.

DEECD. (2013a). *DEECD 2013–17 Strategic plan*. Melbourne: Department of Education and Early Childhood Development. Retrieved from http://www .education.vic.gov.au/Documents/about/department/stratplan201317.pdf.

DEECD. (2013b). *From new directions to action: World class teaching and school leadership*. Melbourne: Department of Education and Early Childhood Development. Retrieved from http://www.eduweb.vic.gov.au/ edulibrary/public/commrel/about/teachingprofession.pdf.

DEECD. (2013c). *Professional practice and performance for improved learning: School accountability*. Melbourne: Department of Education and Early Childhood Development. Retrieved from http://www.education.vic .gov.au/school/principals/management/Pages/schoolperformance.aspx.

DEECD. (2013d). *The compact: Roles and responsibilities in school education*. Department of Education and Early Childhood Development. Retrieved from http://www.education.vic.gov.au/Documents/school/principals/ management/thecompact.pdf.

DEECD. (2013e). *The school global budget and student resource package in Victoria: Twenty years of innovation and refinement*. Melbourne: Department of Education and Early Childhood Development. Retrieved from http://www.education.vic.gov.au/Documents/school/principals/finance/ sgbsrpbook.pdf.

DEECD. (2013f, June). Languages—Expanding your world: Plan to implement the Victorian government's vision for languages education 2013–2025.

Retrieved from http://www.education.vic.gov.au/Documents/about/department/languagesvisionplan.pdf.

DEECD. (2013g, September 28). Induction for beginning teachers. Retrieved September 25, 2014, from http://www.education.vic.gov.au/school/teachers/profdev/Pages/beginning.aspx.

DEECD. (2013h, October 1). Roles and responsibilities: Teaching service. Department of Education and Early Childhood Development.

DEECD. (2013i, December 24). Recruitment in schools. Retrieved from http://www.education.vic.gov.au/hrweb/Documents/Schools_recruitment.pdf.

DEECD. (2014a). DEECD health and well-being priorities. Retrieved from http://www.education.vic.gov.au/Documents/about/department/hawbpriority.pdf.

DEECD. (2014b). DEECD principles for health and well-being. Retrieved from http://www.education.vic.gov.au/Documents/about/department/hwsummary.pdf.

DEECD. (2014c). *Early years strategic plan 2014–2020*. Melbourne, Vic.: Department of Education and Early Childhood Development. Retrieved from http://www.education.vic.gov.au/Documents/about/department/earlyyearsstratplan.pdf.

DEECD. (2014d). *Professional practice and performance for improved learning: Performance and development*. Melbourne, Vic.: Department of Education and Early Childhood Development. Retrieved from http://www.education.vic.gov.au/Documents/school/principals/management/ppilperfdevt.pdf.

DEECD. (2014e). Professional practice and performance for improved learning: Professional learning and support for school leaders and teachers. Retrieved from http://www.education.vic.gov.au/Documents/school/principals/management/ppilearningsupport.pdf.

DEECD. (2014f, July). Summary statistics for Victorian schools. Department of Education and Early Childhood Development. Retrieved from http://www.education.vic.gov.au/Documents/about/department/brochure-2014july.pdf.

DEECD. (2014g, August 4). Remuneration teaching service. Department of Education and Early Childhood Development.

DEECD. (2014h, September 8). Management of excess teaching service. Department of Education and Early Childhood Development. Retrieved from http://www.education.vic.gov.au/hrweb/Documents/Management_of_excess_school_staff.pdf.

DEECD. (2014i, September 30). Teaching academies of professional practice. Retrieved October 7, 2014, from http://www.education.vic.gov.au/about/programs/partnerships/Pages/tapp.aspx.

DEECD. (2014j, October 22). School centres for teaching excellence. Retrieved June 22, 2015, from http://www.education.vic.gov.au/about/programs/partnerships/pages/partnernationalsteach.aspx.

DEECD, & VCAA. (2011). *Victorian early years learning and development framework: For all children from birth to eight years.* Melbourne. Retrieved from http://www.education.vic.gov.au/Documents/childhood/providers/edcare/veyldframework.pdf.

Deloitte. (2015). *Australian Institute of Teaching and School Leadership: Induction environment scan report.* Melbourne. Retrieved from http://www.aitsl.edu.au/docs/default-source/aitsl-research/induction-environment-scan-report.pdf?sfvrsn=14.

DET. (2003a). Blueprint for government schools: Future directions for education in the Victorian government school system. Department of Education and Training.

DET. (2003b). *Quality teaching in NSW public schools: Discussion paper.* Sydney, Australia: NSW Department of Education and Training.

DET. (2005). *Professional learning in effective schools: The seven principles of highly effective professional learning. Melbourne: Deparment of Education and Training.*

DET. (2008). *Quality Teaching to support the NSW Professional Teaching Standards. Part A: Linking the NSW Professional Teaching Standards and the NSW Quality Teaching model.* Sydney, Australia: NSW Department of Education and Training.

DET. (2013, October 2). Performance and development Culture. Retrieved July 6, 2015, from http://www.education.vic.gov.au/school/principals/management/Pages/pdculture.aspx.

DET. (2015a). *Education state: Schools.* Melbourne: Department of Education and Training. Retrieved from http://www.education.vic.gov.au/Documents/about/educationstate/launch.pdf.

DET. (2015b). *Strengthening DET regional relationships and support: Consultation paper.* Melbourne, Vic.: Department of Education and Training. Retrieved from http://www.education.vic.gov.au/Documents/about/department/regionalsupport.pdf.

DET. (2015c). *The education state: Consultation paper.* Melbourne: Department of Education and Training. Retrieved from http://educationstate.education.vic.gov.au/explore-the-consultation-paper.

DFAT. (2013, December). Victoria state economic indicators. Department of Foreign Affairs and Trade. Retrieved from https://www.dfat.gov.au/geo/fs/vic.pdf.

DHS. (2014). *2013–14 Annual report.* Canberra: Department of Human Services. Retrieved from http://www.humanservices.gov.au/spw/corporate/

publications-and-resources/annual-report/resources/1314/resources/annual-report-2013–14.pdf.

Dinham, S. (2013). The Quality teaching movement in Australia encounters difficult terrain: A personal perspective. *Australian Journal of Education*, 57(2), 91–106. http://doi.org/10.1177/0004944113485840.

Dinham, S., Ingvarson, L., & Kleinhenz, E. (2008). *Teaching talent: The best teachers for Australia's classrooms*. Melbourne: The Business Council of Australia.

Dodd, T. (2014, July 14). NSW opposes Teach for Australia program. *Australian Financial Review*. Retrieved from http://www.afr.com/news/policy/education/nsw-opposes-teach-for-australia-program-20140713-j0x8a.

Dowling, A. (2007). Australia's school funding system. *Policy Analysis and Program Evaluation*, 1.

Drabsch, T. (2013). *The Australian curriculum*. (New South Wales Parliamentary Library Research Service, Ed.). Sydney: NSW Parliamentary Library.

Elmore, R. (2002). *Bridging the gap between standards and achievement: The imperative for professional improvement*. Washington, DC: Albert Shanker Institute.

Eltis, K. J., & Crump, S. J. (2003). Time to teach, time to learn: Report on the evaluation of outcomes assessment and reporting in NSW government schools| NOVA. The University of Newcastle's Digital Repository.

Erebus International. (2012). Evaluation of the take-up and sustainability of new literacy and numeracy practices in NSW schools—Final report for phase one, undertaken on behalf of the NSW minister for education. Retrieved from http://www.cese.nsw.gov.au/images/stories/PDF/EvalRpt_121919_NPLN_FinalReport_Phase1.pdf.

Franklin, M. (2012, January 24). We risk losing education race, Julia Gillard warns. *The Australian*. Canberra. Retrieved from http://www.theaustralian.com.au/national-affairs/education/we-risk-losing-education-race-julia-gillard-warns/story-fn59nlz9–1226251791091.

Gable, A., & Lingard, B. (2013). NAPLAN and the performance regime in Australian schooling: A review of the policy context.

Gillard, J. (2012, September). *A national plan for school improvement*. Presented at the National Press Club, Canberra.

Gonski, D. M. (2014, May). Thoughts of a reviewer of school funding, two years on. Presented at the The Australian College of Educators' Inaugural Jean Blackburn Oration, Melbourne.

Gonski, D. M., Boston, K., Greiner, K., Lawrence, C., Scales, B., Tannock, P. (2012). *Review of funding for schooling*. Canberra: Deptartmentof Education, Employment and Workplace Relations.

Gosper, S., & Karvelas, P. (2012, September 5). Biggest teacher strike in Vic history. *TheAustralian*. Retrieved from http://www.theaustralian.com.au/news/nation/vic-teachers-warn-of-further-strikes/story-e6frg6nf-1226465374183.

Graduate Careers Australia. (2013). *Graduate salaries 2012: A report on the earnings of new Australian graduates in their first full-time employment.* Melbourne: Graduate Careers Australia. Retrieved from http://www.graduatecareers.com.au/wp-content/uploads/2013/07/Graduate%20 Salaries%202012%20[secured].pdf.

Hargreaves, D. H. (2010). Creating a self-improving school system. Retrieved from http://dera.ioe.ac.uk/2093/1/download%3Fid%3D133672%26filena me%3Dcreating-a-self-improving-school-system.pdf.

Hargreaves, D. H. (2012). A self-improving school system: Towards maturity. Retrieved from http://dera.ioe.ac.uk/15804/1/a-self-improving-school-system-towards-maturity.pdf.

Harrington, M. (2008). *Preschool education in Australia.* Canberra, Australia: Parliament of Australia. Retrieved from http://www.aph.gov.au/About_Parliament/Parliamentary_Departments/Parliamentary_Library/pubs/BN/0708/PreschoolEdAustralia.

Harrington, M. (2013). *Australian government funding for schools explained: 2013 update.* Canberra: Parliament of Australia. Retrieved from http://parlinfo.aph.gov.au/parlInfo/download/library/prspub/366868/upload_binary/366868.pdf;fileType=application%2Fpdf#search=%22library/prspub/366868%22.

Harris-Hart, C. (2010). National curriculum and federalism: the Australian experience. *Journal of Educational Administration and History,* 42(3), 295–313. http://doi.org/10.1080/00220620.2010.492965.

Hattie, J. (2012). *Visible learning for teachers: Maximizing impact on learning.* Routledge.

Hattie, J. (2015). Can Australian education become self-transforming? *Australian Educational Leader,* 37(1), 8.

Helme, S., & Lamb, S. (2011). *Closing the school completion gap for Indigenous students (Resource sheet No. No. 6).* Canberra: Australian Institute of Health and Welfare.

Hughes, J., Brock, P., & Wales, N. S. (2008). *Reform and resistance in NSW public education: Six attempts at major reform, 1905–1995.* NSW Department of Education and Training.

Ingersoll, R. M., & Strong, M. (2011). The impact of induction and mentoring programs for beginning teachers: A critical review of the research. *Review of Educational Research,* 81(2), 201–233. http://doi.org/10.3102/0034654311403323.

Ingvarson, L. (2013). *A review of Victoria's developmental learning framework for school leaders*. Melbourne: Australian Council for Educational Research. Retrieved from http://research.acer.edu.au/professional_dev/7/.

Ingvarson, L. C. (2012). Comments on DEECD discussion paper: New directions for school leadership and the teaching profession, June 2012. Retrieved from http://works.bepress.com/lawrence_ingvarson1/199/.

Ingvarson, L., Kleinhenz, E., Khoo, S. T., & Wilkinson, J. (2007). *The VIT program for supporting provisionally registered teachers: Evaluation of implementation in 2005*. Canberra: AutralianCouncil for Educational Research. Retrieved from http://research.acer.edu.au/teacher_education/2/.

Mahuteau, S., & Mavromaras, K. G. (2014). Student scores in public and private schools: Evidence from PISA 2009.

Marzano, R. J., Pickering, D., & Pollock, J. E. (2001). *Classroom instruction that works: Research-based strategies for increasing student achievement*. ASCD.

Matthews, P., Moorman, H., & Nusche, D. (2007). *School leadership development strategies: Building leadership capacity in Victoria, Australia*. OECD. Retrieved from http://www.oecd.org/edu/school/39883476.pdf.

Mayer, D., Pecheone, R., & Merino, N. (2012). Rethinking teacher education in Australia: The teacher quality reforms. *In Teacher education around the world*. London: Routledge.

MCEETYA. (2008). *Melbourne Declaration on Educational Goals for Young Australians*. Melbourne: Ministerial Council for Education, Employment, Training and Youth Affairs.

McIntyre, A. (2011). Teacher leader and school learning—What works. Presented at the Australian Council for Educational Leaders National Conference, Adelaide, Australia: Australian Council for Educational Leaders.

McIntyre, A. (2012). The greatest impact for early career teachers. Presented at the Australian Council for Educational Leaders National Conference, Brisbane.

McIntyre, A. (2013). Teacher quality: Evidence for action. Paper developed for the Australian College of Educators conference, Sydney, Australia.

McKenzie, P., Weldon, P. R., Rowley, G., Murphy, M., & McMillan, J. (2014). Staff in Australia's schools 2013: Main report on the survey. Retrieved from http://research.acer.edu.au/tll_misc/20/.

Monash University. (2015, July 7). EDF5099: Education research project. Retrieved September 2, 2015, from http://www.monash.edu.au/pubs/handbooks/units/EDF5099.html.

Moore, R., & Pitard, J. (2012). A longitudinal evaluation of the Career Change Program at Victoria University 2005–2011 (p. 213). Presented at the 2012

Australian Collaborative Education Network National Conference, Perth: Australian Collaborative Education Network. Retrieved from http://acen. edu.au/2012conference/wp-content/uploads/2012/11/ACEN-2012-National-Conference-Proceedings.pdf#page=213.

MPA. (2014). *Plan Melbourne: Metropolitan planning strategy.* Melbourne: Department of Transport, Planning and Local Infrastructure. Retrieved from http://www.planmelbourne.vic.gov.au/__data/assets/pdf_file/0016/131362/Plan-Melbourne-May-2014.pdf.

NCOA. (2014). *Towards responsible government*: National Commission of Audit. Retrieved from http://www.ncoa.gov.au/report/appendix-vol-1/9–7-schools-funding.html.

NCOSS. (2014). *Poverty in New South Wales.* Sydney: Council of Social Service of New South Wales. Retrieved from https://www.ncoss.org.au/sites/default/files/public/ncoss_antipoverty_final_2.pdf.

NSW CESE. (2013a). *International students enrolled in NSW public schools.* Sydney: NSW Centre for Education Statistics and Evaluation.

NSW CESE. (2013b). *Rural and remote education: Literature review.* Sydney: NSW Centre for Education Statistics and Evaluation.

NSW CESE. (2015). *Schools and Students: 2014 Statistical Bulletin* (CESE Statistical Bulletin No. Issue 4). Sydney: NSW Centre for Education Statistics and Evaluation. Retrieved from http://www.cese.nsw.gov.au/images/stories/PDF/2014_Statistical_Bulletin_Sept2015_compressed.pdf.

NSW Department of Education and Communities. (2013). Benefits and incentives. Retrieved January 27, 2014, from http://www.dec.nsw.gov.au/about-us/careers-centre/school-careers/teaching/teach-with-us/benefits-and-incentives.

NSW Education Act (1990). Retrieved from http://www.austlii.edu.au/au/legis/nsw/consol_act/ea1990104/s21b.html.

NSW Government. (2011). *NSW 2021 A plan to make NSW number one.* Sydney: Department of Premier and Cabinet. Retrieved from http://www.ipc.nsw.gov.au/sites/default/files/file_manager/NSW2021_WEBVERSION.pdf.

NSW Government. (2013). *OCHRE—Opportunity, choice, healing, responsibility, empowerment (NSW government plan for Aboriginal affairs: Education, employment and accountability).* Sydney: NSW Government. Retrieved from http://www.aboriginalaffairs.nsw.gov.au/wp-content/uploads/2013/04/AA_OCHRE_final.pdf.

NSW Government. (2014). *Trade and investment report July 2014 (Trade and Investment).* Sydney: NSW Government. Retrieved from https://www.nsw.gov.au/sites/default/files/news/trade_and_investment_report_-_july_2014.pdf.

NSW Institute of Teachers. (2013, June). Manual for applying to become an Institute of Teachers Endorsed Provider of Professional Development. Retrieved from http://www.nswteachers.nsw.edu.au/Continuing-ProfessionalDevelopment/CPD_Becoming-a-Provider/becoming-provider-for-the-maintenance-of-accreditation-at-proficient-teacher-level/.

NSW Teachers Federation. (2016). Retrieved June 1, 2016, from https://www.nswtf.org.au/.

NSW Trade and Investment. (2013). State economies. Retrieved November 11, 2013, from http://www.business.nsw.gov.au/invest-in-nsw/about-nsw/economic-and-business-climate/state-economies.

OECD. (2014a). *Education at a glance 2014*. OECD Publishing. Retrieved from http://www.oecd-ilibrary.org/education/education-at-a-glance-2014_eag-2014-en.

OECD. (2014b). *PISA 2012 results: What students know and can do—Student performance in mathematics, reading and science* (Revised February 2014, Vol. I). Paris: OECD Publishing. Retrieved from http://dx.doi.org/10.1787/9789264201118-en.

OECD. (2014c). *Talis 2013 results: An international perspective on teaching and learning*. OECD Publishing. Retrieved from http://dx.doi.org/10.1787/9789264196261-en.

OECD. (2015). *Education at a glance 2015: OECD indicators*. Paris: OECD Publishing. Retrieved from http://dx.doi.org/10.1787/eag-2015-en.

Parliament of Victoria. (2005). *Step up, step in, step out: Report on the inquiry into the suitability of pre-service teacher training in Victoria: Final report*. Melbourne, Vic.: Government Printer.

Patty, A. (2013, December 7). Australia's report card in the latest OECD snapshot highlights the need for urgent education reform. *The Age*. Retrieved from http://www.theage.com.au/national/education/australias-report-card-in-the-latest-oecd-snapshot-highlights-the-need-for-urgent-education-reform-20131206-2ywoe.html.

Piccoli, A. (2011). NSW Minister for Education's address. Presented at the NSW Department of Education and Communities' Principals Induction Conference, Sydney: NSW Department of Education and Communities.

Piccoli, A. (2014). Transforming education: The New South Wales reform journey. Presented at the Education World Forum. Retrieved from http://www.dec.nsw.gov.au/documents/15060385/15385042/world_edu_forum_paper_minister.pdf.

Pyne, C. (2015, February). The future of teacher education. Presented at the Australian Council of Educational Leaders Hedley Beare Memorial Lecture.

Ramsey, G. (2000). *Quality matters. Revitalising teaching: Critical times, critical choices.* Sydney, Australia. Retrieved from https://www.det.nsw.edu.au/teachrev/reports/reports.pdf.

Reid, A. (2009). Is this a revolution?: A critical analysis of the Rudd government's national education agenda.

Rickards, F. (2012). New course design: Building clinical skills with grounded experience in schools. Presented at the National Forum on Initial Teacher Education, Melbourne. Retrieved from http://www.education.vic.gov.au/Documents/about/programs/partnerships/natforuminitialnoon.pdf.

Rudd, K., & Gillard, J. (2008). *Quality education: The case for an education revolution in our schools.* Canberra: Commonwealth of Australia.

Sergiovanni, T. J. (1984a). *Handbook for effective department leadership: Concepts and practices in today's secondary schools.* Allyn & Bacon.

Sergiovanni, T. J. (1984b). Leadership and excellence in schooling. *Educational Leadership*, 41(5), 4–13.

Sergiovanni, T. J. (2006). *The principalship: A reflective practice perspective* (5th ed.). Boston: Pearson/Allynand Bacon.

Teach for Australia. (2014). Fast facts. Retrieved November 5, 2014, from http://www.teachforaustralia.org/content/fast-facts.

TEMAG. (2015a, February). Action now: Classroom ready teachers: Australian government's response. Deparament of Education and Training. Retrieved from https://docs.education.gov.au/system/files/doc/other/150212_ag_response_-_final.pdf.

TEMAG. (2015b, February). Action now: Classroom ready teachers: Report of the Teacher Education Ministerial Advisory Group. Department of Education and Training.

Thomas, S., & Watson, L. (2011). Quality and accountability: Policy tensions for Australian school leaders. In *International handbook of leadership for learning* (pp. 189–208). Springer.

Thomson, S., De Bortoli, L. J., & Buckley, S. (2014). *PISA 2012: How Australia measures up.* Australian Council for Educational Research (ACER).

Thomson, S., De Bortoli, L., Nicholas, M., Hillman, K., & Buckley, S. (2010). Highlights from the full Australian Report: Challenges for Australian education: Results from PISA 2009. Retrieved from http://research.acer.edu.au/ozpisa/8/.

Topsfield, J. (2012, August 1). Catholic teachers to strike. *The Age*. Melbourne. Retrieved from http://www.theage.com.au/victoria/catholic-teachers-to-strike-20120731–23d70.html.

Townsend, T. (1995). Victoria's Schools of the future: Lessons for community educators. Presented at the National Community Education Association Meeting, Atlanta, GA.

Trioli, V. (2015, March 17). Footscray North Primary School students score high NAPLAN marks. *Star Weekly*. Retrieved from http://www.starweekly .com.au/1834437-footscray-north-primary-school-students-score-high-naplan-marks-2/.

VAGO. (2010). *Managing teacher performance in government schools* (No. 2009–10:22). Melbourne: Victorian Auditor-General's Office.

VAGO. (2012). *Science and mathematics participation rates and initiatives* (No. 2011–12:33). Melbourne: Victorian Auditor-General's Office.

VCAA. (2013a). On demand testing. Retrieved September 22, 2014, from http://www.vcaa.vic.edu.au/pages/prep10/ondemand/index.aspx.

VCAA. (2013b). Overview. Retrieved December 5, 2014, from http://ausvels. vcaa.vic.edu.au/Overview/Strands-Domains-and-Dimensions.

Victorian Government. (2014). *Victoria in future 2014: Population and household projections to 2051*. Melbourne, Vic.: Department of Transport, Planning and Local Infrastructure. Retrieved from http://www.dtpli.vic .gov.au/__data/assets/pdf_file/0009/223110/VIF-2014-WEB.pdf.

VIT. (2013, January 1). Evidence of professional practice for full registration. Retrieved September 29, 2014, from http://www.vit.vic.edu.au/prt/pages/ evidence-of-professional-practice-for-full-registration-36.aspx.

VIT. (2014). *Annual report 2014*. Melbourne: Victorian Institute of Teaching.

VIT. (2014). *Teacher mentor support program*. Melbourne.

VIT. (2014, June). Evaluating the supporting provisionally registered teachers program: 2013 summary report.

VRQA. (2014, August). Guide to the minimum standards and other requirements for school registration. Victorian Registration and Qualifications Authority.

Wasson, D. (2009). Large cohort testing: How can we use assessment data to effect school and system improvement? In *Assessment and student learning: Collecting, interpreting and using data to inform teaching* (Vol. 4). Perth, Australia: Australian Council for Educational Research.

Watt, M. (2009). The movement for national academic standards: A comparison of the Common Core state standards initiative in the USA and the National Curriculum in Australia. *Online Submission*.

Weldon, P. (2015). *The teacher workforce in Australia: Supply, demand and data issues* (Policy Insights No. 2). Camberwell, Victoria: Australian Council for Educational Research. Retrieved from http://research.acer .edu.au/cgi/viewcontent.cgi?article=1001&context=policyinsights.

Weldon, P., McKenzie, P., Kleinhenz, E., & Reid, K. (2013). *Teach for Australia pathway: Evaluation report phase 3 of 3*. Camberwell, Victoria: Australian Council for Educational Research.

Weldon, P., Shah, C., & Rowley, G. (2015). *Victorian teacher supply and demand report 2012 and 2013*. Melbourne, Australia: Department of Education and Training. Retrieved from http://www.education.vic.gov.au/Documents/about/careers/teaching/TeacherSupplyDemandRpt2012and2013.pdf.

Zanderigo, T., Dowd, E., & Turner, S. (2012). *Delivering school transparency in Australia: National reporting through MySchool* (Strong Performers and Successful Reformers in Education). Paris: OECD.

Lightning Source UK Ltd.
Milton Keynes UK
UKHW022303040620
364444UK00008B/723